P9-BIH-520

THE BUSINESS OF BEING A WRITER

The Business of Being a Writer

JANE FRIEDMAN

THE UNIVERSITY OF CHICAGO PRESS

Chicago and London

The University of Chicago Press, Chicago 60637

The University of Chicago Press, Ltd., London

© 2018 by Jane Friedman

Published 2018

Printed in the United States of America

27 26 25 24 23 22 21 20 19 18   2 3 4 5

ISBN-13: 978-0-226-39302-5 (cloth)

ISBN-13: 978-0-226-39316-2 (paper)

ISBN-13: 978-0-226-39333-9 (e-book)

DOI: https://doi.org/10.7208/chicago/9780226393339.001.0001

Library of Congress Cataloging-in-Publication Data

Names: Friedman, Jane, author.

Title: The business of being a writer / Jane Friedman.

Other titles: Chicago guides to writing, editing, and publishing.

Description: Chicago ; London : The University of Chicago Press, 2018. | Series: Chicago
    guides to writing, editing, and publishing. | Includes bibliographical references and index.

Identifiers: LCCN 2017038268 | ISBN 9780226393025 (cloth : alk. paper) | ISBN 9780226393162
    (pbk. : alk. paper) | ISBN 9780226393339 (e-book)

Subjects: LCSH: Authorship—Economic aspects. | Literary agents. | Authors and publishers.

Classification: LCC PN161 .F744 2018 | DDC 808.02—dc23

LC record available at https://lccn.loc.gov/2017038268

♾ This paper meets the requirements of ANSI/NISO Z39.48-1992 (Permanence of Paper).

For my mom,
because when I announced my intention
to study creative writing in college,
she never suggested I pursue
something more lucrative

CONTENTS

INTRODUCTION

Thousands of people dream of writing and publishing full-time, yet few have been told how to make that dream a reality. Working writers may have no more than a rudimentary understanding of how the publishing and media industry works, and longtime writing professors may be out of the loop as to what it takes to build a career in an era of digital authorship, amid more competition—and confusing advice—than ever. Even instructors who are well informed and up to date on the practical aspects of a writing career may believe their job is to teach the art and craft, or feel that students shouldn't allow business concerns to influence their voice or direction as writers.

The Business of Being a Writer takes it on principle that learning about the publishing industry will lead to a more positive and productive writing career. While business savvy may not make up for mediocre writing, or allow any author to skip important stages of creative development, it can reduce anxiety and frustration. And it can help writers avoid bad career decisions—by setting appropriate expectations of the industry, and by providing tools and information on how to pursue meaningful, sustainable careers in writing and publishing on a full-time or part-time basis. Because writing degrees may have little or no impact on earnings potential or industry knowledge, this guide is as much for students—or graduates—of undergraduate or graduate writing programs as it is for writers working outside such programs.

Despite ongoing transformations in the publishing industry, there are fundamental business principles that underlie writing and publishing success, and those principles are this book's primary focus. Writers who learn to recognize the models behind successful authorship and publication will feel more empowered and confident to navigate a changing field, to build their own plans for long-term career development.

One underlying assumption in this guide is that many creative writers—particularly those pursuing formal degrees—want to build careers based on publishing books. It seems like common sense: literary agents sell and profit from book-length work, not single stories or essays; and getting anyone (whether a reader or a publisher) to pay for a book is easier than getting them to pay for an online article or poem. But book publishing is often just one component of a full-time writing career. Perhaps you've read personal essays by debut authors "exposing" the fact that the average book advance does not equate to a full-time living for even a single year. Such essays reveal unrealistic expectations about the industry—or magical thinking: *I will be the exception and earn my living from writing great books.*

This guide does offer guidance on how to get a book published, a milestone that remains foundational to most creative writing careers. But because very few people can make a living solely by writing and publishing books, it goes further, showing why this one pursuit should not constitute one's entire business model. Earnings can come as well from other sectors of publishing, other activities that involve writing and the types of skills one picks up as a writer. Online media and journalism, for example, now play a significant role in even fiction writers' careers, so this guide spends considerable time on skills and business models important to the digital media realm. When combining these skills with the entrepreneurial attitude and knowledge this guide teaches, a writer will be better prepared to piece together a writing life that is satisfying and sustainable. In the end, some writers may discover they prefer other types of writing and publishing—and not just because it's tough to make a living wholly from books.

If you are a writer looking for the business education you feel you never received, I hope this book provides the missing piece. While I try to be encouraging, and want you to feel capable and well informed, I don't sugarcoat the hard realities of the business. When you decide to pursue a writing career, you'll experience frustration, again and again, and not just in the form of rejection letters. But it helps to know what's coming and that your experience is normal. Writers who are properly educated about the industry typically feel less bitterness and resentment toward editors, agents, and other professionals. They are less likely to see themselves as victimized and less likely to be taken advantage of. It's the writers who lack education on how the business works who are more vulnerable to finding themselves in bad situations.

HOW THIS GUIDE COMPLEMENTS OTHER RESOURCES
There are innumerable resources available to help writers with the business side of the writing life:

- books on how to get a book published or how to self-publish
- niche guides, on how to be a freelance magazine writer, how to market and promote your work, how to build a platform, etc.
- annual directories, such as *Writer's Market*, which list thousands of places where writers can get published

While the best of these guides offer deep dives into specific topics, the book you're now reading takes a strategic, high-level look at how writers can establish a lifelong writing career. It includes overviews of the major industries of interest to writers: book publishing, magazine publishing, and online media. When launching a career as an author or freelancer, it helps to understand the business models of these industries, what their pressure points are, and what kind of treatment (and payment!) is to be expected. This guide offers nuts-and-bolts information on how to get published, but its larger purpose is to push writers to apply the idea of a business model to their own careers. Many writers end up teaching, or holding down a day job, to support their writing, which is neither good nor bad—but often it's an accident or shadow career the writer never intended. This guide aims to provide writers with information that will help them make deliberate, informed choices, and consider what kind of compromises might be needed to reach their particular goals for earnings or prestige.

USING THIS GUIDE IN THE CLASSROOM: NOTES FOR INSTRUCTORS

The business aspects of writing and publishing are often neglected in creative writing classrooms, and I think it does students a grave disservice. Few graduates will secure full-time teaching positions, and many will have gone into debt to pay for their degrees; for them, the dream of a writing career may be shunted to the side in favor of reliable, well-paying work to repay their loans.

I do not see creative writing students as too delicate or underdeveloped to handle the business side of the writing life—nor do I view these matters as extracurricular. Rather, I believe students deserve considered guidance on the choices they must make as players in a larger industry. Graduate writing students, in particular, are often people who are well into adulthood, who may have significant responsibilities awaiting them post-degree. If programs want their graduates to flourish, they need to expose their students to the foundations of publishing industry success, and not give the false impression that it all boils down to excellent writing.

The number-one question I've received over my twenty years in publishing has always been "How do I get X published?" or "Where can I publish X?" Students may, understandably, be focused on this question, and if the overriding course goal is to give them the tools to answer it, then part 3, "Getting Published," may be the place to turn to first. This section works well in conjunction with research into publishing markets and opportunities, such as those listed in the back of the *AWP Chronicle* and *Poets & Writers* magazine or in annual market directories. For such a course, each student could choose at least one manuscript (short or long) that they feel is polished and ready to place, then research the market for it, write a cover or query letter, and submit their materials (and wait). However, I think grasping how the industry works is foundational to getting published, which is why I cover it earlier, in part 2, "Understanding the Publishing Industry," Its four chapters cover books, magazines, and online and digital media, as well as literary publishing challenges. These can be read and assigned in any order, depending on how the course is structured.

Most writers, in their desire to get published, put the cart before the horse: They want to see their work accepted and validated before they've thought through what their larger goals are. While not every step (or even most steps) in a writer's life has to be analyzed as to its strategic benefit, no writer wants to wake up one day, after many years of effort, and realize they were mistaken in their expectations about how a particular publishing activity would lead to a particular income or career. Part 1 therefore looks at the first steps in making a life as a writer, and how to be strategic, smart, and efficient. It can be used to complement any type of writing class, even craft-focused classes, since it partly serves as a wake-up call to those who may not realize how little money is earned through traditional publishing, particularly in the literary market.

Part 4, "The Writer as Entrepreneur," can be seen as a continuation of part 1. It explores more advanced territory and is best suited for classes focused on the business of writing and publishing. It deconstructs the components of an author platform, discusses activities related to maintaining an online presence, and presents ways to market, promote, and sell one's books, services, or products of any kind.

Part 5, "How Writers Make Money," looks at how writers ultimately make a living, either full-time or part-time. (Writers who dream of starting their own publications or presses should look at this part closely, along with the applicable chapters from part 2.) I can imagine students cherry-picking methods that complement their strengths, and beginning to sketch out business models for their careers. Looking at my own model, I mix freelance writing, online writing, editing, online teaching, and affiliate income. The combinations are endless, and part 5 drives home that a writer's income is almost always cobbled together from many different sources.

Finally, this book has a companion website, businessofwriting.org, that offers examples of submissions materials (queries, synopses, and book proposals), as well as links to supporting resources and information.

Using This Guide in a Craft-Focused Class

As mentioned earlier, part 1 is the most important reading for students whose expectations for their writing go beyond treating it as an enjoyable hobby. While writers young and old can have trouble even *calling* themselves writers (the term "aspiring writer" is used far too much!), I find that many aspirants, if pressed, will confess to dreams of publication and a life centered on writing. Whether they admit it in public or in a classroom is another matter. That's why I advocate spending at least one class period in upper-level craft-focused writing courses discussing issues related to the business of writing, encouraging students to share what surprised them or what questions were raised by their reading of part 1 and perhaps part 2. It can also be eye-opening for students to research the career trajectory of a contemporary, living writer (especially one on the syllabus) and to look for interviews where the writer offers any transparency as to their earnings, business model, or frustrations with the publishing business.

Part One
FIRST STEPS
MAKING A LIFE AS A WRITER

In the history of professional writing and authorship, there have been several revolutions in how writers get published and get paid: the invention of the printing press (mid-1400s), the legislation of copyright (early 1700s), the growth of literacy (1800s), and the expansion of the internet and digital publishing (2000s).

Some believe the digital era is making it increasingly difficult for authors to earn a decent living from their writing. I don't agree: it has always been difficult. Every revolution, including the one we're living through now, stirs up excitement, but also confusion and fear of change. In the late 1800s, during what some now consider a golden age for publishing (for magazines especially), you could find disgruntled writers. One complained to a US congressional committee that he did not know any author who made a living by writing literary work. Of all the learned professions, he said, "Literature is the most poorly paid."[1] The truth is that many writers' careers, during every era, have been gifted into existence by birth, by privilege, by marriage.

Throughout history, authors have laid the blame for their less than desirable economic situation on publishers, but such accusations almost always betray ignorance of how publishing works. In the digital era, it is also common to blame authors' suffering on Silicon Valley giants, such as Google. Neither industry deserves most of the blame we heap upon it. During each revolution, authors (and publishers as well) typically seek to preserve the existing system, even if new methods of publishing and distribution have rendered it unworkable. Today, authors' organizations express overarching pessimism: author earnings are lower than ever, they dubiously claim. But this is no reason to be dissuaded from a writing career if that's what you want. It remains possible to make a decent living from writing if you're willing to pay attention to how the business works, devise a business model tailored to your goals, and adapt as needed.

Many serious writers take for granted that art and business are antithetical to one another. Before a word is published—before they've encountered any aspect of the business of their art—they assume that they are bad at business or that attending to business concerns will pollute their creative efforts. Too few are open to the possibility that the business side calls for as much imagination as the artistic process itself. Industry expert Richard Nash once tweeted, "Business & marketing are about understanding networks and patterns of influence and behavior. Writers can handle that."[2] To be sure, business can and does ask for compromises, but that's not always to the detriment of art. A bit of friction, some kind of barrier—a net on the tennis court!—is healthy.

In the literary community, there's a persistent and dangerous myth of the starving artist, a presumption that "real art" doesn't earn money. In fact, art and business can each inform the other, and successful writers throughout history have proven themselves savvy at making their art pay. Dana Gioia, both a celebrated poet and former vice president at General Foods, said, "There is a natural connectivity, at least in American culture, between the creative and the commercial."[3] An open attitude toward business can provide focus, discipline, and, sometimes most importantly, self-awareness about what you want and expect from your writing career.

The following chapters will help you take the first steps toward a writing life based on your own strengths, rather than some unattainable ideal. To that end, they focus on the big picture of building your career. Details about specific types of writing and publishing will follow in later parts of the book.

1 : CAN YOU MAKE A LIVING AS A WRITER?

The ability to make a living by the pen was rare before the emergence of the printing press, the subsequent growth of a literate middle class, and the resulting demand for reading material. Even then, it wasn't customary for printers (who also acted as publishers) to pay authors, and they owned authors' works outright. For their part, writers resisted payment even when it was offered: it was considered crass to accept money for something many saw as sacred. Writers who were able to focus on their art were either of high birth or benefited from the generosity of patrons. It wasn't until around the mid-eighteenth century, not long after the first copyright laws were enacted, that it became feasible and socially acceptable for writers to live solely off book sales or payments from publishers. Samuel Johnson, in what one historian calls the "Magna Carta of the modern author," was able to reject support from a patron because his work was so commercially successful.[1]

But exceptionally few writers have ever been able to make a living solely off what they wished to write. While F. Scott Fitzgerald made good money writing short stories for magazines, he also pursued Hollywood writing stints, which he didn't really enjoy. William Faulkner also wrote scripts. Chekhov wrote newspaper articles. Beckett translated for *Reader's Digest*. And so on.

To make your writing the foundation of a sustainable living will likely involve compromise. If you want to realize monetary gain, you have to be willing to treat (some of) your art as a business. No writer is entitled to earn a living from his writing, or even to be paid for his writing; once you seek payment, you have to consider the market for what you're producing, especially during a time when supply outpaces demand. This is one of the most difficult tasks writers face: to adopt a market-driven eye when necessary—to see their work as something to be positioned and sold. It helps to have psychological distance from the work, which comes with time and training. Writers who see this as a creative challenge rather than a burden are more likely to survive the cycle of pitching and rejection without sinking into hopelessness.

While there are far easier ways to make a living than as a writer, that is not because good writing is at odds with commercial success. It's because most people are not willing to learn the business and do what's required to make writing pay. They're looking for what's easy. And writing for publication isn't, at least not for most writers at the start of their careers.

That said, some types of writing are more beholden to marketplace concerns than others. Expecting to make a living through freelance writing or journalism is a very different proposition than expecting to make a living through creative writing (such as novels, short stories, or poetry). Freelancers and journalists *must* pay attention to the market. They are often writers for hire, and don't typically expect—or shouldn't expect—to make a living just from writing what they want. Creative writers, on the other hand, are usually presumed—and often told—to focus on their craft and mostly disregard trends, though what they write may of course be influenced by what can be sold to a commercial publisher. Either type of writing may be sustainable only with some form of patronage, whether from individuals or from institutions—as has been the case throughout history. But there is definitely a bigger challenge ahead for the creative writer who expects to make a living by writing, because there are few paying opportunities for such work outside of book publication, and the landscape is competitive.

Creative writing instructors sometimes claim that focusing on business too soon is dangerous. It's true that it can cause unproductive anxiety, but that's mainly because of bad information and gossip that passes from writer to writer. For example, some writers are led to believe they have to develop a readership before they sell a book, or "build their platform" to become more desirable to agents or publishers. That's true only in a small percentage of cases, and rarely does it apply to the types of work produced in creative writing programs. This persistent whirlpool of misinformation about the industry is yet another reason business issues ought to be addressed up front and early.

Here's where the biggest danger lies, if there is one: Business concerns can distract from getting actual writing done, and can even become a pleasurable means of avoiding the work altogether. No one avoids writing like writers. Producing the best work possible is hard, and focusing on agents, social media marketing, or conference-going feels easier. Writers may trick themselves into thinking that by developing their business acumen, they are improving as writers—but all the business acumen in the world can't make up for inferior writing.

It's also possible that too much attention to business concerns could stymie experimentation. Ideally, creative writers are always experimenting, failing, and improving in some manner. An overbearing focus on work that leads to a paycheck can derail less commercial work that, over the long term, might break boundaries or be more meaningful artistically.

IS IT BETTER JUST TO HAVE A DAY JOB?

If thinking about the business of writing causes you to feel, at best, uncomfortable, then it may be better to keep your pursuit of it unadulterated by market concerns. Some literary legends have never experienced conventional employment, pursuing a writing life underwritten by existing wealth or family support (Gertrude Stein and Jane Austen, for example). But many held day jobs: Franz Kafka worked for an insurance company, Herman Melville as a schoolteacher and customs inspector, and Louisa May Alcott as a seamstress and governess— to name but a few. For some writers, the day job actually fosters their creative work. (Elizabeth Hyde Stevens's essay on Borges's life and work as a librarian offers one example.)[2]

When agents, editors, and other writers say, "Don't quit your day job," it is simultaneously the best advice and the worst advice. On the one hand, it helps moderate one's expectations and acknowledges the most common outcome for writers: you'll need another form of income. But it also perpetuates the misconception that writing can't or won't make you a living. It can, just probably not in the ways you would prefer.

If your idea of the writing life centers on a remote garret in which you scribble away in quiet isolation and then deliver your genius unto the world—then yes, you'll need a day job, or wealth. However, if your idea of the writing life allows for community engagement, working with different types of clients, or digital media prowess, then you're in a better frame of mind to make a full-time living as a writer.

THE DIFFICULT EARLY YEARS

Many early-career writing attempts are not publishable, even after revision, yet are necessary for a writer's growth. A writer who has just finished her first book or short work probably doesn't realize this, and may take the rejection process very hard. That's why publishing experts typically advise that writers start work on their next project: move on, and don't get stuck waiting to publish the first one.

In his series on storytelling, Ira Glass says:

All of us who do creative work, we get into it because we have good taste. But there is this gap. The first couple years that you're making stuff, what you're making isn't so good. OK? It's not that great. It's really not that great. It's trying to be good, it has ambition to be good, but it's not quite that good. But your *taste*, the thing that got you into the game, your taste is still killer, and your taste is good enough that you can tell that what you're making is kind of a disappointment to you. . . . You can tell that it's still sort of crappy. A lot of people never get past that phase. A lot of people, at that point, they quit.[3]

If you can't perceive the gap—or if you haven't gone through the "phase"—you probably aren't reading enough. Writers can develop good taste and understand what quality work is by reading writers they admire and want to emulate. Writers improve over time by practicing their craft in addition to getting focused feedback from experienced people who push them to improve and do better.

As a young editor, recently out of school, I asked professor and author Michael Martone if he could tell which of his students were going to succeed as writers—was there a defining characteristic? He told me it was the students who kept writing after they left school, after they were off the hook to produce material on a deadline or for a grade. The most talented students, he said, weren't necessarily the ones who followed through and put in the hours of work required to reach conventional publishing success.

Similarly, when Ta-Nehisi Coates was interviewed by the *Atlantic*, he said, "The older you get, that path [of writing] is so tough and you get beat up so much that people eventually go to business school and they go and become lawyers. If you find yourself continuing up until the age of thirty-five or so . . . you will have a skill set . . . and the competition will have thinned out."[4]

Few demonstrate the persistence required to make it through the difficult, early years. Some people give up because they lack a mentor or a support system, or because they fail to make the time, or because they become consumed with self-doubt. They don't believe they're good enough (and maybe they aren't) and allow those doubts to become a self-fulfilling prophecy.

I used to believe that great work or great talent would eventually get noticed—that quality bubbles to the top. I don't believe that anymore. Great work is overlooked every day, for a million reasons. Business concerns outweigh artistic concerns. Some writers are just perpetually unlucky. But don't expect to play the role of poor, starving writer and have people in publishing help you out of sympathy or a sense of moral responsibility. They're more likely to help writers they see as indefatigable and motivated to help themselves—since they know that's what the job of a working writer requires. If you find yourself demonizing people in the publishing industry, complaining as if you're owed something, and feeling bad about your progress relative to other writers, it's time to find the reset button. Perhaps you've been focusing too much on getting published.

No matter how the marketplace changes—and it always does—consider these three questions as you make decisions about your life as a writer:

What satisfies or furthers your creative or artistic goals? This is the reason you got into writing in the first place. Even if you put this on the back burner in order to advance other aspects of your writing and publishing career, don't leave it out of the equation for long. Otherwise your efforts can come off as mechanistic or uninspired, and you're more likely to burn out or give up.

What earns you money? Not everyone cares about earning money from writing, but as you gain experience and a name for yourself, the choices you make in this regard become more important. The more professional you become, the more you have to pay attention to what brings the most return on your investment of time and energy. As you succeed, you won't have time to pursue every opportunity. You have to stop doing some things.

What grows your audience? Gaining readers can be just as valuable as earning money. It's an investment that pays off over time. Sometimes it's smart to make trade-offs that involve earning less money now in order to grow readership, because having more readers will put you in a better position in the future. (For example, you might focus on writing online, rather than for print, to develop a more direct line to readers.)

This book helps you sort through questions 2 and 3—that's where writers lack guidance. The first question is a personal decision that I assume most writers have already considered. It's unlikely that every piece of writing you do, or every opportunity you pursue, will advance artistic, monetary, and readership goals. Commonly you can get two of the three. Sometimes you'll pursue projects with only one of these factors in play. You get to decide based on your priorities at a given point in time.

A book that strongly influenced how I think about my writing career is

The Art of Possibility by Rosamund Stone Zander and Benjamin Zander. In it they write, "Many of the circumstances that seem to block us in our daily lives may only appear to do so based on a framework of assumptions we carry with us. Draw a different frame around the same set of circumstances and new pathways come into view."[5] Consider, for example, the assumptions that art can't pay, that great writing is created in isolation, or that serious writers never consider the reader. These are all frameworks that can hinder you. An open attitude about what the writing life might look like—based on your own, unique goals, not someone else's standards—is an invaluable asset. While some may consider the Zanders' perspective to be hopelessly idealistic or naive (or both), writers rarely coast into a paying, satisfying career that's free of trouble and frustration. So the ability to reframe dilemmas rather than viewing them as dead ends is like rocket fuel to continued progress.

Finally, I've witnessed many writers hit their heads against the wall trying to publish or gain acclaim for a particular type of work, even as they succeed wildly with something else—that they don't think is prestigious or important enough. Getting caught up in prestige is perhaps one of the most destructive inclinations of all. Paul Graham has written elegantly on this, comparing prestige to a "powerful magnet that warps even your beliefs about what you enjoy. It causes you to work not on what you like, but what you'd like to like."[6] Avoiding this trap is easier said than done. Most of us live under the weight of expectations put upon us by parents, teachers, peers, and the larger community. Breaking free of their opinions can be liberating, but what others think of us also contributes to how we form our identities. It's not a problem you can solve as much as acknowledge and manage. Still, if you can at least let go of the many myths about writing, and pursue what you truly enjoy with as much as excellence as possible, you can shape a writing life that is not only uniquely your own, but one that has a better chance of becoming a lifelong career.

2 : THE ART OF CAREER BUILDING

It is no great thing to publish something in the digital era. Many of us now publish and distribute with the click of a button on a daily basis—on Twitter, Facebook, and retail websites such as Amazon. The difficult work lies in getting attention in what professor and author Clay Shirky calls a world of "cognitive surplus." Cognitive surplus refers to the societal phenomenon where we now have free time to pursue all sorts of creative and collaborative activities, including writing.[1] While rarely called by this rather academic term, it's a widely remarked-upon dynamic. Arianna Huffington has said, "Self-expression is the new form of entertainment,"[2] and author George Packer wrote in 1991, "Writing has become one of the higher forms of recreation in a leisure society."[3]

A writer today is competing against thousands more would-be writers than even a couple of decades ago. Still, committed writers succeed in the industry every single day, especially those who can adopt a long-term view and recognize that most careers are launched, not with a single fabulous manuscript, but through a series of small successes that builds the writer's network and visibility, step by step.

BRAND BUILDING

A reliable way to upset a roomful of writers is to promote the idea of "brand building." Unless you are already comfortable with the idea of running your writing career like a business, it goes against literary sensibilities to embrace the idea that you, or your writing, might be boiled down to something so vulgar. It can also feel suffocating—who wants to feel beholden to their "brand"?

I use the word "brand" to indicate strategic awareness about what type of work one is producing, how and where that work is being seen, and who is seeing it. Brand is about how you and your work are perceived. In a word, brand is *expectation*. What do readers expect from you? Like it or not, they *will* form expectations. You can wait and let it happen by accident, but it's better to consider how you can shape expectations yourself—or decide when and how to work against them.

If you haven't given this the slightest thought, a good starting exercise is to inventory everything you've written or published. What topics or themes emerge in those pieces? Where have they appeared, or who has read them? What patterns can you identify? Almost every writer is preoccupied with something, and it shows up in their work. Awareness of these preoccupations is the start of identifying your brand. Hopefully the type of writing you're doing now—whether it's published or not—bears some relation to the work you want to be known for. (If you find there's a disconnect, ask yourself why. Do you lack confidence to tackle the work that feels most important to you? Are you distracting yourself with easier writing work?)

One of the keys to building a strong brand as a writer is producing more work, and getting it out there, continually and frequently. The explanation is simple: You get better the more you practice and receive feedback, plus it helps you avoid the common psychological traps of creative work—such as waiting for the muse or for your skills to match your ambition. (Such a time never arrives!) When Ira Glass describes that problematic gap between your good taste and the quality of your early work, he also offers a solution: "The most important possible thing you can do is do a lot of work."[4]

Once you've identified patterns in your work, you have the start of a brand-related statement that you can put in your bio (discussed later in this chapter). But you want to go beyond simply listing ideas or themes; you want to tell a story about *why*. There is tremendous creative power *and* marketing power in forming a narrative around yourself and your work. Regardless of whether you're a poet or a businessperson, everyone recognizes the allure of story. To help spark the story you want to tell, consider these three questions:

- Who are you?
- How did you get here?
- What do you care about and why?[5]

Deceptively simple questions! Some people spend the greater part of their lives answering and reanswering them, so don't expect to solve this puzzle in one night. The truth is, your story (or brand) will evolve over time—it's never meant to be a static thing. It's something that grows, it's organic, and it's often unpredictable.

Another interesting exercise is to come up with a brand statement that gets at the essence of what you do without using external signifiers.

For example, creative writing students from selective programs may be tempted to say, "A graduate of [prestigious MFA program] . . ." and lean on that credit to telegraph who or what they are. This is also a common tactic if you've worked for well-known publications or won awards. Set those qualifications aside for the moment, and dig deeper: How does your creative work transcend markers of prestige or transient characteristics, such as your current job title? It's not that you should leave out signifiers (which may be an important part of your identity); rather, this exercise pushes you to think beyond resume accomplishments.

Once you have a partial handle on who you are and what you're about, you can benefit more from connecting with others and talking about others who have a similar *why*. This helps you build up a network not only of good will but of genuine relationships that will support your writing career. And relationships are key.

RELATIONSHIP BUILDING: ONLINE AND OFF

Building relationships is an activity that's largely unquantifiable, but it's foundational to every writing career. When you see a successful writer and try to trace their path to success, keep in mind that what you see are only the *visible* aspects of what they have done. Behind the scenes are mentors, other relationships, and communities that contributed to their success. (When considering the benefits of an MFA program, ask yourself, How will the relationships I develop during my studies affect my future success? If it's a good program, it most certainly will affect your trajectory for years afterward.)

There are two types of relationships to pay close attention to: (1) influencers or gatekeepers and (2) readers, fans, and evangelists. Sometimes the two groups overlap, which can provide an amazing career boost—if, for example, an editor at a prestigious publication takes a liking to you and can't stop assigning you work or talking you up to her colleagues.

Let's start with influencers. Many writers want to meet or get friendly with such people but don't know how, without appearing like a leech. One approach is simply to find ways to be useful to them—even to try to solve their problems. Follow them on social media or community sites and get a sense for where you can contribute. Respond to their calls for conversation or engagement. Write thoughtful comments on their blog if they have one. Bring things to their attention that you think merit their interest. In short: be helpful but not overbearing. At the very least, share what they're doing with your community.

If you end up at a real-life event that presents a networking opportunity, and you find yourself tongue-tied, here are two questions (proposed by author Michael Ellsberg)[6] to help you start a meaningful conversation:

- What's the most exciting thing for you right now?
- What's your biggest challenge right now?

Ask, then listen to the answers—that's the most important part by far. Perhaps there will be an opening for you to offer help or suggest further interactions. At the very least, you can draw on the conversation if you find yourself emailing or connecting with the person at another time.

But what if such opportunities rarely present themselves? One of the greatest gifts of the digital age is the ability to connect with people we wouldn't ordinarily be able to reach in person. Social media can offer immediate access to people who will actually respond and notice you. Don't forget, though—the consideration you would put into real-life interactions is also needed online. Taking the time to engage on social media is exactly like taking time to attend readings, community events, and parties where you can meet influencers or established authors. Rather than being so goal-oriented that everyone moves far, far away from you ("*Please* like me!"), you should be there to have a good time, to listen and learn, to stay in touch with like-minded people. That's why social media works best for long-term awareness and networking, not the hard sell.

Fortunately, writers—as imaginative, unique, and expressive people—have an advantage over those who use communication tools with a more antiseptic or corporate approach. Just as your work has a distinctive voice and footprint, so does (or so should) your expression online. By consistently showing up, you build awareness in the community of who you are and what you stand for. You become more visible and identifiable. (Yes, this is classic brand building!) As recognition and trust develop, you'll find that people more often think of you for opportunities, or more readily think of you, period—because they're seeing your name more often than that of someone who's not around.

When does social media reach its limits of utility? That's kind of like asking how many relationships, or how many friends, is too many. If it's starting to drag on your resources, consuming time needed for things more important to you (such a writing), then it's time to reassess. While I don't recommend analyzing your social media use when you're focused on its being, well, social, it's helpful to check in with yourself on how the activity is making you feel. Energetic or drained? Positive or anxious? Empowered or jealous? Whenever you experience more negative emotions than positive, it's time to step back and perhaps take a social media sabbatical.

As you begin to establish a name for yourself—especially by putting more work out there—social media becomes an important means of communicating with readers between book releases or publications. It helps you stay engaged with your audience and nurture your readership for the long term. We'll discuss these marketing activities more in part 4. But when you're early in your career, with little or no established readership, don't worry about engaging with readers for work that doesn't yet exist. Instead, you'll likely be focused on literary citizenship.

LITERARY CITIZENSHIP

Early in his career, writer Chris Guillebeau spent two hours every day on activities that could be described as "building relationships." He spent half a year reading the work of authors with whom he identified, and wrote them personal letters of admiration, asking for nothing in return. He also talked them up to the small audience he had. When he managed to attract a new reader, he sent a short personal message of acknowledgment. As a result, when he started producing his own work in earnest, he had a group of people supporting him and spreading the word.[7] This was not only good relationship building but good literary citizenship.

"Literary citizenship" is a term thought to have originated with Rob Spillman, editor of *Tin House* literary journal. It's widely used to refer to activities that support reading, writing, and publishing in the literary community. The thinking is that if one wants to build a life that's sustained by the literary community, one should be a good citizen of that community by promoting or bringing attention to others' work in some form. In other words, much of your public activity (online or off) should be *other*-focused, not centered on your own stuff.

I find this to be a more palatable (or friendly) way for some writers to think of career building. What I've always liked about the literary citizenship movement is that it's simple for people to understand and practice— it's easy to talk about the writers or books one loves—and it aligns well with the values of the literary community. Furthermore, it operates on an abundance mindset, as opposed to a zero-sum game where your gain is someone else's loss, so we must hoard resources and attention. In an abundance mindset, there's plenty of both to go around. If I'm doing well, that's going to help you, so let's collaborate rather than compete.

There have, however, been moments of backlash. Writer Becky Tuch suggests that literary citizenship puts a positive spin on the lack of marketing support from publishers, passing off marketing activities as "enrichment," and thus exploiting writers. She asks us to question and challenge this system and the corporate publishers that make literary citizenship necessary.[8]

My take on this problem is quite different: the backlash clearly demonstrates the negative attitude literary writers have toward the business of writing. The default belief is that marketing activities are undesirable and should be handled by someone else—they suck time away from the more valuable activity of creating art. Consider the prevalence of the literary author who proclaims, "I don't write for readers." In other words, engaging with or even thinking of an audience is seen to lessen the art. This strikes me as a problematic stance for anyone who wishes to make a living through their writing. Financial success depends on reaching a readership, and the belief that serious writers don't market their own work, and would lose more than gain by doing so—and thus should rely on publishers to do the "dirty work"—is unhelpful and misguided.

Most of us don't buy books because of who published them; we buy them because of the author. If we don't know the author, we may be intrigued by the book's premise or topic—or buy based on word of mouth. Publishers try to encourage this word of mouth, but few of them have brand recognition with readers, because they haven't traditionally been direct-to-consumer companies. Instead, they've sold to middlemen—bookstores, libraries, wholesalers. In the last ten years, authors have gained tools to connect directly with readers—tools they never had before—which give them tremendous power amid the disruptions now unsettling the publishing industry. Publishers are catching up in their use of these tools as well, but their efforts will never be as effective as when they can build on an author's outreach and involvement with readers.

When teaching at the University of Virginia, I require students to collaborate on a publishing project. The projects can be difficult to administer in a traditional classroom environment and aren't typical of writing classes, but the challenge is worth the effort. Early on, I require that each student research people who might have a natural interest in the content or goals of their publication—identifying an online or offline community who cares. I also encourage them to speak up to the first and most important circle of relationships for any writer: friends and family who want them to succeed and are willing to spread the word about their project. But by semester's end, they always express the same regrets:

CHAPTER 2

- "I should've posted more often to my friends what I was writing."
- "I wish I'd done a better job connecting with people who could've helped."
- "I didn't start spreading the word soon enough."
- "It was so hard to get readers. I wish I had tried different tactics sooner."

Always remember Shirky: to publish is easy; to get attention is hard. To secure the attention they desire, writers are often advised to "engage with the community," or "be an authentic member of the community," or "share valuable content with the community." But what does it mean to engage with a community? Bottom line: it means talking about stuff you care about. Writers who are not prolific, whose careers may move more slowly, can benefit most from practicing literary citizenship, becoming more visible to their community primarily by never shutting up—on social media and elsewhere—about the ideas and issues they care about. Remember: literary citizenship isn't about focusing on yourself; it's about focusing outward. You don't "own" or control a community, and you don't necessarily build one. You participate or engage with one. To be a recognized community member means operating so as to generate respect and trust. If you try to use the community to fulfill only your own goals (like selling a book), the community will respond less enthusiastically over time.

THE ART OF PITCHING

I use the term "pitching" very broadly, to include any communication where you're trying to obtain an opportunity. It could be publication, a writing fellowship, or simply fifteen minutes of someone's time. Learning how to pitch yourself and your work is a function of several variables:

- understanding the needs or motivations of the person or business you're targeting
- having something desirable or being someone desirable (or faking either)
- approaching at the right time
- reflecting confidence (or charm)
- being lucky

The biggest pitching mistake by far is *wasting someone's time*, and there are many ways to do this, such as sending inappropriate or overly detailed material, or approaching the wrong person entirely. The best safeguard against wasting someone's time is doing your homework and truly understanding—to the best of your ability—who you're approaching. If you can *show* that you've done your homework, your target may be more inclined to consider you thoughtful and respectful. Even if an initial pitch fails, a positive first impression will work to your benefit in any future interaction.

The shrewdest networkers look for opportunities—whether at conferences, at bookstore readings, or online—that offer more insight about potential targets than might be available through official channels. (The best opportunities offer a chance to ask questions.) Observant writers take note of the personalities and preferences of people they meet, so they can make their pitches more effective—even if a pitch happens five years down the road. Few things impress me more as an editor than a personalized note that expresses specific knowledge about where I've been and what I do. But it's not common. Most people who approach editors do little homework but expect big gains. It's not an endearing quality.

Some people can get away with little to no knowledge of their target because they have something to offer that is highly desirable in the marketplace. (Note that I'm avoiding the word "quality." First, quality is subjective. Second, even high-quality work doesn't always succeed, often as a result of market concerns. That said, a great salesperson may overcome objections by framing their work to emphasize the most desirable qualities. That's not lying; that's good pitching. Don't dwell on what is not advantageous to you.) But how do you know if what you have—say, a book idea—is desirable in the market? While you can read trade publications such as *Publishers Lunch* or *Publishers Weekly*, you can stay in touch with the publishing zeitgeist by simply being well-read in your genre and aware of what's regularly getting published at the biggest literary websites (e.g., *The Millions*, LitHub). What pieces are people talking about? What's on the best-seller lists? Immersion in what's getting published gives you a feel for whether you're with the trends or against them.

Timing is mostly out of your control; it works on both a macro and a micro level. Macro level: something about your writing is currently out of fashion. Micro level: a publication just accepted something that's too similar to your proposed work. The latter is an issue of luck, which we'll get to later. The former is unfortunate, but not a deal breaker. I believe what Paul Graham says: "If you do anything well enough, you'll *make* it prestigious."[9] When you commit yourself entirely to the pursuit of something, that produces excellence, and that is intoxicating for people who want to be close to excellence. Excellence takes time to develop, and time for people to notice. No one was publishing boarding school fantasies for middle-grade and young adult readers at the time J. K. Rowling was submitting the first *Harry Potter* manuscript. But publishers became deluged with such work once her series became successful.

You might be tempted to ask agents and editors at conferences, "What's selling right now? What are the trends?" They are accustomed to hearing that question and will try to answer, but they'll also issue a warning: By the time you complete your trendy manuscript, the trend will likely be over. And while it can be helpful to educate yourself about market demand for certain types of work, I don't recommend you chase trends, because your heart isn't likely to be in it.

Even when everything else is in place, writers have to learn to pitch in a way that's relaxed but confident. Some writers labor over their pitch, or experience sky-high anxiety, but that's *not* something you want the pitch to convey—unless it comes off as charming. (Some writers are able to pull this off, but it requires acute self-awareness.) Unfortunately, I don't find most writers to be intrinsically charming when it comes to pitching. Part of the problem is that writers lack exposure to a wide variety of pitches or submissions; without having read a great many good and bad ones, it's hard to know where you're at on the spectrum of detail, voice, and persuasion. One solution is to find an environment where you are exposed to pitches, such as working for a magazine or journal; it's by far the best training to improve your own. But the solution for most writers is simply to pitch a lot. You get better the more that you do it, as with so many things.

It's helpful if you're a lucky person—or *believe* yourself to be a lucky person. Richard Wiseman, a psychologist at the University of Hertfordshire, studied groups of people who strongly identified themselves as either lucky or unlucky. He found that one's own belief or mindset creates one's luck. The so-called unlucky people restricted what they were looking for and missed chance opportunities, whereas the lucky people remained more relaxed and open, more likely to see the opportunities that sprang up in front of them.[10]

Finally, it's useful to remember the famous line from Seneca: "Luck is what happens when preparation meets opportunity." Writers tend to get increasingly lucky the more work they produce (preparation) and the more work they submit (opportunity). Too many writers throw in the towel after a few bad experiences or rejections, believing that's the final verdict on their work—giving up just before a potential win. That's why resilience in the face of rejection and disappointment is perhaps the biggest key to success in pitching. You can't let "no" stop your progress. A single no is rarely meaningful. Even a thousand no's might not be. Take time to regroup and reflect—even to wallow when a pitch fails—but then get back to work.

THE ART OF THE BIO

It's such a small thing, an innocuous bit of copy that can be passed over quickly, even ignored. But when your writing makes an impression, one of the first things a reader will ask is "Who wrote this?" Your biographical note thus represents an opportunity to establish a meaningful connection and potentially draw opportunities to you—and this is just scratching the surface of your bio's importance. A brief bio accompanies nearly everything you do: the publication of your work, your appearances, your social media profiles, your website, and so on. Whenever you're in a position to be noticed, people will see your bio. What story do you want to tell?

Some writers don't say anything substantive—and this is true of both emerging and established writers. So be careful. You won't necessarily learn how to write a better bio by modeling yours on those of successful writers. As I write this, one of the most popular and recognized literary writers uses a bio note that says, "X is a writer." Tendencies toward brevity and understatement can often be chalked up shyness or modesty. (Women especially need to rethink this approach, but I've found men using the modest bio as well.) But for some writers with short bios, it's an attempt to convey status. Famous authors are known for the one-liner—and, of course, when you're Toni Morrison, what's needed except your name? Other writers may be buying into the romance of the introverted author whom one should never know *too* well.

While there may be good reason to appear mysterious, it's still possible to say something meaningful and helpful for your career. Especially if you're emerging, getting noticed is part of the game, and unless more amazing opportunities are landing in your lap than you can possibly accept, it's not to your advantage to be overly coy. That's not to say it's easy to write about yourself. Most writers find it painful to write even fifty words without sounding overly earnest or terribly self-important. But the challenge is worth your attention.

Writing the Bio

If you're tackling a professional bio for the first time, start by listing the most important facts about your writing career, what topics or themes interest you, and where people can find more of your work. While the information may seem boring or rote, your delivery or style doesn't have to be.

The facts provide the foundation for your bio, but don't limit yourself to the facts. Make your short-term or long-term goals apparent. If you're working on a book or collection, mention it. If you're hoping for freelance gigs, then give us a sense, or tell us explicitly, that you're a freelance writer, and do so in the first few lines. It's also acceptable to flat-out describe your dream job or aspirations. One well-established journalist puts in his bio that his dream sponsor is Campari. This both demonstrates what work he's seeking and gives us a glimpse of his personality.

Because one of the main purposes of the bio is to encourage people to contact you with opportunities or follow your updates, provide a link to your website, online portfolio, or anywhere else you're active. You don't have to offer a laundry list of all your social media accounts. In most cases, you'll refer people to your website (see chapter 20), where they can further explore your work and background. And this brings us to the first bio you should write, the kitchen-sink bio.

The *kitchen-sink bio* includes all the detail you are willing to offer on your experience and background. This bio is usually reserved for your author website only. I recommend 200–300 words, if not more, depending on your career history. Try to answer the questions discussed under "Brand Building," particularly the first two: Who am I? How did I get here? It helps if you think in terms of telling a story or building a back story, which writers happen to be good at. While there are many ways to write such a bio, it should convey something of your voice, personality, or point of view. This detailed bio is primarily for the most interested people—editors, agents, or influencers who have read your work somewhere and are now scoping out your website or blog.

The *capsule bio* is often easy to write once you have a long version to work from. Create a 50–100 word bio that would be appropriate to run with your published articles. In this short bio, it's important to offer an explicit statement of your writing goals, and include external validators—where you've been published, where you've worked, awards you've won, anything that lends social proof. For example, a regional freelancer's bio might include, "Focused on issues of poverty and the disenfranchised in Virginia and the winner of three SPJ awards."

As best you can, retain a point of view or voice, and offer one or two human touches, details with the potential to create that "something in common." For example, when I was invited to sit on a panel at the National

Endowment for the Arts, I was told that the mention of being a "late-sleeping editor" in my bio added a bit of personality that indicated I was probably not so bad to work with. If you're looking for inspiration on the task ahead of you, it's worth getting a copy of *Michael Martone: Fictions* by Michael Martone, comprised entirely of contributors' notes.

Social media bios work best if they're customized by channel. Every social media site has a slightly different demographic, and you may have differing goals or patterns of behavior at each one. Many people forget to put a public bio on their Facebook profile, which is a mistake—you never know who might read the public parts of that profile.

If you have a book launch coming up, or if you find yourself receiving frequent media or publicity requests, you should write a *professional bio*, in which the first 100–150 words nail the most important aspects of your career. That's crucial because this bio will be cribbed by third parties for marketing and publicity purposes. If it helps, think of the newspaper journalist's "inverted pyramid," where you pack the opening with the hard-hitting facts, and leave the least important information for the end. A professional bio can be very long (500 words or more), but busy people won't read it all. Interviewers, journalists, and especially publicists will often grab copy from your site and paste it right into whatever document they're working on. If you've already done the work of concisely summarizing your career in the opening lines, you've done them, and yourself, a favor: they can lift it word for word, giving you more control over how you're presented. But beware: they may crib just your first sentence or two, even if it does not present you well or even intelligibly.

THE ELEPHANT IN THE ROOM

It's common to hear writers objecting to career building activities on the grounds of introversion or the idea that serious writing requires solitude. In the literary community—especially creative writing programs—it is more or less accepted at face value that brand building and social communications are detrimental to the writer's work. Maybe, maybe not. Such thinking reflects a romantic approach, not to mention privilege. It is a luxury to have time to write but not bear responsibility for bringing attention to one's writing. It is a luxury not to market and promote oneself, to leave such matters to publishers or hired help. Most writers do not have that luxury, especially if they're emerging, and especially if they intend to pursue writing as a full-time living. Always pay attention to who is criticizing career-building activities. Is it an author who is already established, now choosing between more opportunities than they could possibly accept? An author who established themselves in the days before the internet was an active force? Once you're established, you too can be selective about how and where you'll spend your time.

3 : GENERATING LEADS, GAINING EXPOSURE

A sustainable writing career, not buffeted by the winds of luck and chance, requires a business model. And one of the fundamental steps in developing a business model is creating (or identifying) demand and finding leads. Creating demand for your work isn't easy early in your career. If you've ever felt invisible to editors and agents, and frustrated by their lack of response, then you know what I'm talking about.

Generating "leads" helps alleviate this problem, but it's not a practice writers are likely to have been taught. The term comes from the sales and marketing industry: a lead is a prospect, anyone with the potential to advance your business. For writers, a lead may be someone in a position to buy your work (an editor or publisher), to share your work with the right people, or to otherwise hook you up with an opportunity that might become a paycheck.

Writers tend to be short on leads, especially when they're unpublished, working outside of the publishing industry, or unaffiliated with a writing program or mentor. Worse, such writers may lack the kind of authority that would help them command desirable assignments or good rates of pay. This encourages greater acceptance of opportunities that are about "exposure" rather than pay.

Working for exposure has a bad reputation across all creative professions. In the writing community in particular, it's seen as exploitative and devaluing of the cultural work writers do. But everything depends on context. Writing for free is not intrinsically bad, and neither is writing for exposure. Demonizing every instance of "writing for exposure" does a disservice to writers whose best and most ready tool for establishing their careers may be, in fact, writing for free. If such activity leads to paying work (if it is *successful* lead generation), then it's a smart move. If it leads to insufficient career opportunities, then it should be abandoned.

Even established writers may write for exposure. Most commonly, it happens in the service of book marketing or promotion. Writers in demand may be able to score twice: they can get paid for their writing *and* use it to promote a new book. At other times, though, a well-known writer may work for less than usual, or for free, to reach a new audience or further some larger goal.

To be clear, this discussion isn't meant to excuse editors or publishers who seek quality writing for free; the truth is, most publications get exactly what they pay for. There is a very wide spectrum of legitimate publishing practice, and while writers may choose not to work with publications that don't pay—so as not to encourage that model—as long as writing supply outpaces demand, the practice will continue. I don't believe the value of writing is approaching zero, or that it's meant to be distributed for free or as a gift. However, some writing does indeed have a *market value* of zero; the reason may be general, because there's more supply than demand, or because neither readers nor publishers are willing to pay for the particular product. Writers can avoid frustration by not trying to sell something of low perceived value in the marketplace, especially if their name holds no weight. For such work, it makes more sense to find a method of patronage (grants, fellowships, crowdfunding) or self-distribution that attracts a readership—a form of currency in itself.

Successful lead generation requires writing and sharing things, emblematic of you and your work, that have the potential to reach a large or influential audience. I like to call such things "cheese cubes"—a tasty sample of what you're capable of producing.[1] The people who become most invested will want the premium cheese basket: the highest value offering you have, customized just for them. Publishing expert Richard Nash often talks of how each writer has a "demand curve." At one end of the curve, you offer something for free to the largest possible audience; at the other end, you provide something that's expensive to a small number of individuals.[2] Writers need to envision their *entire* demand curve, and all the potential price points for the work they do, not just the part of the curve that's most obvious (the book sale, the freelance article fee, and so on). What could you charge 99 cents for, and how many people would show up at 99 cents? What could you charge $4.99 for? What could you charge $1,000 for? This kind of exploratory thinking gets you outside of the conventional ways writers have earned a living, and into territory that will more likely benefit how you need to work and want to work to earn a livelihood.

Bottom line: it's smart for writers to make some amount of content available for free—whether through their own platform, social media, or publications—as part of a strategy of continually generating leads. In the remainder of this chapter, I'll introduce some of the key avenues for lead generation and familiarize you with the ideas behind the concept. The nitty-gritty details can be found later, primarily in part 4. If you don't fully understand some of this now, you will later.

These lead generation activities won't work well, however, without due diligence on other aspects of your platform. For example, lack of an author website can prevent leads from contacting you, while cryptic social media profiles that don't even use your real name can hamper your efforts. The foundation of a writer's online presence is explored more fully in chapter 20.

MICRO-PUBLISHING ON SOCIAL MEDIA

Very often, I'm asked to speak on social media at writing conferences. Sometimes, even when I'm *not* speaking specifically on social media, audience questions focus on the topic because it remains an area of anxiety—something writers feel they "ought" to do but don't know how to do without it becoming a distraction or burden.

While I don't think using social media is mandatory, you may cut off significant opportunities if you exclude it from your arsenal. Many consider social media a marketing and promotional tool, but it is just as much a creative writing and publishing tool: each post shares a tiny bit of a story, message, or perspective. Social media posts can spark or contribute to a larger work, as in the case of Roxane Gay, whose posts on Tumblr about eating healthier and finding a tolerable form of exercise led to a book deal for *Hunger*.[3] Because social media work is usually, by default, in the public eye, it's an excellent form of lead generation. Sharing aspects of your work in public for free can help you gain insight into how your audience thinks and engages with your work, which can inspire more excitement and enthusiasm to pursue a project—and enlighten you as to market demand. Some examples to consider:

- Children's author and illustrator Debbie Ohi posts a daily doodle on social media; it's part of her creative practice.[4]
- Poet and editor Robert Brewer issues a poem-a-day challenge in April to get himself and his community producing poetry.[5]
- I post infographics on Pinterest to keep tabs on industry change, and use them as reference points in my talks, and also to benefit others.[6]

Far from a burden, for some writers these activities are inseparable from their creative pursuits. Social media doesn't have to feel like a drag if you shift your perspective; rather than seeing it as isolated from (if not competing with) your writing work, it can be approached as a creative practice that shares aspects—as it takes shape. Austin Kleon, in *Show Your Work!*, argues for the benefits of such activity: "If you want people to know about what you do and the things you care about, you have to share." Doing so isn't necessarily about self-promotion. By using your voice, and using it more often, you find it. "Talk about the things you love," Kleon urges. "Your voice will follow."[7]

Whatever goals you have, meaningful social media activity can draw upon the same creativity and imagination that fuels your "serious" work. And if not, it can provide a much-needed break from it. In an interview, I asked Richard Nash how he responds to writers who say, more or less, "I just want to write," undistracted by what they see as trivial "sharing" activities online. He said, "No one wants to just sit and write! Even Beckett didn't want to just sit and write—seriously! If Beckett can't abide just sitting down and writing, then any writer can find emotional and cultural stimulation by engaging with society. The two are not mutually exclusive."[8]

BLOGGING

Blogging is one of the most common forms of lead generation, particularly for nonfiction writers. But it can also be one of the least successful methods of lead generation. It's no easy task to make your blog visible to the right audience, and few people pursue blogging with the consistency required to generate a meaningful return. Expectations can also be misguided: if one sets out strictly to land a book deal, disappointment is likely to follow. The most lauded blog-to-book deals (such as *Julie & Julia* and *Humans of New York*) were rarely initiated with that outcome in mind, and it's a hard process to intentionally engineer. While it can be done, most writers don't have a clue how to build an audience large enough that an agent or editor is likely to come calling.

That said, my blog, now in its eighth year, is one of the most important ways I make money and my number-one method of lead generation. The value of my blog content attracts hundreds of thousands of visitors every month, and ranks at the top of Google searches for how to write and get published. Significant opportunities come from that, from all directions— I attract businesses and publishers who want to hire me, and I attract people who want to buy my books and courses. Blogging is further discussed in chapter 18.

WRITING FOR FREE

For those who don't have the stamina or personality to blog successfully, writing articles for well-regarded websites is usually the next best thing, if not the best thing. The key is careful selection and targeting—the same scrupulous research you direct toward publications that pay for your writing.

While it's common for writers (and advertisers) to place higher value on a venue with significant traffic, a better way to evaluate potential sites is to look at the engagement of the readership. Are there active comment threads or Facebook pages? Do people spend a lot of time on the site—is the site "sticky"? (You can figure this out by using a free tool such as SimilarWeb to check average time spent on the site—ideally, two minutes or more.) Usually the more focused and niche the site, the more engaged the readership, which is what you're looking for. Blogs by a single person or small organization can be among the most effective places to appear because the content is well curated and promoted.

With very large sites, where the publication model is advertising-based and driven by quantity—such as the *Huffington Post*—it can be a crapshoot as to whether your freely offered content will achieve your goals. Your piece might be buried under an avalanche of other free content, and whether it surfaces depends on a combination of your own effort and the strength of the headline—as well as the publication's placement or promotion of your piece.

So do your homework on the sites you might contribute to. Study the number of shares as well as the comments on its pieces. Check out the publication's social media feeds, and see how well they support contributors' published pieces. Study other guest contributors to the site, as well as its editors and staff, and see if becoming a contributor yourself might open doors that would further your career. Writing for free often requires *you* to make the most of the opportunity, rather than sitting back and waiting for good things to happen.

WRITING RELATED TO LITERARY CITIZENSHIP

Under the umbrella of "literary citizenship," you may write, discuss, or curate things related to what you're reading. There's a near-avalanche of excellent sites, blogs, and social media accounts that offer regular book reviews (formal and informal), roundups of new book releases, and interviews with authors of all kinds. (Examples include LitHub, *The Millions*, and BookRiot.) Sometimes, producing such content isn't so much a means of generating leads (unless you want to produce interviews and reviews that you get paid for) as it is of building relationships and connecting to potential influencers. When you review an author's book or interview them, they're going to take notice of you, likely thank you, and perhaps pay back the favor when your book releases.

If you'd like writing about books and reading to be a primary and perhaps profitable activity, try to narrow your focus to a particular theme, genre, or type of author—ideally, this focus will have something in common with you or your work. This helps distinguish your activity from everything else out there. Positioning your online writing (or blogging) is discussed further in chapter 18.

PUBLISHING IN LITERARY JOURNALS

Writing and publishing in print-based literary journals that don't pay is among the weakest types of lead generation because few people may see the publication, the content is rarely available to be shared online, and it's typically incumbent on the writer to spread the word that they've recently had a publication success. That doesn't mean it's a bad strategy to publish in such journals—only that it's not likely to lead to a string of paying work, unless one is trying to build up a CV for a teaching position.

One important caveat: if you publish in a journal avidly read by literary agents, editors, or influencers, it can serve as a stepping-stone to a book deal or other paying opportunities. Also, placing work in a publication that regularly has pieces selected for anthologies or awards increases your chances of making that credit *really* count, and being seen by more people. That prompts the question of which journals are the "important" ones. Several writers, including Clifford Garstang and John Fox, tabulate and post rankings of literary journals based on the number of their pieces that receive accolades, such as the Pushcart Prize. While the results are highly variable, they can point you in the right direction.[9]

Award-winning fiction writer Yiyun Li placed her first short story in the *Paris Review*, prior to becoming an MFA student in the Iowa Writers Workshop. She had been circulating the story for two years before the acceptance. In an essay about her publishing success, Yi writes:

The story was soon in print, and that, along with a few other pieces published in 2003, started my career—I was signed up by an agent, and at the end of the year sold my first two books. When the story was awarded the inaugural Plimpton Prize, for a while it became the center of a controversy, as it seemed improbable that a story from the slush pile, unaccompanied by a recommendation from an established author or a series of pressing phone calls from an agent, could see itself in print.[10]

I find this story remarkable not because Li lacked connections, but because she landed book deals so quickly as a literary novelist—and became so immediately acclaimed. Of course, Li herself emphasizes the hours of work that prefaced this success, but that notwithstanding, the likelihood of other writers copying her trajectory is about zero. Such well-publicized cases unfortunately can become the secret expectation for other creative writers. While you may end up being an exception like Li, don't base your career plan on it.

OFFLINE OPPORTUNITIES

For writers who prefer to avoid online activity, then organizing or least attending community events can provide connections that lead to paying work. For example, in nearly every region—especially where universities are nearby—it's possible to find a regular reading series. Urban centers may have a literary center where writing classes are taught (such as The Loft in Minneapolis) or an annual book festival. Being the instigator or leader of any community literary activity puts you in a position to connect with more people, particularly influencers, and become better known as a writer. But it requires far more social grace and extroversion than social media—which should call into question the prevailing myth that social media is somehow best for extroverts!

BE PATIENT

Each writer will be different as to how they best generate leads. Some will pursue writing for free or perhaps blog, others will do better with social media, and another group may excel by participating at networking events. The challenge isn't a lack of opportunities to generate leads but the average writer's lack of time, patience, or stamina. Some strategies, such as blogging, take time to pay off—it's rarely a quick win—and not all lead generation will be successful, so tolerance for failure is necessary. I would have considered my blogging or Twitter use a failure had I stopped after the first eighteen months. But I stuck with them because I genuinely enjoyed the activities, and they paid off as essential building blocks to my livelihood as a writer.

As the Zanders discuss in *The Art of Possibility*, we can fail to see opportunities right in front of us because we're focused on the shortcomings of the system—maybe we find it exploitative or antithetical to our values.[11] But abundance for writers exists out there—if you can frame the situation so that you see yourself as a proactive player on a path to writing success, not someone passively waiting to be discovered.

4 : PURSUING AN MFA OR
OTHER GRADUATE DEGREE

Deciding to pursue a master of fine arts (MFA) in creative writing means you are largely committing to one thing: you want to devote serious time and attention to your craft. When MFA programs advertise the success of their graduates, that success is predicated on one, overarching belief: that they produce writers who accomplish great things because they produce writers who have achieved artistic excellence.

Accomplishment, however, does not always follow from artistic excellence. There are also commercial factors, salesmanship, timing, luck, and connections. MFA programs can provide valuable connections. But they have no control over timing or luck and, until recently, haven't devoted much attention to helping students navigate the publishing industry and sell what they create.

Perhaps more importantly, accomplishment does not equate to earning a full-time living from writing. The majority of graduates of MFA programs earn little from the writing they produce, rarely a living. So an MFA program is not necessarily the best choice to advance a writing career, given that the average student will be thousands of dollars in debt when they graduate, and likely pressured to finding paying work of the nonwriting variety.

However, there can also be excellent reasons to invest in an MFA program. First, as mentioned, they afford you precious and required time to focus on craft, often to the exclusion of all else. There may be teaching requirements or a graduate assistantship, but you're there to get writing done and be among people who value writing and writing time above all else. That kind of unwavering devotion to the craft can lead to creative breakthroughs, important relationships with career-long mentors and peers, and—yes—publication.

Second, for writers interested in teaching, an MFA is a terminal degree that can lead to tenure-track positions in creative writing programs. But—and this is critical to understand—there are thousands more graduates of creative writing programs than there are teaching positions available. Especially tenure-track positions, which are becoming rarer at nearly every university, while the proportion of adjunct and part-time positions increases. The competition for a permanent position, even at a small, unknown school, is stiff. Candidates must have a strong track record of publication—usually at least one book from a well-known press—and satisfy other considerable requirements, such as a record of teaching excellence. Furthermore, MFA programs may prefer or demand candidates with PhDs in creative writing, which calls into question whether the MFA is truly a terminal degree. Bottom line: an MFA alone won't lead to a sustainable teaching career; it's merely the first step.

Third, it can be worthwhile to enroll in an MFA program based solely on its faculty and networking opportunities. If faculty members are invested in seeing their students succeed; if you hope to achieve what they have achieved; if you're confident it will move your career to the next level to study under a specific writer—those are relevant and motivating factors to pursue an MFA. But it's wise to schedule a visit or series of appointments before committing, to confirm there's good chemistry between you and the faculty members. Don't take it on faith that you'll love any program or faculty sight unseen—get as much exposure as possible beforehand.

Finally, if you're interested in an MFA program and obtain full funding—or can otherwise ensure you'll have no debt when you graduate—you'll find few (if any) other opportunities during your lifetime as a writer to spend two or three years focused full-time on developing your art.

MFA programs have largely focused on producing writers who would be considered "literary" in the marketplace. "Literary" in publishing speak is sometimes code for "doesn't sell," although cream-of-the-crop literary novelists (e.g., Jonathan Franzen, Zadie Smith, Donna Tartt, Jonathan Safran Foer) can bank on reaching the *New York Times* best-seller list with each new book. But these are outlying cases, and no writer should count on being an outlier. Rather, assume you'll be among the majority of literary writers who do not enjoy sufficient commercial success to earn a full-time living. Poets, short story writers, and personal essayists in particular need to prepare themselves to earn next to nothing as they begin their careers.

If you're not interested in producing literary work, or if you want to pursue a career as a freelancer or journalist, an MFA makes less sense, although a handful of MFA programs offer concentrations in popular or commercial categories such as young adult fiction. Both freelancers and journalists might improve their craft in an MFA program, but they won't learn a thing about the business or the marketplace for selling their work, which is just as important (if not more so) than the writing itself. It's not an exaggeration to say that an MFA could even be detrimental to a successful freelance career, because it trains you to be aware of how writing succeeds, not on a commercial level, but only on an artistic one—which you may then need to be trained *out* of.

If you have little interest in teaching as part of your living, think hard about why you should obtain a degree. If its sole purpose is to allow you to focus on your writing, is there some other approach that would help you achieve the same outcome? Could you pursue a series of fellowships or grants instead (see chapter 26)? What if you sought a degree with a more practical slant, but with writing still at its core—such as a professional writing degree?

This brings us to the alternatives to an MFA in creative writing, such as master's degrees in publishing, professional writing, and journalism. These degrees are intended not just for writers but also those interested in working in the publishing industry as editors, marketers, and business leaders. These programs can be useful for learning the art *and* the business, but evaluate them carefully. Does the faculty have industry experience, and do they actively produce work for the current market? What partnerships does the program have with publishing companies or publications? Do graduates land at companies you envision working for? Be wary of programs that appear to focus on producing work for the university community; the best experience involves writing, editing, and publishing for more mainstream or commercial audiences. Professional writing programs should also offer training related to digital forms of writing and publishing. If the graduate program seems to fetishize print, prioritize literary work, or minimize commercial forms of publication, look elsewhere.

While such degrees can be useful, they are not required. You don't need a journalism degree to work as a journalist, and you don't need a degree in publishing to work at a magazine or book publishing house. The majority of employees currently working in publishing don't have specialized master's degrees, nor is it expected that applicants will have them. By far the best way to learn about writing and publishing is to go out and find as many opportunities as possible to write and publish in real-world situations. Never forget this when considering degree programs: if a paid job opportunity becomes available that would put you in the middle of what you want to be good at—or what you want a full-time career doing—take the job and forget the degree. For more on publishing careers, see chapter 30.

Part Two
UNDERSTANDING THE
PUBLISHING INDUSTRY

The chapters that follow provide an overview of the major sectors of the publishing industry that you'll likely work in as a writer. Each reinforces the fact that publishing is a business, not so much because that is in question but because writers often forget what drives decision-making at the end of the day: the bottom line. All publishers use P&Ls, or profit-and-loss statements, to evaluate the health of their business and determine what publishing projects have the best chance of succeeding in the market. We'll take a look at simplified versions of P&Ls and how they work, which is often an eye-opening exercise for writers with limited business skills.

However, not *every* decision is driven by the bottom line or *only* the bottom line. In fact, the deepest, most persistent tension in the publishing industry, no matter where you go or whom you talk to, is art versus commerce. If you ask any editor or publishing industry professional, "Why do you do it?" they almost respond that they believe their work is important to society, art, or culture. People in publishing believe that what they do fundamentally *matters* to life as we know it. And if you're reading this book, you likely agree.

Still, there's a broad range of material produced across the publishing industry. Some of it might qualify as art, but some is produced purely for profit. More often than not, the profitable work helps subsidize what's considered art. If I had to choose a symbol to represent publishers, it would be Janus, the two-faced god, with one eye always on art, and the other always on commerce. Most publishers can't survive long unless they balance the two.

The last chapter in this section takes a special look at literary publishing and the challenges it faces during the digital revolution. Literary work has often been gifted into existence by patronage of one form or another, and some patrons (such as universities) aren't as reliable as they once were. Basing one's operations on the continued good will of a patron can be a perilous situation; thus, literary ventures are under pressure to establish sustainable business models (either nonprofit or for-profit), the same as every writer.

Understanding how the business models of publishing work will help you make better-informed decisions about your own career—plus this section will provide a critical foundation if you're considering whether and how to launch a publishing operation of your own. While the industry information is current as of this writing, the publishing industry is ever evolving. Details may change.

5 : TRADE BOOK PUBLISHING

While some people imagine there was a golden era of book publishing where selecting and producing the best literature took priority—when art was more important than commerce—today's book publishing industry has its roots in Gutenberg-era printers, a distinctly commercial lineage. Since the invention of printing, publishers have remained fairly consistent in their profit-driven approach, even as authors' business models and attitudes have shifted over time. As discussed in chapter 1, in the early days of authorship, you had to be of high birth or have patrons to support your writing. It wasn't until the eighteenth century, with the spread of literacy, that authorship became tied to the commercial success of a book.

Since the days of Gutenberg, authors have complained about the money-grubbing tendencies of book publishers and booksellers, who until the nineteenth century were typically one and the same. Even Horace, a Roman poet in the first century BC, warned writers of the Sosii, the brothers who published his work and were, in his view, less than honest in their business dealings. Yet he also acknowledged that without their efforts, his work would never have become so well known throughout the Roman Empire.

In publishers' defense, authors have historically held unreasonable expectations. When authors' complaints reached a critical mass in the late nineteenth century, publisher G. H. Putnam wrote a "manual of suggestions for beginners in literature" that outlined operating standards and sought to improve the PR surrounding publishing companies. In 1897, he argued that when literary workers complain, it's because they don't understand the business of making and selling books, nor their actual rights and obligations.[1]

When most people think of book publishing, what they're envisioning are the Big Five. These New York–based publishers, all owned by media conglomerates, produce the majority of "trade" books in the United States, or books meant for a general audience. Publishing wasn't always

THE LARGEST US PUBLISHERS

These are the top companies publishing books for a mainstream, general audience in the United States.

1. Penguin Random House. With more than 250 imprints worldwide, PRH releases 15,000 new titles every year, or 25 percent of the world's English-language books. It is easily twice the size of the next four publishers on this list combined. Owned jointly by Pearson and Bertelsmann, with Bertelsmann soon expected to buy out Pearson's share.[a]

2. HarperCollins. Of its more than 65 imprints,[b] one of the best known is Harlequin, which it acquired in 2014. Owned by News Corp.

3. Simon & Schuster. Publishes about 2,000 titles per year under 35 imprints, including Atria, Pocket, and Scribner.[c] Owned by CBS.

4. Hachette Book Group. A subsidiary of the French media company Hachette Livre, releases about 1,000 books per year.[d] One of its best-known imprints is Little, Brown.

5. Macmillan. The smallest of the Big Five, its imprints include Farrar, Straus and Giroux and St. Martin's Press.

6. As of 2017, Scholastic is the sixth-largest publisher. It has rights to the *Harry Potter* series in the United States, one of the best-selling series of all time.

a. Penguin Random House (website), "Imprints," accessed July 4, 2016, http://www.penguinrandomhouse.com/imprints.

b. Erin Crum, "Harpercollins Publishers Forms Harpercollins Germany: Plans Expansion of Foreign Language Publishing," HarperCollins Publishers (website), October 8, 2014, http://corporate.harpercollins.com/us/press-releases/414/HarperCollins%20Publishers%20Forms%20HarperCollins%20Germany.

c. "Simon & Schuster," Wikipedia, June 30, 2016, https://en.wikipedia.org/w/index.php?title=Simon_%26_Schuster&oldid=727740357.

d. Carolyn Kellogg, "Amazon and Hachette: The Dispute in 13 Easy Steps," *Los Angeles Times*, June 3, 2014, http://www.latimes.com/books/jacketcopy/la-et-jc-amazon-and-hachette-explained-20140602-story.html.

---

consolidated into the hands of a few media companies, but consolidation began in the 1980s and 1990s and has never really stopped. Larger publishers have bought smaller ones, and multimedia companies have bought the big publishers. Eventually, the Big Five are expected to become the Big Four, or perhaps even the Big Three.

One might ask whether all this consolidation has been good for authors. It does reduce competition, since imprints within the same house won't bid against each other for books. Also, in part due to consolidation, the Big Five have been accused of producing homogenous work.[2] Whether that accusation is fair or not (what some call a drift toward mediocrity others defend as "risk aversion"), publishers are reliably interested in work that demonstrates commercial potential from the outset. The bright side is that the Big Five's focus on mass-market, commercial work provides an opening for quality midsize and small publishers to operate in the markets they've abandoned or neglected.

While Big Five imprints fill probably 75 percent of the shelf space in the average bookstore you walk into, and have significant distribution power, smaller and more independent presses can and do compete, particularly when they have strong and recognizable brands. Graywolf Press, for instance, is well known in literary publishing circles for producing some of the highest quality poetry and fiction, and some of its books have hit the *New York Times* best-seller list.

Beyond the Big Five, it's nearly impossible to generalize about publishers. New York trade publishing is quite different from K–12 educational publishing, which is quite different from scholarly publishing. Even within trade publishing, considerations vary across categories—for example, romance imprints often publish in high volume at low prices, while publishers of heavily illustrated titles produce fewer books at higher prices.

Industry estimates put the number of publishing companies in the tens of thousands, but many don't even sell through bookstores. With the relative ease and low overhead of digital and print-on-demand publishing, small presses have proliferated. A good number of these new small presses have little trade publishing experience, avoid investing in print runs, and focus on publishing books that primarily get sold on Amazon.

That brings us to one of the most critical transformations in today's publishing landscape: it's now possible for authors or small presses to publish books on an even footing with the Big Five, because they have equal access to distribution at Amazon, the number-one retailer of books. It's estimated that across all formats—print, e-book, and audio—more than 60 percent of book sales in the United States are now made through Amazon. Looking solely at e-books, Amazon is believed to account for 70 to 80 percent of all US book sales.[3] Appearing on an Amazon best-seller list or gaining better visibility on its site due to high sales rank can lead to a sales boost that doesn't happen in quite the same way through physical distribution or bookstore placement. Amazon is one of the ten most visited websites in the world, with some 180 million visitors every month. Publishers' marketing and sales strength pales in comparison; most of them have limited consumer data, while Amazon has data on millions of book buyers.

So it's hard to overstate Amazon's effect on the book business at every level, not to mention its role in the shift to digital book consumption. The launch of the Kindle in 2007 changed the face of book retailing forever, not only affecting how books get sold and at what price, but encouraging authors to self-publish and sell their work in just a few clicks—while earning much higher royalties than in traditional publishing deals. Between 2006 and 2011, the number of self-published titles tripled, to nearly a quarter million a year. By 2013, that number had risen to nearly half a million.[4] By comparison, traditional publishers in 2013 turned out about 300,000 titles. Yet even these incredible numbers miss much of the self-publishing activity out there. They only account for books that have ISBNs, or International Standard Book Numbers. Many self-publishers choose to publish through Amazon or other outlets without one.

While more books are being published than ever, the bad news is that book sales have remained more or less flat, with slight gains in some sectors.[5] Modest growth and stability has been possible only through the addition of digital audio sales, e-book sales, and flash-in-the-pan trends (such as adult coloring books in 2015 and 2016). According to data from Nielsen (now renamed NPD), the US print book market peaked around 2008 to 2009; print book sales have been on a slow decline ever since.[6]

In recent years, publishers have had to more actively defend their value to authors, in response to successful self-published authors speaking out against what they call "legacy publishing." They like to portray the Big Five as slow-moving, low-paying, and generally working against authors' interests. But all of this is just a new take on a very old story line: the love/hate relationship between author and publisher. Throughout the history of publishing, you will find a mixture of loyalty and vitriol, of partnership and violent disagreement. Some in the media may now promote a story about the irrelevance of gatekeepers, yet the line of people knocking on the doors of traditional publishers is as long as ever.

Agents and publishers often say their rejection rate is 99 percent, even 99.9 percent. Yet, as selective as publishers are, their approach tends to be "let's throw it at the wall and see what sticks." They don't market everything they publish, and they have minuscule marketing budgets compared to other consumer products. The lucky author who gets a publishing deal often realizes, after the fact, that their book is just one among thousands of titles released every year. In bookstores, it will likely sit spine-out on a shelf, rather than on display. Unless it quickly establishes a track record of success, every print book sitting on a store shelf is at risk of being returned or pulped to make room for the next season of new titles.

THE BOOK P&L

Writers often overestimate the amount of money a book deal might bring them, so let's be up-front: most authors will earn little, or at least nothing close to a living wage, from their books. While advances vary depending on the size of the publisher, trends in the market, and the publisher's enthusiasm for a project, a book advance for an unknown author may not go beyond $20,000 even at a major New York house. Small and midsize publishers commonly offer advances in the four figures.

It's not unheard-of for an unknown author to land a six-figure book deal, but should you be so lucky, understand that the advance is always divided into a few installments, and that even $100,000, portioned out over two years or more, isn't much to live on—especially after your agent takes a cut and you pay taxes on what's left. Furthermore, because it's an advance on royalties, you won't receive more money after publication until you earn back that amount through sales.

To determine whether to publish your book—and the size of your advance—publishers first decide if the book is an appropriate fit for them, the flip side of the judgment you (or your agent) made in pitching the book to them in the first place. Then any large publishing house runs the numbers. In a widely shared excerpt from his memoir, *My Mistake*, publishing industry veteran Daniel Menaker describes his first experience trying to acquire a book at Random House. His boss told him, "Well, do a P-and-L for it and we'll see."[7]

P&L stands for "profit and loss." It's a publisher's basic tool for deciding whether a book makes financial sense to publish. It's a mixture of the predictable (such as manufacturing costs) and the unpredictable (namely, sales). Nearly every publisher uses a proprietary P&L that it doesn't disclose. When I worked as an acquisitions editor, it was my responsibility to put together the P&L for every title I proposed and to make sure it would hit the target profit margin before wasting the pub board's time with a proposal. "Pub board" was a weekly assemblage of key company players in editorial, sales, and marketing who gave the green light to contract authors and titles. When I started negotiating author contracts, my marching orders were to ensure the author advance didn't go beyond what the P&L indicated would be earned out through sales of the first print run. (This isn't the case at every publisher, but I worked for a fiscally conservative house.) If you'd like to look at a stripped-down version of a P&L, I've posted one you can download at the URL provided in the footnote.[8]

You often hear about celebrity or blockbuster titles subsidizing the other titles a publisher produces. Publishers typically look at each title as part of a larger "season": each season is a strategic mix of titles expected to produce relatively high earnings and "quieter" books that carry more risk.

The industry has changed dramatically since I saw my first P&L. For starters, more than half of book sales now happen online—but the underlying math remains the same. While no author will be offered a look at her own book's P&L, understanding how a book deal comes together can help you appreciate what financial pressures publishers are under, and why an advance might look low to you but high to a publisher.

ESTIMATING A BOOK'S SALES
(AND THUS THE AUTHOR ADVANCE)

It is nearly impossible to separate discussion of an author's advance from sales projections. In fact, you should be able to make an educated guess as to how many books the publisher thinks it will sell based on your advance—with one caveat, to be explained in a moment.

As mentioned earlier, the author's advance is an advance against royalties. As books sell, authors earn a percentage of the price for each copy sold (a royalty), but they receive no further payments until the advance is fully "earned out." That may sound like paying back a loan. But industry insiders estimate that 70 percent of authors do not earn out their advance,[9] and authors do not have to return or repay the advance if that happens. So the advance represents a true risk on the part of the publisher. In fact, it's fairly common for Big Five houses to offer advances they know up front won't earn out. If you want to look at these transactions in an altruistic light, by offering an advance that won't pay out, publishers are essentially agreeing to pay a higher author royalty rate than what's stated in the contract. The dark side of this, however, is that some publishers may pay larger advances because they refuse to increase royalty rates, particularly on e-books—which may hurt authors' earning potential over the long term.

Publishers' projected sales for a book are based on several criteria:

- past sales of books by the author (or comparable authors, for a debut title)
- recent performance of the book's genre/category for the publisher
- subsidiary rights deals (such as foreign rights and sales) or the potential for such

There is one wild card that affects this calculation: irrational enthusiasm. Building buzz and excitement about your book is part of your agent's job. If an agent sells a book at auction, it forces publishers to compete against one another, which may push the price much higher than a P&L would indicate is appropriate. As you might guess, agents like running auctions. If a publisher overpays, that means more money up front, but it also helps ensure the publisher's commitment to marketing and promoting the book in order to recoup the investment.

Midsize and large publishers have an in-house sales force that secures retail and distributor orders, as well as in-store placement and merchandising for books. The challenge for most authors seeking publication is to bring a project to publishers' attention that merits this physical retail sales push. Most major publishers need to anticipate sales in the thousands of copies, on a national level, to make it worth the time and investment. At pub board meetings, the sales and marketing team may commit to specific sales figures by channel—Barnes & Noble, Amazon, libraries, special sales, discount stores, and so on. These numbers are often based on sales of a comparable title in the publisher's list or a competitor's list. As you might imagine, sales projections reflect the optimism and enthusiasm of the sales and marketing staff for your book. They may also reflect the editor's ability to pitch your book effectively to their colleagues—we'll address this issue at length in chapter 14.

Once an author has at least one book published, they have a sales track record that can be found and researched by anyone in the publishing industry with a subscription to Bookscan. Bookscan collects sales data on print books in the United States across many types of retailers, on a title-by-title basis. It also shows sales data patterns for specific authors, categories, genres, regions, and types of retailers. If your first book is a dud and doesn't sell well, that may depress enthusiasm for your next book—and not just at the publishing house, but at bookstores and other retailers who place orders prior to publication. This is why it can be difficult for an author with a poor sales record to get another book deal—the publisher is handicapped from the outset when trying to pitch your book and must provide reasons why your new book will perform better.

AUTHOR ROYALTY RATES

An author's royalty rates vary based on format (hardcover, paperback, or e-book) as well as the sales channel or method of distribution. Most book deals include escalators: when specific sales thresholds are reached, the royalty rate goes up. For example, royalties for a trade paperback sold in a bookstore might look like this:

- 1–5,000 copies sold: 8.0%
- 5,001–10,000: 10.0%
- 10,001–20,000: 12.5%
- 20,001 and higher: 15.0%

Hardcover royalties typically start at 10 percent, paperback royalties at 8 percent, and mass-market (an inexpensive and small format) even lower than that—but as always, much depends on the publisher. When evaluating royalty rates, it's important to know whether they're based on the list (retail) price of the book or on net receipts. For example, a $20 hardcover with a 10 percent royalty based on list price will pay the author $2 per copy sold. But if that royalty is based on net receipts—the net amount the publisher receives—the payment may be much less. If that same $20 book sells at 50 percent of list (most common), the net royalty would be $1 per copy sold. Agents typically expect and want royalties based on list, but smaller publishers often pay based on net.

E-book royalty rates at most traditional publishers have been "stuck" at 25 percent of net for years, to the frustration of both agents and authors. Agents would like to see e-book royalties paid on list price, like print, but publishers have resisted.

The table below contains a sample royalty breakdown for a book across three formats. The publisher's revenue indicated in this chart is an industry average, but can vary depending on the size of the publisher and the sales channel. Publishers negotiate specific discounts and co-op costs with each account or retailer. (Co-op costs are the fees retailers expect from publishers for in-store marketing and promotion of books, to be explained in chapter 14.) I've applied a generic 50 percent here, since most traditional bookstore channels receive a 50 percent discount, give or take a few points.

Table 5.1 Example of author royalty payments

	Hardcover	Paperback	E-book
Retail price	$25.00	$16.00	$12.00
Publisher's revenue	$12.50	$8.00	$8.40
Author royalty (%)	10% of retail	8% of retail	25% of net
Author royalty ($)	$2.50	$1.28	$2.10

Table 5.2 Example of publisher profit per copy sold

	Hardcover	Paperback	E-book
Retail price	$25.00	$16.00	$12.00
Average cut to wholesaler or distributor	−$12.50	−$8.00	−$3.60
Author royalty	−$2.50	−$1.28	−$2.10
Manufacturing cost	−$2.00	−$1.00	—
Distribution/freight	−$0.75	−$0.50	—
Cost of returns	−$1.00	−$0.50	—
Profit per title (before overhead, staffing, marketing costs)	$6.25	$4.72	$6.30

THE TOUGH LOVE ABOUT BOOK PUBLISHING

There's not a whole lot of money to be made in book publishing, for either the author or the publisher. John Steinbeck famously said, "The profession of book writing makes horse racing seem like a solid, stable business." Furthermore, to achieve decent sales as a book author, almost no one can expect to "just write" and leave the marketing and promotion to the publisher. While authors complain that the marketing workload has unfairly shifted to them in recent decades, it's hard to find a successful author in history who didn't market, promote, or innovate in order to sustain their writing career. During the Renaissance, Erasmus organized a network of agents across Europe to actively distribute his works and collect his rewards.[10] Mark Twain's most successful work was sold by traveling salesmen going door to door—at a time when this form of marketing was considered extremely impolite.[11] And everyone knows how Charles Dickens released his work in multiple formats, modified his stories based on audience feedback, and masterfully used the serial to garner attention and publicity.

If you're committed to pursuing a career primarily focused on book publication, then you'll be faced with the challenge of staying competitive, current, and discoverable in a shifting digital landscape; of having the right tools to be effective and in touch with your readers; and of developing strong partnerships to help you market and promote your work. (All of these skills are covered in part 4.) A publisher may or may not assist you with these challenges, based on a range of factors, including how large an advance you receive (the greater the advance, the more the publisher should be motivated to recoup it); how well your editor advocates for you to the publisher's sales and marketing staff; what sales the publisher anticipates for your book; who you're competing against for the publisher's time and attention; and how much each of these people likes working with you (yes, really).

The right publisher for you should be a long-term partner and resource. The best publisher will help you produce better work and ensure more sales over the long term. Sometimes an agent fulfills this role alongside or instead of the publisher. The wrong publisher will leave you feeling as if your career has been derailed and wishing you hadn't signed a contract. In chapters 9–14, we will dive further into what every author needs to know about getting a book published. Regardless of how you view traditional publishers' strengths and weaknesses, they undeniably remain the best path to seeing your book distributed nationwide in print form. Publishers excel at packaging and marketing the print book, and they offer a business partnership that is invaluable to most authors at some point in their careers, even if some aspects of the relationship can be disappointing or frustrating. Having the right expectations (or even low expectations!) helps tremendously.

6 : MAGAZINE PUBLISHING

The book publishing industry, even in the throes of the digital revolution, feels relatively staid and reliable when compared to the volatility prevalent in the magazine publishing industry. In 2010 industry leaders decided to rebrand their business as "magazine media" rather than "magazine publishing,"[1] clearly motivated by future survival and sustainability. Today, magazines need to be seen as something more than just a print product; they need to engage and reach readers wherever they are—through mobile devices and digital advertising, social media, and events.

But the current challenges facing magazines may not be so different from those in the past. From the very start, the magazine business has suffered a bit of an identity crisis. When the first magazine in America was published in Philadelphia in 1741, it was out of business within three months.[2] Nearly all early magazines suffered the same fate, mainly due to insufficient paying readership. People lacked leisure time and were able to satisfy their informational needs through newspapers. In fact, it was hard for magazines to distinguish themselves from newspapers until the 1800s, but by the mid- to late nineteenth century, magazines had become a distinct class of publication served by a distinct type of editor and writer.[3] (For the purposes of this chapter, "magazine" refers primarily to consumer magazines found on the newsstand, and does not include literary journals, sometimes known as "little magazines.")

During the 1800s, increased literacy and leisure time increased market demand for magazines—just as they did for books—but most publications struggled to turn a profit until their prices were lowered, making them mass-market products and viable advertising vehicles. It was then—in the final decades of the nineteenth century—that the prevailing business model for magazines was born: sell the product below cost to gather a readership, and become profitable by selling advertisers access to that readership. Before radio, film, and TV, magazines were the only way for advertisers to reach a national market, and business boomed. One of the

THE TRADITIONAL PRINT MAGAZINE BUSINESS MODEL

The traditional magazine business model has three areas that require close attention: editorial, circulation, and advertising. Understanding the basic performance metrics of magazines can be essential if you hope to work in the business.

Advertising-editorial ratio. Every magazine (with rare exception) has a mix of editorial pages and advertising pages, and has a target ratio of advertising to editorial pages. For example, a 20–80 ratio means a magazine has 20 percent advertising pages and 80 percent editorial pages. This ratio is important because editorial pages represent cost (content typically costs money to acquire, in the form of staff time or freelance writing fees), while advertising pages represent income. If advertising pages consistently decline, then the magazine's total page count may have to be decreased.

Average advertising revenue per page. In a magazine's advertising kit, standard rates are quoted for display ads—which include back cover or inside cover ads, interior full page ads, half-page ads, quarter-page ads, and so on. Some magazines run classifieds in the back, which are usually text-based and much cheaper than display ads. While advertisers pay variable rates based on the quantity and type of advertising purchased, most magazines can reliably calculate average revenue per page of display and classified advertising. There is also a cost per advertising page, which includes sales staff salaries, commissions, and meals and entertainment.

Average cost per editorial page. Before printing costs, a magazine should also be able to estimate the average cost for producing one page of editorial content. This could be an all-in cost (including editorial staff) or just the costs of acquiring content (freelance fees, art and illustration fees, and so on). Most magazines have a fixed editorial and art budget for each issue that must not be exceeded.

Print run per issue. A publisher decides how many copies to print per issue based on subscriber rates and newsstand sales history, in addition to copies needed for back-issue sales, sales and marketing, and in-house purposes.

Cost per new subscriber. For much of magazine publishing history, subscribers have been acquired through direct mail. The circulation department sends a subscription offer to a list of names—often acquired through other magazines or direct-to-consumer companies—and the cost of that effort is divided by the number of new subscribers acquired. There is almost always a cost, not a profit, associated with acquiring a new magazine subscriber. Today, direct mail is the most expensive way to acquire a new subscriber but is still common. Other approaches include email marketing, online advertising, and cross-promotional efforts with other brands or products.

Conversion rate. This is the percentage of new subscribers who renew their subscriptions for the first time.

Renewal rate. This is the percentage of subscribers who renew their subscriptions again, after the initial conversion. Both conversions and renewals typically involve a direct mail or email marketing campaign to ensure the subscriber doesn't forget to renew. This entails costs, but the cost is much lower than a new subscriber cost.

A magazine's publisher always knows at what moment in the cycle of renewals a subscriber becomes profitable, that is, when the cost to acquire and keep the subscriber falls below the subscription fees paid. A reliable renewal rate is essential to keep a magazine profitable. When a magazine has high "churn," that means its subscriber base turns over frequently, which leads to higher circulation costs.

Single-copy sales (newsstand). For magazines distributed to newsstands, revenue also comes from single-copy sales. A distributor or wholesaler manages the process—delivering, billing, and collecting money from newsstands for the magazines sold—and the distributor takes a cut of sales. A publisher can expect to receive about 50 percent of the cover price for a newsstand sale. Unsold copies are destroyed.

The *draw* is the total number of magazine copies delivered to the distributor; *sell-through* is the number of copies sold through newsstands. Sell-through figures vary tremendously, but, as of this writing, about 25 percent is average. Magazines almost never achieve 100 percent sell-through. The number-one factor in newsstand sales is the cover, so distributors often advise publishers on designing covers that will maximize sell-through—a combination of compelling cover lines and a catchy image (often a celebrity photo).

Magazine P&L

A bare bones magazine profit-and-loss statement would include the following:
Revenue
    advertising revenue
    subscription revenue
    single-copy or newsstand revenue
Expenses
    magazine printing and postage
    circulation costs (subscriber acquisition, renewal, and fulfillment)
    advertising sales costs
    editorial costs (staff, freelance, and art)
Profit = Revenue − Expenses

leading magazines of its time, the *Saturday Evening Post*, earned $6,993 from advertising in 1897; by 1907, it was pulling in $1,266,931.[4]

Thus most magazines have, for more than a hundred years, served two customers: the reader and the advertiser. While all types of publishers are sensitive to changing economic conditions, magazine publishers can find themselves unprofitable and out of business in a quick instant if advertisers abandon them, or if they fail to balance the "three-legged stool" of the traditional business model: advertising, circulation (subscription and newsstand distribution), and editorial.

When television overtook magazines as the biggest and best way for businesses to launch mass-market advertising campaigns, the industry had to reassess its role and value for advertisers—not to mention how it competed for people's time. Ironically, high-circulation magazines were often the most vulnerable. Subscription revenue was never meant to cover a magazine's publishing costs, and the expense of servicing a high number of readers can become a severe liability on the balance sheet if there is not sufficient advertising revenue. To compete, many magazines targeted narrower demographics—offering advertisers the benefit of specialized audiences—and raised cover prices.[5]

This history is necessary to understand the current predicament that magazines find themselves in. In 2007 US magazine print advertising exceeded $25 billion;[6] by 2016 it had fallen below $17 billion with no prospects for improvement.[7] It's not TV that's the problem this time; it's the rise of digital media, which surpassed TV ad spend by the end of 2016.[8] Video, social media, and mobile are currently the most popular vehicles for internet advertising—and the beneficiaries of those digital ad dollars are largely Google and Facebook.[9]

It used to be acceptable for magazines to maintain a high circulation even if it meant signing up subscribers at a loss, because it was more important to guarantee that advertisers would reach a promised number of readers with each issue of the magazine. Today, it's more common for magazines to cut their *rate base* (the number of readers guaranteed to advertisers) rather than inflate the numbers with low-quality subscribers, because of the unreliability and continued decline of advertising dollars. However, if the rate base declines, so do advertising rates. To save the rates as much as possible, magazines have focused on selling advertising packages that combine many different types of exposure: print ads, digital edition ads, website ads, email newsletter placements, event sponsorships, and more.

Longtime industry observers predict a great shakeout yet to come, where many magazines fold. Aside from declining ad dollars, there are additional pressures on magazines, such as increased costs for postage and paper and shrinking newsstand sales. But advertising is the most critical and faltering piece, and isn't necessarily solved by simply swapping out print advertising revenue for digital. Not only does advertising inventory online reach nearly unlimited quantities; it can also be more highly targeted and personalized than ever before, with performance immediately measured. A new form of advertising has emerged—programmatic advertising—which uses software to purchase ads automatically, in an efficient and economic manner, bypassing the traditional, human-driven process that involves a magazine's advertising sales rep or director.

Many websites—including those of magazines—serve up ads through an advertising network, and the technology that delivers such ads can slow down the site or otherwise prevent easy reading, which frustrates readers. As a result, ad-blocking technology has become increasingly popular, to the great dismay of magazines, which not only struggle to get digital ad dollars in the first place, but must now entreat readers to turn off their ad blockers, or even restrict access to those unwilling to do so.[10] The next chapter discusses these issues in greater depth.

Advertising revenue will not bounce back to the levels that magazines once enjoyed—and of course it's not only the magazine industry that's affected. Newspapers have been hit even harder, and there's no sign of recovery for them either. Some magazines are attempting to modify their business models by becoming even more specialized and focused in their approach—to reach a truly loyal and dedicated readership—and increasing per-issue and subscription prices.[11] Of course, this approach is the same one they took when TV stole away ad dollars. Others are taking more radical steps. In summer 2016, *Prevention* magazine, published by Rodale since 1950, with a circulation of nearly two million, eliminated all print-based advertising, in addition to increasing the cover and subscription price. By eliminating print advertising, the company was able to shed employees and related costs of securing such advertising.[12]

Another popular but controversial solution is to follow in the footsteps of internet media companies that accept or produce "native advertising." Native advertising is paid content made to appear similar to the publication's editorial content, and delivered to readers in the same manner as that editorial content. (It may or may not be labeled as paid placement.) Native advertising also goes by the name "sponsored content." With print magazines suffering continued erosion of advertising revenue, and online publications looking for paths to sustainability, some of the best-paying opportunities are now in the area of native advertising. There is considerable disagreement about the ethics of running pieces that aren't disclosed as paid articles, but it has become a profitable business model for one of the most successful online media start-ups, BuzzFeed.[13]

Content marketing is yet another potential profit area. Content marketing refers to any kind of material that a corporation, business, or organization produces to help market and promote its products or services. Blogs were one of the earliest forms of content marketing (and are still popular), but content marketing comes in many different forms: white papers, digital books, slide presentations, surveys and reports, infographics, and more. Businesses don't often have the time or the skills to produce the content, so hire freelancers or companies that are already in the content business, such as magazines. The *Atlantic* has a content marketing arm, called Atlantic Media Strategies, as does the *New York Times*, with T Brand Studio.

TYPES OF MAGAZINES AND MAGAZINE CONTENT

When the average person envisions a magazine, they tend to think of the glossy, pop-culture titles on newsstands or grocery checkouts. Often a celebrity is featured on the cover, and the cover lines tell and sell the content inside. These are known in the industry as consumer magazines, and some have a reputation for prestige and glamour—although shrinking advertising revenue has led to shrinking budgets for maintaining their glamorous appearances. The best-known consumer magazines pay freelance writers very well, often one to two dollars per word—possibly more for brand-name journalists.

Within the consumer magazine sphere, there are several overlapping categories:

- general interest magazines covering a wide range of topics, such as the *New Yorker* and *Time*
- women's service and lifestyle magazines covering family, relationships, and home, such as *Ladies' Home Journal*, *Real Simple*, and *O*
- style and design magazines, usually upscale publications, covering fashion and food, such as *Bon Appetit*, *Garden & Gun*, and *Vogue*
- active interest magazines focusing on health and fitness or outdoor recreation, such as *Runner's World*, *Outside*, and *Men's Journal*

- special-interest magazines serving niche audiences, such as *Modern Farmer, The Modern Scholar,* and *Mother Jones*

There tends to be a significant divide between magazine writers who focus on service, how-to, or lifestyle content and those (typically journalists) who provide original news and reporting. Magazines may carry both types of content, but you can tell which way a publication leans by simply looking at the cover lines. An issue of the *New Yorker* will inevitably feature in-depth reporting on a current event and profiles of important people in society. *Real Simple,* on the other hand, will feature stories on how readers can better organize their homes or get dinner on the table in twenty minutes on a weeknight.

It probably goes without saying, but writers themselves tend to put a higher value on reporting and journalism, while how-to or service content (including this book) is seen as a lesser form of writing. However, service content has a long and proud history in both book and magazine publishing, and also plays an important a role in influencing culture. From a business perspective, service publications are typically more sustainable than those focused on reporting and journalism—which isn't any different than in other types of media, such as TV and radio. Quality journalism is expensive to source, expensive to edit and fact-check, and expensive to find a devoted readership for—and controversial editorial content can also put advertising at risk. For that reason, publications devoted to quality reporting can be quite vulnerable. Even the *New Yorker*, often cited as the highest-quality publication in terms of artistic and journalistic excellence, is said to have operated at a loss for many years, although its figures have never been made public (and it's now said to be profitable).[14] *Harper's Magazine* transitioned from a for-profit enterprise to a nonprofit one in the 1970s to protect its uncertain future.[15] And the *Atlantic* was considered to be a lost cause in the mid-2000s, until it refocused its efforts on digital media and posted its first profitable year in 2010 after a long period of multimillion-dollar losses.[16]

THE CHALLENGE POSED BY DISAGGREGATION

Before the internet, if you subscribed to a newspaper or magazine but were only interested in one aspect of the publication, you didn't have a choice—you bought all of it or none of it. Journalism has been sustainable in part because the most profitable or popular parts of the media operation have subsidized the reporting.

In the digital era, this model doesn't work as it once did. People no longer have to buy a whole publication to acquire just the one or two types of content they really want. Think of all the newspaper content you can now obtain free online: top news headlines, Associated Press wire reports, weather forecasts, sports scores, classified ads, entertainment listings, reviews, and so on. Maybe you used to subscribe to food magazines for new recipes; now you can search for and acquire thousands of recipes for free through blogs and websites (and from the websites of the magazines themselves).

Today's print readers have to desire the whole experience or package, or consider it part of their identity or community—to feel they would be missing out on an important shared experience if they didn't subscribe. At the same time, more and more content is discovered and consumed through social media channels; friends and online relationships play an increasingly dominant role in what types of content we're exposed to. Rather than an editor curating content for us, we're each curating our own "publications" based on who we connect with and what we like—and social media or search algorithms fill in the gaps. This phenomenon has been criticized as a "filter bubble"—a media environment that excludes divergent views and opinions. However, people have always selected and supported media that appeals to their viewpoints and interests; online media simply makes such behavior more evident, and perhaps more extreme.

Regardless of how you view the phenomenon, there's no going back. We won't be returning to an age where we consume entire publications because that's what the editors would prefer. Instead, readers will continue to cherry-pick, becoming aware of a range of outlets or media brands, gravitating toward some of them more often, and supporting a handful.

THE ERA OF MAGAZINE MEDIA

The *Atlantic* offers a case study in how a magazine that was once focused on delivering a single experience—the print magazine—can become a media-agnostic operation, driven by a philosophy or set of values associated with the brand we know as the *Atlantic*. That brand is now expressed in many ways, and profit arises from types of content and experiences that aren't related to receiving the print artifact.

The *New Yorker* has also become profitable in recent years with what looks more and more like a media-agnostic strategy. While it has made some traditional changes to its business model—such as increasing subscription prices—it is also pursuing other channels of profit and engagement. Its Cartoon Bank allows readers to buy any cartoon—or cover—from the magazine, at a range of price points. Its podcasts and mobile apps provide additional advertising and sponsorship opportunities. It runs an annual festival with ticketed events that sell out weeks and months in advance, as well as a special one-day tech conference with a $1,500 price tag. The magazine has partnered with Amazon Prime Video to produce and distribute a TV series.[17] If a reader wants to experience the *New Yorker* beyond its pages, there's no shortage of opportunities to do so. Of course, the big question might be: Do readers really want *more* to consume or have *time* to consume it? (How many subscribers can even keep up with the weekly issues?)

But such a question is beside the point if the new channels and forms of media attract a new or different audience that expands the footprint of the *New Yorker* brand and offers more potential for advertising and long-term revenue. Rather than stubbornly insist on profiting only from print or online advertising, the *New Yorker* is exploring the entirety of the demand curve for its voice, style, and brand. This is what it means to operate in the era of magazine media, and what most magazines have to look toward to remain sustainable. Eventually, it will become impossible to distinguish "magazine media" from media that originated online or as digital-first.

THE EMERGENCE OF CONTENT

In the mid-2000s, as digital media became more central to every publishing company, the word "content" took center stage. There were proclamations such as "content is king," and new professional positions emerged in the field of "content strategy," including chief content officers. The more business-oriented and consumer-facing the publisher, the more likely you'll hear the word "content" used instead of "writing." This change has been unsettling for the writers, who rarely want to be seen as "content creators," which sounds about as desirable as "widget maker."

But here's the reason "content" is preferred: it's a broader, more inclusive term that includes writing, visuals, infographics, audio, video, user-generated material, and more. Writing is a specific type of content, and most publishers—recognizing that what they do is about much more than writing—are ready to adapt to whatever form of media is preferred by their audience. "Content" can be reshaped, reconfigured, and reimagined for many different people, places, and purposes.

This, too, can upset writers, who may have a more artisanal outlook on publishing. In this view, writing (or the content) is specifically imagined and created for a particular container or mode of delivery—historically and traditionally, a printed book, magazine, or journal. If one takes that writing and excerpts it, serializes it, or condenses it, the integrity of the experience is lost, or the intent of the author may be undercut.

Publishers with an artisanal philosophy do exist, particularly in the literary publishing community. An excellent example is *McSweeney's*, a publishing venture that began in 1998 with a quarterly literary journal that changed format with each and every issue, which was part of the excitement and charm. One memorable issue arrived in a large plastic bag, packaged as a bundle of mail. *McSweeney's* dedication to the integration of form and content motivated people to be collectors, not just subscribers. For publishers that single-mindedly take on such an artisanal approach, and are unwavering in their devotion to it, it can work—if there's a strong "why" or mission that attracts a following. However, it's far more common in commercial and digital-age publishing to focus on adaptability. That's not to say that it's not important how the writing is presented—it is—but that today's magazine business model is more robust and sustainable when media agnosticism is part of the approach: the content can be reconfigured and repackaged wherever there's an audience to serve.

7 : ONLINE AND DIGITAL MEDIA

The previous chapter focused on magazine media that have print legacies. This chapter is devoted primarily to media that came into being as digital-only or digital-first. The distinction is not without significance, since print publishers have overhead, staffing, and workflows that have been defined by print revenue—their expertise and instincts still lean toward preserving print and a print business model. New media companies start with a clean slate and nothing to preserve—which doesn't, however, mean they start with a sustainable business model, as we'll see.

When compared to print, the most striking quality of digital or online publishing is that there is little barrier to entry and low overhead cost. Anyone, anywhere, at any time, can launch an online publication that costs little aside from their time and energy, and can distribute it through the same channels used by established publications. This is at once a blessing and a curse. It allows for publications to exist that would've never been possible before, and it allows for dramatic failure as people with little to no experience try to gain attention or revenue for their efforts.

If we judge a publication on its success as a business, then more online and digital publications have failed than succeeded. One of the earliest and best-known of them, *Salon*, has yet to turn a profit, as of this writing, and remains alive because of continued investment.[1] Countless other online publications have folded and disappeared, even though they had loyal followings. Why is it so hard to keep an online publication alive when it's never been easier to get started—and when the digital world makes it possible to build a niche audience? Aside from the fact that new publishing enterprises throughout history have often failed, regardless of medium, here are the most talked-about factors.

THE DIFFICULTY OF ADVERTISING-BASED MODELS
A traditional ad-driven model for online publishing requires a high volume of free content to generate traffic. Only with a high number of visitors can

a publication attract sufficient advertising revenue to cover the cost of producing that content. Some online publications have succeeded with this model; one of the best known is the *Huffington Post*. But it's easy to end up in a race to the bottom, creating headlines that entice people to click on low-quality content (clickbait), producing stories or slideshows that require visitors to click multiple times, or aggregating content from other sources to increase the number of articles published—and thus traffic. There's also continual demand for "hot takes": to be among the first to produce a reaction to breaking news. The hotter, the better for traffic, which doesn't necessarily lend itself to quality, but that's not the point. Complicating matters is the popularity of ad blockers, which make it harder to earn advertising revenue, since they erase as much as a third of traffic. (A website visitor who doesn't see ads doesn't count when a publication adds up the total number of ad impressions for an advertiser.)

Online advertising can be measured, targeted, modified, and redistributed in an instant based on a variety of factors, such as click rate—the percentage of people who click an ad out of the total number who see it. Advertisers quickly discovered that the value of many online ads is exceedingly low because they aren't effective, a devastating blow to publications. In a digital world with millions of potential ad placements, the low-quality advertising inventory is practically infinite. The most valuable type of online advertising as of this writing is original video—expensive to produce and in high demand—while website banner advertising has one of the lowest values because it is so common and ineffective.[2]

Furthermore, online advertising money is largely not captured by stand-alone publications. In 2016, Google and Facebook accounted for more than 65 percent of digital ad revenue.[3] Most online publications don't work with advertisers directly and instead work through ad networks, which programmatically place ads based on demographic considerations, and have little or no interest in any publication's survival. It is, in short, a numbers game that only the largest publications or media corporations can effectively play. Niche publications are more likely to seek out sponsorships that aren't based on site performance (or ad performance), which are sometimes driven by community or PR relationships important to the sponsor.[4]

FREE CONTENT

If an online publication seeks ad dollars, then the content usually has to be free to ensure sufficient traffic. When two of the earliest online publications—*Salon* and *Slate*—faltered in their efforts to sustain themselves through advertising alone, they transitioned to a paid-subscription model. Traffic plummeted, advertising declined, and the subscription revenue wasn't enough to make up for the advertising revenue lost. Both sites eventually abandoned their paywalls and made the content freely available again.

Once a readership has been developed based on free content, it is difficult to turn back the clock and make that same content pay-only. One successful example is the *New York Times*, but even it uses a "leaky paywall" that allows readers up to ten free articles per month. If the transition from free-to-pay is to succeed, the content has to be unique, in demand, and hard to replicate. Otherwise, most readers will simply find another source that remains free.

One popular alternative to a paywall for publications seeking a financially supportive readership is to offer premium access or content to those who pay to become "members." Benefits might include first-look opportunities at new stories, direct engagement with the publication staff, access to a members-only area, ability to comment, and so on. Such models, instead of developing a punitive paywall, offer a "positive" paywall that rewards loyalty. Memberships and paywalls are discussed further in chapter 28.

For years, media observers have suggested a micropayment system as the solution: virtuous readers could devote a set dollar amount each month to the publications they read online, then the pool would be divided among the sites visited. So far these systems have not been widely adopted and appear to be driven by wishful thinking. It's hard to change established behavior, and people mostly act in their own self-interest, not in the interest of sustaining someone else's business.

SOCIAL MEDIA

Of greater concern to all publications is the growing dominance of social media as a destination where people spend the majority of their time online. Facebook, Snapchat, and others are no longer just places where people talk to each other. They're places where content itself is hosted, effectively creating a "walled garden" that people need never leave. In 2015 Facebook launched Instant Articles, basically a means for delivering content from publications without sending users outside of Facebook. While Instant Articles still allows publications to profit from views inside Facebook, it's yet another step that puts more control into the hands of Facebook, and offers both print and online publications less information and access to their readership.

In 2015 BuzzFeed saw its website traffic flatten, but consumption grew steadily in channels outside of the site—particularly videos posted on Facebook.[5] BuzzFeed now distributes its content in more than forty different places online and plans strategically for a time when the website matters little to its business model. Some new online publications aren't even bothering to build a site as a first step; they begin by developing a following on a specific social media channel, such as Instagram, then expand from there. The increasingly prevalent philosophy is, Go where the people are already gathered because it's getting harder to get anyone to come to you. This is yet another facet of the disaggregation challenge discussed in chapter 6.

LACK OF A BUSINESS MODEL

It is now a cliché in start-up culture to talk about gathering an audience first and worrying about the business model later. Silicon Valley has faith that if you've gathered many thousands of people to your site, service, or app, then *of course* you'll find a way to monetize that attention. How could you not?

But the reality is more complicated, especially in the writing and publishing industry, which is not an easily scalable business. Scalable means that as the audience grows, the business becomes more profitable without added expense. Publishing can be difficult to scale because producing high-quality content consumes considerable resources, and investing in more content always means more cost, but not necessarily more readers or more revenue. Many start-ups have gone into publishing thinking they could "revolutionize" the industry, only to fail within a few years with little to show for their efforts. Or even if revolution wasn't on their mind, they didn't remain sustainable, even with significant readership. (See Byliner, GigaOm, and Medium, just to name a few.)

It's not impossible to make online publishing pay; it's that deciding you'll figure out the business model at some later date can doom the venture from the start. The goal shouldn't be to secure the largest readership but to reach a readership that supports the business model envisioned. Here are some examples:

- *The Information* is a premium subscriber publication, online-only, that offers high-quality journalism and analysis on the tech industry. It's considered an essential read for tech insiders due to the value and relevance of the information, which is unmatched by competitors.

- *Stratechery* is another tech-industry site, run by Ben Thompson, which features his analysis of breaking news and long-term trends. People pay for full access as well as discussion privileges.[6]
- *The Skimm* is an email newsletter that targets young women, delivering news summaries with a distinctive voice and personality. It's free for readers to subscribe, so it runs on an advertising and sponsorship business model. For anyone who thought email was dead, *The Skimm* is an important reminder that understanding your audience is more important than chasing trends.
- Purchased by the *New York Times* in 2016, *The Wirecutter* is a review site that is the digital-age cousin of *Consumer Reports*. It helps people cut through the noise and confusion of purchasing decisions—especially for high-ticket electronics—and delivers what it believes to be the absolute best purchasing option, with an in-depth report on why. The publication is free and makes money from Amazon affiliate marketing.
- BuzzFeed has become, as the years pass, a serious publication with big-name journalists that reaches a demographic beyond that of young adults. Its business model is based on native advertising and sponsored content, discussed more in chapter 31.

LOW-QUALITY CONTENT

Writers sometimes express frustration at what they perceive to be the flood of low-quality work now online, particularly at ad-driven sites. (I'm referring not to political "fake news" but to content that is poorly written or of little substance.) How do serious writers compete against the tidal wave of dreck? This question comes up at almost every talk I give these days, but each person is making a different statement or asking a different question. It can mean:

- I am appalled at the quality of work published today.
- I am worried that low-quality work will push out high-quality work.
- What will happen to us as a society if we allow low-quality work to proliferate?
- I am overwhelmed and anxious about all the horrible stuff out there. Will I lose what I love?
- I am tired of people talking about what they had for breakfast.

Such concerns have been expressed literally since the beginning of publishing. After the printing press was invented, and the world started filling with books, intellectuals worried that the abundance would negatively affect people's consumption of the worthiest content. When novels emerged, they were disparaged as light entertainment that would rot the mind. Johann Adam Bergk, an intellectual dismayed at the quality of literature being produced in the 1700s, commented, "Reading is supposed to be an educational tool of independence, and most people use it like sleeping pills; it is supposed to make us free and mature, and how many does it serve merely as a way of passing time and as a way of remaining in a condition of eternal immaturity!"[7] An identical passage could be written about the dynamics of reading in the digital age, and the quantity of cat videos you'll find in the average social media newsfeed. By nearly all accounts, young people are reading more now than they ever did, but *what* they read and *how* they read has changed.

Once you recognize this pattern—the same concerns about media consumption recurring throughout history—you can take consolation in it. It's natural to be wary and dismissive of new forms. It's normal to feel overwhelmed when confronted with change. But are the problems we face today any more dire or pernicious than those our predecessors faced? (For more on this, I highly recommend "Why Google Isn't Making Us Stupid . . . or Smart" by Chad Wellmon.[8])

When it comes to low-quality operations disrupting high-quality operations (such as the *Huffington Post* disrupting the *New York Times* or, farther back, *USA Today* disrupting city papers), people forget that these low-quality operations often evolve and mature into high-quality operations. Outlets like BuzzFeed are implementing journalistic standards and getting closer to what traditionalists consider quality journalism.[9] So arguments about quality aren't productive or taking us anywhere new. There is an audience for all levels of quality; know your market and serve the quality that's appropriate—and remember that the price reflects the quality.

When I interviewed longtime magazine industry insider Bo Sacks in 2014, he discussed how survival of the fittest is the rule both in print and online. Regardless of medium, the success rate has always been low in publishing:

> If you do not have excellence, you will not survive in print. There's plenty of indifferent writing on the web—it's free entry, and it doesn't matter. But quality will out there, too. Really well-written, well-thought-out editorial will be the revenue stream. You must have such

worthiness that people give you money when they don't have to, since they can get entertained elsewhere for free.[10]

Too often we equate content with its container. For much of our lives, quality content—especially journalism—has appeared in newspapers and magazines, so we equate the decline of that particular industry with the decline of journalism. But the survival of quality writing or journalism is not tied to the future of the newspaper or magazine business. Those are delivery and distribution mechanisms, they are services to readers, and they have become less useful to us in the digital era. Many valuable digital-era operations give us plenty to be optimistic about. In addition to those mentioned above, there are journalistic efforts such as ProPublica, a nonprofit, and *Pacific Standard*, a nonprofit online magazine run out of the Miller-McCune Center for Research, Media and Public Policy.[11] (Nonprofits and for-profit publishing operations often face the same issues of sustainability.)

The challenge, of course, is that we know how to monetize a print newspaper or magazine—and it's easier to charge for their perceived value. We're still figuring out how to monetize digital forms. But amid this challenge, I'd argue we're not seeing less quality journalism today, we're seeing more, because there are fewer distribution barriers and low start-up costs. I'd also ask if we really think the system pre-internet was producing quality journalism, or if we merely prefer the devil we know. By the mid-twentieth century, media was operated by handful of conglomerates with significant control over the mass media of radio, TV, newspapers, and magazines, a system that was hard for outside voices to access. To be sure, these major media conglomerates are being disrupted by another set of powerhouses (Google, Apple, Amazon, Facebook), but the latter provide distribution and publishing opportunities to those who have traditionally had to work outside the mainstream media.

8 : LITERARY PUBLISHING IN THE TWENTY-FIRST CENTURY

Literary publishing of books, journals, and other media, generally distinguished from commercial publishing, is lauded as being almost wholly concerned with artistic excellence. Big Five New York publishers and consumer magazine publishers seek excellence as well, but they have to weigh whether a given project will earn back its investment in the marketplace. Just about every major publisher relies on blockbuster hits to offset losses on smaller books that may sell a modest number of copies. Editors generally won't stay in the business long if they don't pick books that enjoy some level of commercial success.

Literary publishers are more often run as nonprofits and support their artistic mission by applying for grants or seeking donations. *McSweeney's*, a literary publishing stalwart since 1998, became a nonprofit organization in 2014 to remain sustainable. Other stars of literary publishing, such as Graywolf Press and most university presses, are also run as nonprofits.

But literary publishing doesn't *have to* mean nonprofit publishing. In the nineteenth century, two of the most venerated literary publications in history, *Harper's Magazine* and the *Atlantic Monthly*, began as commercial enterprises within years of each other, and built their reputations on publishing the most excellent writing for an upper-class, educated audience. Their contributors read like a Who's Who of the time: Charles Dickens, Anthony Trollope, Mark Twain, Ralph Waldo Emerson, Herman Melville, and many others. These publications were sustainable at first because of the growth of literacy and the middle class, lack of competition, and tremendous reader interest in short fiction. But in the twenty-first century, each took a different path to survive: the *Atlantic* became a savvy digital media enterprise; *Harper's* became a nonprofit.

The audience for quality literature has always been small, in both the magazine and the book publishing industry. Authors' and publishers' complaints about the lack of audience for serious literature date back to at least the eighteenth century, when ghost stories sold better than formal poetry.[1] More recently, Hamilton Nolan of Gawker wrote, "The audience for quality prestige content is small, even smaller than the actual output of quality prestige content, which itself is smaller than most media outlets like to imagine."[2] Although Nolan was speaking specifically about journalism, the same applies to all "prestige content" produced primarily for an upper-class, educated audience. And what constitutes "prestige" has changed over time. Short stories, venerated by those who value literature today, once served as light entertainment and were published heavily in magazines in the eighteenth and nineteenth centuries. Many of those early pieces have more in common with today's soap opera story lines or romance novels than with an F. Scott Fitzgerald story. Short fiction did not become unprofitable (and transform into something considered almost entirely "literary") until well into the twentieth century, after TV became the primary vehicle of both entertainment and advertising.[3]

The greatest challenge facing literary publishers is that the audience they imagine for themselves has barely progressed beyond the audience captured by those first literature-focused magazines like *Harper's* and *Atlantic Monthly. Harper's* was fortunate to have a loyal and diverse audience: "Some were poor scholars, some farmers with the advantage of an education, some rich and cultured people, but the one thing they all held in common was a passionate interest in culture, not only for themselves but for their children."[4] But it is next to impossible to publish for that audience today. The digital age has brought fragmentation of audiences and markets. Broad, general-interest publishers that have been around for decades, or even a century or more, struggle to stay afloat in the new environment, and literary publishers are not spared this challenge.

At a 2014 Association of Writers & Writing Programs conference panel, Morgan Entrekin, president and publisher of Grove/Atlantic, a well-respected and independent literary publisher, identified two primary challenges facing literary publishing going forward: distribution and discoverability. Entrekin argued that publishing needs diversity in distribution channels, largely because opportunities for books to be discovered by readers are disappearing and those that remain rely upon a few big companies, such as Amazon, Apple, and Google.[5] He's right that it's largely Silicon Valley companies and the tech industry that are shaping the future of book distribution and discoverability. But there's not really a distribution problem here at all. Indeed, that problem has gone away entirely in the digital age. Anyone, anywhere, can get their hands on any nearly any title if they're willing to make a purchase through an online retailer. That leaves the issue of discoverability, where the problem isn't so much that readers have a hard time discovering new things to read, as that publishers have a hard time making their works visible to the right readers.

As discussed in chapter 5, one of the primary advantages a publisher can offer an author has been getting her book distributed to every bricks-and-mortar bookstore or retailer. As physical retail become less important to an author's discoverability, what purpose does a publisher serve? For literary publishing in particular, the imprimatur of a house remains important. It's not enough to simply publish; literary authors must be published by a credible someone to attract the "right" types of reviews, awards, and attention. Literary authors are also concerned with quality editorial relationships that will nurture their careers for the long term, which presumably a literary publisher cares about too.

In this sense, literary presses can be in a better position to serve authors' needs than commercial publishers. Without the imminent pressure for profits, they can play the long game, be happier with small or "quiet" books, and focus on cultivating what is increasingly imperative in the internet era: a sense of shared values or community among readers. Unfortunately, a prevalent attitude in the literary community, particularly among authors, is that the work should "speak for itself"—that engaging in brand building or reader engagement can subvert one's credentials as an authentic writer or publisher. As literary novelist Will Self said in a *Guardian* interview, "I don't really write for readers. I think that's the defining characteristic of being serious as a writer. . . . And if people like it, great, and if they don't like it, well, that's that—what can you do? You can't go round and hold a gun to their head."[6] (A couple years later, without any sense of irony, he wrote in the same publication, "The literary novel as an art work and a narrative art form central to our culture is indeed dying before our eyes."[7])

But not everyone finds literary publishing incompatible with effective marketing and a strong brand that engages readers. The *Paris Review* is perhaps one of the most remarkable examples. Travis Kurowski observed, in his essay "In Exile and Against Criticism: *The Paris Review* and the Branding of Contemporary Literature":

The editors saw that, in order for any readers in America or abroad to notice it during a time both color television and the hydrogen bomb came to fruition, when advertising had begun its stronghold on culture, they had to work hard to develop interest and trust in the magazine through the magazine's content, image, and overall concept. . . . For the majority of literary magazine editors, the content *itself* was supposed to be significant enough. And for the early *Paris Review*, the content of the magazine was still primary, but to get that content into the minds and hands of readers they had to do various things to make the magazine a marketable venue . . . [and] make new and experimental literature a part of the culture.[8]

A successful brand isn't a sign of pandering to readers; rather, it evokes and emphasizes the *why*, or what the publication or publisher stands for. Perhaps the most important reason this is now so critical—putting aside the fact that we live in a time where we need not struggle to find something of quality to read, even if we limit ourselves to what is free—is disaggregation, as discussed in chapter 6. Being able to cherry-pick an essay from *ABC Review*, a poem from *DEF Journal*, then a short story from *GHI Quarterly*, and consume it on a device of our choosing, leads to dramatic changes in reading behavior. Readers are less committed to any single publication if it doesn't interest them from cover to cover, or if they're not interested in its larger reason for being.

While disaggregation has a particularly powerful and immediate effect on literary journals, magazines, and online publications, book publishers face the challenge too: the proliferation of (quality) digital content that we can save and read for later can take us away from the to-be-read pile on the nightstand. One can easily fill all available reading time with a self-curated list of articles saved to Pocket, friends' links from Facebook or Twitter, or breaks to play Candy Crush. The less visible and immediate physical books are in our lives (because bookstores disappear, because books become digital, because of the competition from other media), the less likely any book will find its audience through patience or serendipity.

Without a framework and context for what is published, literary publications can feel virtually indistinguishable from one another, with no criteria guiding the selection of work aside from artistic excellence. Many submission guidelines and editors' letters talk about seeking "quality" work, but what does that really mean—to the staff and the publication's supporters, the readers, or the community at large? Journals especially can be guilty of making work available but not known.

Fortunately, the digital era has made it easier to succeed with a niche publication and target a narrow readership. Through digital marketing and distribution, it is possible to identify and directly reach a potential audience, without special distribution, a large advertising budget, or even physical shelf space. But doing this requires a publisher that knows its intended market and how it's different from other publishers. Even once this is known, it takes time to develop an ongoing connection with readers, and it's a very different game than the one that is (and will be) played by the Big Five in New York. In 2009 Richard Nash theorized:

> Basically, the best-selling five hundred books each year will likely be published like Little, Brown publishes James Patterson, on a TV production model; or like Scholastic did Harry Potter and Doubleday Dan Brown, on a big Hollywood blockbuster model. The rest will be published by niche social publishing communities.[9]

Literary publishers produce niche work, and as such are poised to become leaders of the community of readers and writers who have matching missions and belief systems. Literary publishers can add value and credibility to niche communities, through the act of publishing, of course, but also through forms of leadership and support that go beyond print and extend into events, services, grants, fellowships, reading groups, and more. Coffee House Press is one example of a literary publisher that has reconsidered its activities to encompass more than just releasing new books. Its publisher Chris Fischbach wrote:

> We think of our role as catalyst and connector, driving various kinds of cultural and community engagement. Sometimes that takes a solid and sellable form, and sometimes it's performative, electronic, participatory, or even culinary. This is the kind of publishing we're interested in, and what we think literature, and publishing, needs more of.[10]

Building community is primarily about intimate knowledge of and respect for that community, combined with creativity and imagination in serving it. Publishers that survive, whether they focus on traditional publications or digital media, must be indispensable to the communities they serve. While at one time a publisher might have been indispensable by communicating quality ideas and stories by remarkable authors, a publisher who does that today—and nothing more—can be seen as merely adding to the burden we all now face. There are too many wonderful things to read, and too few sign posts as to what's worth our time. Thus, the literary publisher needs to be a beacon, a strong signal amid all the noise, and organize ideas, content, and stories within an identifiable and useful context. Otherwise, many of us will turn away because we simply can't find the time to understand or discover the meaning or the quality of what's presented to us.

THE CHALLENGE FACED BY LITERARY JOURNALS

Good luck trying to find (or run) a profitable literary journal. Nearly all of them are supported by universities or by individuals who love literary publishing and are willing to put their own time and money into them. A literary journal's costs are rarely, if ever, covered by subscriptions, but rather by a combination of grants, institutional funding, and donations. Even extremely well-regarded, award-winning journals—such as the aforementioned *McSweeney's*—have found themselves on the edge of a precipice, and continue in part due to dogged persistence and commitment from their founders and staff, who repeatedly raise the funds needed to continue.

A sustainable model for a new print literary publication likely requires a combination of crowdfunding, grant writing, and traditional fundraising, in addition to the usual business of ginning up subscriptions and renewals. If a founder can't identify at least a few initial patrons willing to underwrite the publication for its initial year or two, or some kind of institutional sponsor, then a digital-only start is the smarter option. In other words, first build the audience that might support a print publication later on. Some literary journals survive because staff members work with little or no pay (or as part of a faculty position), or interns work for free in exchange for experience and connections.

In recent years, public expressions of frustration with literary journals have been on the rise, particularly when it comes to reading or entry fees. Writers feel exploited and taken advantage of, especially those struggling to find full-time jobs under a load of student debt.[11] But writers don't seem to realize that their struggles and literary journals' struggles are two sides of the same coin. The journals rarely have sufficient funding or support and rely on writers, whose own lack of funding or support affects their ability to prop up literary journals' fragile business model. Someone has to pay—so who should it be? Writers should hesitate before pointing the finger at publications that are struggling just as hard as they are to stay afloat. There is a difference between publications that have the ability to pay (or absorb costs) and those that don't, but writers have trouble appreciating the difference between the two, understanding the business model of the average journal or magazine, and recognizing the dramatic change underway in all types of publishing business models.

THE ROLE OF THE GATEKEEPERS

Well-known literary journals and publishers aren't shy about publicizing an acceptance rate of 1 percent or less. Scarcity is the assumed rule; many must be rejected and only a few can be accepted. If getting published is not difficult, how do we know who or what really matters, or that quality is being represented?

However, except for a few elite publications, literary journals (and many literary books) reach a couple thousand people at best. Gaining entry into the club still means something, of course—it's a respected rite of passage for emerging writers who want to be taken seriously by a particular literary community. A literary journal's influence and prestige is presumed to outpace its actual reach, and thus it can retain its relevance to the writing community as well as the broader culture. Even if very few read the publication, and it is a failure in commercial respects, if people have heard of it and equate its name with respectability and exclusivity, then isn't publication in its pages worthwhile?

Still, important questions have been raised about this model in the current publishing environment—an environment where there is an overabundance of content, increased competition from digital media, and many high-quality reading options. Before the days of the internet, something published in a literary journal would be amplified and would reach more people than it might through self-distribution or self-publishing. That's not the case today, and placing work in a well-read online publication—whether inside or outside the literary community—often can be done more quickly and with more perceptible impact than gaining acceptance in a print literary journal.

In an absurd twist, literary journals premised on great literature must now play the exclusivity game even harder, and manufacture what is ultimately a false scarcity—which usually means posting little or none of their content online. In 2013 Richard Nash wrote an essay for the *Virginia Quarterly Review* on the disruption of publishing's business model, arguing that the gatekeeping function was never that effective in the first place. While he is speaking of book publishers, the same principles apply to any publisher or editor of literature:

> The skill that is commonly associated with the pinnacle of editorial talent—picking the right book—is, frankly, nonsense. Success, in terms of picking things, is a hybrid of luck with the non-self-evident and money with the self-evident, and even the self-evident often

requires luck. . . . The advent of self-publishing has rendered this ever more visible. . . . Publishing has no particular ability to discern what is good or not, what is successful or not. This is true not just at the level of predicting commercial success, but also at predicting critical success. . . . This is not a knock on publishing. There's no evidence that stockbrokers can pick good stocks, or touts good horses.[12]

Nash doesn't see this as evidence that publishing will die—quite the contrary. But he does call for publishers, if they are to survive the disruption to their business, to focus on other valued functions. Again, publications have to stand for something more than "we publish great work" if they want reader support. Still, few literary journals have responded to the new publishing environment by setting aside or de-emphasizing their gatekeeping function.

In 2015 Michael Nye, then managing editor of the *Missouri Review*, wrote about a staff discussion where one editor explained to an intern why they wanted writers to keep submitting after getting rejected multiple times:

Getting rejected by a magazine repeatedly and then, finally, getting work accepted is, actually, fairly normal. It's a little frustrating for an editor, she said, when a writer submits to us five times and then just stops and we never get the chance to read the writer's work again. To emphasis this point, she noted that TMR has published several writers who sent manuscripts to us for over a decade before we published their work.[13]

While Nye was trying to be encouraging, his post provoked a significant backlash from writers who felt tired of banging their heads against the wall—pursuing success within a system that never seemed to work that well in the first place. Many writers commented via social media on the futility of waiting years to be published in a journal that very few would read or see in any case. One said:

At last count, I had 24 respected literary journals request to see more of my work, but just couldn't get there. I was at it for 12 years before I gave up with a serious hit to my self-esteem as a writer. I indie published a collection of my Southern short stories . . . and it is the readers now who are reminding me why I write. They love good stories and some of them even let me know. AND they don't charge me $2–$18 to get read. They actually pay me![14]

CHAPTER 8

When the number of visits to a publication's submission guidelines page is greater than that for its content—but there's no interaction with those writers, and in fact writers are asked to pony up to subscribe or submit—that sets up a dynamic in which the people who should value you come to either hate you or ignore you. And that is what is happening among young and old writers alike.

A FINAL WORD

Too many literary publishing efforts launch with the expectation that quality automatically sells. It does not. Anything that requires good will and charity to survive is a risky enterprise. But for a publisher with patience to see an audience grow, and with a strong vision, it's possible to survive on sales or subscriptions if a specific readership is targeted. Rather than pursue a general audience, it's imperative to go after a defined one—people must feel inspired by the vision. Because the audience for literature is so fragmented, this approach is nearly essential unless a publication possesses vast resources to draw upon for years or decades.

Today's public reads more than ever and has more access to literature than ever. A lot of the anxiety and concern surrounding literary publishing today is a concern about changing media consumption habits and discovery habits. We don't need to read the traditional journals or magazines to discover the next great writer. We can discover that person through a blog, Twitter, Tumblr, or a newsletter. Traditional publishers and journals may be right to be nervous about such changes, but they have no reason to be nervous about the demand for literature. It's the same as it's ever been, but its distribution and discovery will no longer be reliant upon them. This is a win for the writers, and an identity crisis for the publishers.

Part Three
GETTING PUBLISHED

Part Two grounded you in the business models of the publishing industry, across print and digital, books and periodicals. Now, with a holistic understanding of the artistic and financial concerns at play in the industry, you are better equipped to meet the challenge ahead: to successfully position and pitch your work.

Getting published doesn't depend on who you know. You can get editors, agents, magazines, and literary journals to consider your work even if they've never heard of you, by following a traditional, cold submissions process. That said, it doesn't hurt to get your portfolio started by working through whatever connections you have in hand, to score a few easy acceptances. My first pieces were published in an undergraduate literary journal, as well as in a journal edited and published by one of my writing professors. Early wins build confidence and give you something to put in your cover or query letters to other publications. As your career advances, you may submit cold less often, and secure new credits based on relationships. This can be ideal, but doesn't push you to stretch beyond your comfort level, and risk rejection—a key to growth.

Some say you're not really a writer until your work has been rejected. I tend to agree. Rejections will come from people you know, from strangers, and from publications that later accept you. Stick with it long enough, and you'll receive form-letter rejections, personalized rejections, rejections that contradict each other, and rejections that give you strength to continue.

If you're actively producing work but have never been rejected, it's likely you aren't sending your work out frequently enough or widely enough. You might be playing it too safe, trying to avoid the sting of rejection. That's understandable, but not helpful for a writing career. You don't have to develop a thick skin, but you do have to find the wherewithal to keep your work in circulation—to keep trying—especially early in your career. If you aren't actively submitting, you will not get published. Period.

As you gain more publishing credits, it becomes easier to ride this wave. You start to understand that no single rejection means anything, that rejections happen for a million reasons, and are only sometimes related to the quality of the work. The more you can see rejection as a business response, and not an attack on your ability as a writer, the better mindset you're in. So avoid giving up on your work after only a handful of rejections. Too many writers get discouraged early in the process and abandon an effort before they've given it a fair chance.

While this section addresses getting published in many forms, it predominantly emphasizes books, as they're the aspirational form for most creative writers and involve the most complicated procedures for getting published. Chapters 16–18 cover the basics of publishing shorter forms. Later, in part 5, we'll look at publishing opportunities that are more entrepreneurial and digital in nature, as well as how to seek funding to support your writing projects, particularly prior to publication.

9 : BOOK PUBLISHING
FIGURING OUT WHERE YOUR BOOK FITS

Before we begin this very in-depth exploration, a brief warning: Getting a book published is a significant accomplishment that sometimes doesn't happen for years into a writing career, and securing a book deal for your very first manuscript is extremely unlikely. Still, "published author" is the expressed goal and dream for the vast majority of creative writers. So that's where we'll start.

The first step on the path to book publication is understanding how a publisher would categorize your work. You should be able to define your book's genre or category, and have some insight into how commercially viable it is. This will help set, or moderate, your expectations of your work's potential, plus help you submit it to the right agent or publisher.

If you consider your work so unique that it can't be categorized, that's not a selling point for a publisher. To market a product, publishers need to be able to identify an audience and point to comparable work that's been successful. If your work is truly cross-genre or mixed genre, then you'll have to approach publishers that expressly accept that type of work (hint: there aren't many). Ultimately, if you're unsure, pick the genre that best aligns with your story or content. Then, once the book secures interest, you can further discuss how to best position it. Here's a high-level overview of fiction and nonfiction categories.

FICTION: LITERARY VERSUS COMMERCIAL

Fiction publishing can be broadly divided into two areas: commercial fiction and everything else. Commercial fiction encompasses well-known genres such as romance and women's fiction; mystery, crime, and thriller fiction; science fiction and fantasy; historical; and young adult fiction.

What defines commercial fiction is a matter of great debate, but most people agree it focuses on delivering a compelling story—a priority is to keep readers turning the page. There's a clear hero or set of heroes, and probably a villain or other characters who get in the hero's way. There's a traditional narrative arc: rising tension that culminates in a thrilling climax, with a satisfying or definitive ending.

This basic structure has been around since humans first gathered around the campfire to tell stories. And, with adjustments to fulfill the requirements or expectations of the various genres, it's a "formula" you'll see repeated across commercial fiction. Such work is not boring or derivative, but it does build on narrative techniques proven to work time and time again. Joseph Campbell compared myths and religions over time and across cultures, and wrote several works arguing for the existence of a "monomyth," a basic pattern that underlies narratives from around the world (he borrowed the term from James Joyce's *Finnegan's Wake*). This monomyth is (at least in the film industry) commonly summarized as "the hero's journey." You can find writing instruction books, such as *The Writer's Journey*, that teach you how to apply its principles to your own stories.

Work that doesn't fall under the rubric of commercial fiction is often referred to as "literary," a category discussed in chapter 8. What literary means depends on who you ask. If you were to pose the question to a panel of editors or agents, you'd likely hear a chorus of sighs; no one likes to define it, especially in front of an audience of writers. That's because the distinction is based on stereotypes. Literary writing is sometimes regarded as more complex, artful, and nuanced than commercial fiction, work written by smart or deep people for other smart or deep people—with the obvious implication that commercial fiction is for simpletons who probably don't even notice bad writing. That's a stereotype you need to be aware of, and one commercial writers especially hate having to do battle with.

Neither literary nor commercial fiction has a monopoly on being complex, artful, and nuanced, or on being "good" writing. However, those who write and read literary fiction do tend to have a more pronounced concern with language. They care deeply about not just the story, but exactly how that story is expressed. The aesthetics of the writing are as important as what happens.

Some people read to be entertained, as an escape; others read to be intellectually challenged. Either commercial or literary fiction can accomplish these goals. But commercial fiction does tend to focus on entertaining readers, while literary fiction is more likely to challenge them. Literary novelists may be less inclined to satisfy readers than to discomfort them. Literary authors may take five or ten years to write a book that they hope will be carefully read and analyzed for its many layers of meaning.

As the very name indicates, "commercial fiction" is work that's positioned to make money. Literary fiction is notorious for selling few copies and not making publishers much of a profit. It usually reaches a large readership only if the author is a household name or the book receives national recognition.

Most writers don't choose to write literary work or commercial work. They're simply drawn to produce one or the other. Creative writing programs, however, tend to favor literary work and aim to produce literary writers, not commercial novelists. Perhaps not surprisingly, most commercial authors are not graduates of writing programs. As is well known, John Grisham was a lawyer before he became a full-time novelist, and James Patterson worked in advertising when he produced his first novel.

When pitched a short story collection from an unknown writer, most agents or commercial publishers will immediately say no and ask if a novel is available instead. Short story collections, as distinctly literary work, are most appropriate for small and nonprofit presses that specialize in publishing and promoting the art of the short story. Most are based outside of New York and offer little money, but there can be prestige and opportunities with well-recognized presses.

As for poets: You'll find the commercial market even less receptive to poetry collections than short stories—unless you're a social media celebrity. (See Rupi Kaur's *Milk and Honey*, first self-published, then picked up by a commercial publisher. Kaur has more than 1.5 million Instagram followers.) Still, as with short stories, there are literary publishers and university presses devoted to publishing collections. But even if you interest one, don't expect to earn much money or see your book widely available in stores.

NONFICTION: NARRATIVE VERSUS PRESCRIPTIVE

According to industry estimates, nonfiction makes up a large majority of published work in the United States, perhaps as much as 70 percent.[1] That's not surprising if you study the layout of a large bookstore. Shelf space in stores may be divided among dozens and dozens of nonfiction categories, but here it will be more useful to think of two broad areas: narrative nonfiction and prescriptive nonfiction.

Prescriptive nonfiction is driven by information and advice. If you're teaching lessons, cultivating skills, or helping someone improve their life, then you're solidly in the realm of prescriptive nonfiction. These are practical books: The reader is trying to achieve something or derive a specific benefit from their content. As such, prescriptive nonfiction books are most often sold on the basis of an author's platform—their visibility in the field or to their target readership. You don't have to be a highly skilled writer to produce a best-selling prescriptive nonfiction book; rather, the book has to deliver on its promise to readers, with clarity and directness. While great writing is certainly a bonus, and a merely satisfying prescriptive book can become transcendental when written with great artistry, that's not the goal. The reader is not primarily interested in being entertained or delighting in what an artful writer you are; they want the benefit of your knowledge, experience, or unique insights.

Narrative nonfiction tells a true story, often using the techniques of fiction, such as narrative tension, well-crafted scenes, and character development. Memoirs fall into this broad category, as do biographies and autobiographies. If you've seen the movies *Seabiscuit* or *Unbroken*, both were based on best-selling narrative nonfiction books by Laura Hillenbrand. Sometimes narrative nonfiction is called creative nonfiction, although the terms aren't quite synonymous. The latter term is most often used within academic settings and literary publishing communities—not commercial publishing—and often refers to essay-length works that use techniques of both fiction and poetry.

Unlike prescriptive nonfiction, you need some experience or skill as a writer to produce a memoir, history, or other fact-based work that's meant to entertain through storytelling as much as it is to inform. Also, don't expect that you can research and write a nonfiction book from the comfort of your home office, relying solely on an internet connection and the local library. Armchair reporting isn't likely to pass muster with a New York publisher. Most successful narrative nonfiction work involves serious legwork, some amount of travel, and plenty of interviews. If you want to build a career in this nonfiction category, staying at home probably won't be an option. At the very least, you'll have to become skilled at using the phone or online video conferencing to get at information that is otherwise unavailable.

A Word about Memoir

Many people—especially those new to writing and publishing—attempt a memoir as their first book-length writing project. This sets up a significant challenge: the writer usually hasn't developed sufficient skills to tell the story, and—complicating matters—memoir is one of those categories where good writing doesn't necessarily seal the deal. The writer must have something new to say that sets her book apart from many similar stories. It can't just be about how hard her life has been and how others can survive a hard life too—which sums up the majority of memoirs being pitched in today's market.

You should be able to sum up the story in a couple sentences, in a way that encapsulates your unique and compelling perspective, but it must go further than just "growing up in a small town" or "overcoming addiction." For example: a New York City cop tells how he became a Bronx detective after being a bartender (*NYPD Green*). Or a woman tells about becoming a new mother while her parents are being sent to prison (*This Is Not My Beautiful Life*). Or a young woman recounts a six-month adventure with her dying 160-pound English mastiff (*Gizelle's Bucket List*). Notice how these stories zero in on a particular period in the writer's life. Don't expect to sell a memoir that begins during your childhood and ends in the present day. That's not actually a memoir so much as an autobiography. A memoir tells the story of a specific time, a span of months or a few years. Trying to tell your entire life story is a giveaway that you don't have a focused or cohesive narrative.

Also, it's best to avoid the book idea that combines elements of narrative or memoir with elements of advice or self-help. For example, you might want to tell the story of advocating for your special-needs child, while giving parents of similar children information they desperately need but can gain only from someone who's been through the same experience. Such hybrid narrative/self-help works can be difficult to sell because they don't firmly land in one category or the other. If the primary goal is to help others and build a reputation as an expert in the subject matter, commit to the prescriptive angle. If your motivation is to tell your story or build your career as an author, commit to memoir.

ESSAY COLLECTIONS, ANTHOLOGIES, AND HUMOR

File all of these under "difficult to get published," similar to short story and poetry collections. Few publishing goals are more difficult to achieve than selling a book-length work as an essayist, humorist, or satirist without first establishing a track record of publishing shorter work. Although there has been a resurgence of interest in essay collections, with the best-selling examples of *Bad Feminist* by Roxane Gay and *The Empathy Exams* by Leslie Jamison, both writers had years of experience before their collections were published. It's best to focus on small presses to land a book deal for a collection, and the same goes for anthologies with multiple contributors.

While children's publishing could command an entire book of its own, there are usually three areas of interest to creative writers: picture books, middle-grade books, and young adult books. The age of the target reader is often critical when pitching children's work, since the work should address issues that would be most appropriate for the child's age, as well as use language that fits their reading level.

A picture book is meant for younger children, typically pre-readers or beginning readers. It features pictures on every page and tells its story through both the text and the picture. The traditional picture book is thirty-two pages and has no more than a thousand words. Generally, the shorter the better.

Middle-grade books are for young readers, ages eight to twelve, who aren't yet ready for young adult novels. They might include a few illustrations, but the story is told solely through the text. A well-known middle-grade series is Encyclopedia Brown. (If you've heard of chapter books, those are for a slightly younger audience, usually have larger type and illustrations, and make a point of not being intimidating. An example is the Captain Underpants series.)

YA, or young adult, has experienced astronomical growth and is currently one of the most commercially successful genres. In 2004 adult fiction comprised about a third of all books sold in the United States. By 2014 it had dropped to 23 percent, partly as a result of gains in the young adult market. More adults are reading young adult fiction; if you're an adult who's read *Harry Potter*, *The Hunger Games*, or the *Twilight* series, then you're part of this trend. YA has many subgenres (such as paranormal or "realistic" YA), but their unifying quality is that the protagonist is a teenager, with parents in the distant background, if they're around at all.

These categories are all related to what we would consider leisure reading for children, or reading that happens outside of school requirements. Writers tend to have considerable leeway in how the stories are told and what vocabulary is used. If you intend instead to write children's books that will be used as school texts, then you need to study the very specific requirements and guidelines that are available from educational publishers.

Some writers think that, since children's work is often short, it must be easier to write and publish. The opposite is probably true. Especially when it comes to children's picture books, you'll find an extremely competitive market. It seems that every parent, grandparent, teacher, and caretaker has a picture book they want to publish. But picture books are among the most

WHAT'S YOUR WORD COUNT?

Publishers think about the books they're considering in terms of word count, which they translate into printed page count. The average book in today's market is 80,000 words, or somewhere between 200 and 300 published pages. The average for some genres, such as science fiction and fantasy novels and histories, can be longer, perhaps 100,000 or more. But once you reach 120,000 words or longer, you're decreasing the chances that an agent or editor will be interested in your work.

Word count for nonfiction widely varies—an illustrated book may have fewer than 10,000 words, while a reference book might be well beyond 100,000 words—but you can use 80,000 words as a rule of thumb for any type of nonillustrated narrative. Prescriptive nonfiction often runs shorter than 80,000 words.

Upon hearing these recommendations, some writers rightly point out that best-selling books can be very long indeed. *The Da Vinci Code* is nearly 200,000 words, almost three times the length of a typical novel. As J. K. Rowling passed the midway point of the *Harry Potter* series, the books were exceeding 500 published pages. So what gives?

If you're a first-time author, you're an unknown quantity. The longer your book is, the more it will cost to edit, manufacture, and ship. Therefore, the financial risk increases. No editor wants to be responsible for a 500-page commercial failure. Not that they want to publish failures of any length, but the longer the book, the more it will hurt. While there are always exceptions to length rules, don't count on being one of them. In most cases, a very long manuscript indicates a work the writer hasn't been disciplined enough to edit down.

If you have a manuscript that's between 20,000 and 40,000 words, you haven't written a book. If it's fiction, you've written a novella, and you'll have to look for publishers or journals that accept them; one example is Nouvella. If it's nonfiction, depending on the category, your work might be called a "single" by digital-only imprints and publishers; see Amazon's Kindle Singles program for an example. Generally, it's better to avoid this manuscript length given the publishing difficulties you'll encounter, assuming you want to publish traditionally.

difficult to get right. You have very few words, not to mention a limited vocabulary, in which to tell your story. Plus you must know what children are like today—what situations and difficulties they face in current times—and not write only from your childhood memories.

BEFORE YOU BEGIN THE SUBMISSIONS PROCESS

There are different levels of commercial viability: some works are suitable for Big Five traditional publishers, while others are better suited to midsize and small presses, as discussed in chapter 5. Most writers find it difficult to be honest with themselves about their work's potential, but the most important thing to remember is that not every book is cut out to be published by a New York house or represented by an agent. Remember that the Big Five's hope is to sell each book they publish in every bookstore across the nation. Does your work merit national distribution and promotion?

Once you've determined what type of book you have, you can begin researching agents or publishers for your work, preparing your submissions materials, and pitching your work via snail mail or email—or even at a conference. (These topics are covered in the chapters that follow.)

Fiction writers should finish and polish their manuscripts before approaching editors or agents; it is nearly unheard of for a debut novelist to secure a book deal based on a partial manuscript. Nonfiction writers, however, can secure a deal by writing a book proposal (usually including at least one sample chapter, as discussed in chapter 13) instead of the full manuscript; this way, they can receive an advance up front to support the time and research required to produce the manuscript.

Before you embark on the process of submitting your work, be confident that you've made it the best you can, and can see no further way to improve it. Don't expect agents or editors to act as your coach on a problematic manuscript or book idea, and, most important, don't proceed through the submissions process as if you're running a race. One of the biggest mistakes new writers make is rushing to get a book published. In 99 percent of cases, there's no reason to rush.

CHAPTER 9

10 : UNDERSTANDING LITERARY AGENTS

Within the more than five-hundred-year history of book publishing, literary agents are a recent phenomenon: they started appearing in late nineteenth-century Britain. The publishing landscape was growing in both size and complexity, so writers had greater need of a representative to navigate the market, protect their interests, and negotiate more lucrative contracts.

Publishers weren't initially pleased with this development. William Heinemann, who founded one of the oldest imprints still operating in the UK, wrote, "This is the age of the middleman. He is generally a parasite. He always flourishes. I have been forced to give him some little attention lately in my particular business. In it, he calls himself the literary agent."[1] Soon enough, these so-called parasites became valuable to both the publisher and the author. While agents served as authors' representatives, placing their clients' work at the best possible publishing houses, they also became talent scouts and a trusted filter for publishers. The biggest publishers stopped accepting unagented work, and the gatekeeping responsibility passed to the agents.[2]

Then, as now, agents might be former editors, or they might be lawyers—or neither. There isn't a formal industry credential for literary agents; anybody can call themselves one. Similar to editors, they have their own subjective tastes and opinions, and many specialize in certain types of work.

Whether you need an agent depends on several factors. Probably the most important is whether you want your work considered by the Big Five New York publishing houses, which generally don't look at material unless it's sent by an agent. But there are other benefits. Today, as was the case 140 years ago, agents know the market better than authors. They have relationships with specific editors at many publishing houses. They're experts in what's selling and how to pitch your work to the right place at the right time. They bring many years of experience, along with a network of contacts—and hopefully a reputation for uncovering talent. They're trusted by publishers to bring marketable projects to the table. When an agent represents you, you're getting the benefit of their insider knowledge and contacts.

The advantages don't stop there. Once they've negotiated the best deal for you, the agent should remain closely involved as your book progresses on the path to publication, running interference during any disagreements you might have with your editor or publisher. If there's ever a contractual dispute, your agent is the one who will handle it; if there's a problem with payment, your agent should be the first to spot it. Most authors appreciate how an agent allows them to focus more on writing, confident that the agent will take care of business and raise red flags if they see something amiss.

The very best agent serves as an author's career manager, taking an interest not only in the first book but in how to best strategize and sell future books. The agent alternates between roles: coach (pushing you to get your work done), therapist (helping you cope with the inevitable bad reviews), cheerleader (celebrating every win), and sharp-nosed accountant (ensuring you get every dime that's due). Some even become active in your book's marketing campaign. The best agent for you is someone who truly understands and believes in your work, and is committed to looking out for your long-term interests. You should trust your agent implicitly.

Before we discuss how to find an agent in chapter 11, you should first understand the standard business practices of a traditional literary agent, what their legal responsibility is, and what commitment you're making when you choose to be represented by one.

First, agents are supposed to make money only when they sell your work. Their standard commission is 15 percent of everything the author receives. That means 15 percent of your advance, 15 percent of any royalties you earn, and 15 percent of other earnings that come from selling rights to your work. This of course gives them incentive to find the best opportunities for selling your work and to negotiate better deals.

A small number of agents charge a fee for reading your work, but this isn't standard practice. Generally you should avoid anyone who charges up-front fees, because this is how publishing scams typically operate. Watch out as well for the agent who offers paid editing service, or refers you to an editing service in exchange for representation. While it is common for agents to say they'll consider representing your work if you revise it according to their specifications (known as a "revise and resubmit" request), it is *not* usual for them to do this work themselves and charge you for it, or to send you to a specific person they approve for help. In such cases, the agent may receive a kickback for referring you, which is considered unethical.

While agents have traditionally worked based on handshake agreements with their authors, they now often formalize the relationship in writing. The author-agent contract spells out how long the representation lasts, how it can be renewed or terminated, the agent's commission, and how disputes will be resolved. While the agent has the right to be your exclusive agent of record, your relationship should give you the freedom to represent yourself or market your own work when desirable. In other words, if and when you negotiate a deal for your own work without the agent's assistance, she shouldn't earn a commission on it. But for any and all works that the agent sells and negotiates a contract for, she is entitled to earn a commission for as long as that contract remains in effect. In fact, the publishing contract you sign with a book publisher will include what's known as an "agency clause"—which is written and provided by the literary agent. This clause binds the agent to the book deal as the agent of record, who receives all payments and distributes them to you, the author, until the contract terminates. Even if you break up with your agent, she will continue to receive a 15 percent commission while the publishing agreement remains in effect.

So, you should sign only with an agent you trust. Your agent oversees and double-checks your royalty statements from the publisher, and is responsible for sending you payments due. If either of you suspect the publisher isn't being accurate or honest in its financial reporting, it will be your agent who oversees the auditing process.

HOW TO EVALUATE AGENTS

In the following chapters, I'll discuss in detail how to research potential agents and how to submit materials to them. Assuming your search is successful, when an agent offers you representation, you should receive an email, and likely a phone call, to discuss the arrangement. Don't feel pressured to agree to the offer of representation immediately—it's OK to (respectfully) play hard to get. If your manuscript is under active consideration by other agents, you should say so and ask for at least a week or two to see if the other agents are also interested. You'll also want to ask if the agent requires you to sign a contract, which you'll need time to review.

Finally, you'll want at least a day or two to go back to your research notes about this agent, formulate a list of questions about how they work, and ask about next steps.

If you find yourself in the lucky position of being courted by two or more agents, then your phone conversations—which should give you the first signs of good or bad chemistry—may be the determining factor in which agent you ultimately choose. But also consider the following criteria.

First, look at the agents' track record of sales, or their client list and the publishers they have recently sold to. (You should be able to find this information on their website.) Are the publishers they sell to the types of publishers you consider appropriate for your work? Ensure that your agent has success in representing the type of work you're trying to sell. If she doesn't have the experience or connections you would expect, then ask her about it—again, respectfully. Publishing tends to be driven by relationships and reputation, and if your agent is trying to break into new business territory with your book, you should know prior to committing.

Sometimes it's easier to get represented by a new agent who is trying to build a roster of clients, someone who may not have a lot of sales under their belt. If an agent's track record is still developing, take a look at their previous experience in publishing. For example, were they formerly an editor at a New York house? What's the experience and reputation of the agency they're associated with? If they're working at a solid agency with an identifiable track record, or have a long history in the publishing world, these are good signs.

The second thing to look for is industry professionalism. This can be tough for a beginner to gauge, but the agent should be treating you in a way that inspires confidence. They should get back to you in a timely manner and communicate clearly. Their business operations shouldn't be cloaked in secrecy, and they should treat you as an equal. If you feel you're being treated shabbily, others might feel the same way—and that includes editors at publishing houses.

I should note here that I've observed some unpublished writers who can be very demanding and cling to expectations that are exceptional and outside the norm for the publishing industry. So be reasonable. You can't call your agent at any hour and expect to have a lengthy discussion, or demand daily contact, or count on near-instant responses to your emails. Remember: Most agents work for free until your book is sold. Their most immediate responses go to established clients whose continued book sales pay their bills.

The final thing you're looking for is enthusiasm. Do you get the feeling that the agent genuinely believes in you and your work? While agents are certainly interested in a sale, they're also interested in projects that excite them and clients they are proud to represent. While it's not possible to quantify "enthusiasm," think of it this way: Your agent represents your cause to the publisher throughout the life of your book's publication, and helps to resolve conflicts. Does this agent feel like your best champion? Having an agent you're not confident is doing the best job for you is often worse than having no agent at all.

One thing you shouldn't worry about too much is the size of the agency, which doesn't necessarily correlate with the size of the deals it negotiates. Some reputable agencies consist of only one or two principals, with perhaps a few associates—you might call these "boutique" agencies. Midsize and large agencies may have many agents on board, as well as specialized staff, such as a contracts manager or foreign rights specialist. Finally, there are mega-agencies, like William Morris Endeavor or ICM Partners, that have far greater scope than just literary talent—they also deal with actors, singers, and other performers.

WHAT HAPPENS AFTER YOU'VE SIGNED WITH AN AGENT

Once you've secured an agent, that doesn't mean your work will be sent out to publishers immediately. Agents' practices vary widely in this regard: some will help you further refine your manuscript or book proposal, some will ask you for revisions, and others might rework your submissions package to increase its chances of success. Only when the agent is satisfied with your materials and their presentation will they start contacting editors.

You've probably heard that publishers spend less time on editing than they once did, sometimes shifting pressure to agents to fulfill the role of nurturing editor. While you will find some agents who are very hands-on editorially, this isn't true of all agents. They aren't supposed to take the place of the editor at the publishing house. If you want to know if your agent is a hands-on type, look closely at their website, read any interviews they've done, or simply ask them directly if they make an offer of representation. There isn't really a right or wrong level of editorial involvement, but agents who are new to the business may be more inclined to put in substantial editorial work. That's because early on, while they're still establishing themselves, they're probably not attracting cream-of-the-crop projects. If you're seeking an agent who will take an active hand, it can be smart to target these "hungry" agents who may have more time to spend on nurturing talent.

Before the agent sends your work out, she'll probably discuss her pitch strategy with you—typically a round of submissions to the most desirable editors, or sometimes an auction. Auctions take place when an agent has what she thinks is a hot property. She might establish a floor price—the minimum for which she will sell the book—and then make submissions to potential editors, giving a deadline for responses. If one publisher's bid is topped by another's, the first publisher is given the opportunity to top the competitor's offer. Obviously, this process hinges on one factor: the book must be one that the industry believes will be a big seller. Nothing is more embarrassing for an agent than holding an auction and finding no bidders.

Sometimes, before the auction starts, a publisher issues something called a preempt, an offer conditioned on the agent immediately taking the project off the market. If the publisher and author are a good match for each other, and the offer is good enough, then a preempt can be a satisfying deal for everyone. Preempts often happen when an editor loves the project and doesn't want to compete with other publishers for it. If the preempt is declined, the agent and author then take their chances with the auction process.

However the process plays out, an agent can never force you to accept a deal or work with a publisher you're uncomfortable with. It's not uncommon for authors to turn down better money with one publisher to go with another house, or another editor, that offers a better fit.

WHEN THE AGENT CAN'T SELL YOUR WORK

Having an agent doesn't guarantee a book deal. These days it's common to hear from agents, after several failed rounds of submissions, "I could have sold it five years ago." Today's market is tougher than ever. So if this is what your agent tells you, hopefully they can offer more specifics about why. Is the market saturated? Are publishers demanding authors with bigger platforms? Have the publishers cut back on the number of titles they're signing?

Agents should specify what imprints or publishers they've contacted and been rejected by. It's your right to know this information, especially after a long period of time has passed. You can also ask for the rejection letters, though your agent is under no obligation to provide you with specific contact information of editors and publishers.

Don't assume that your agent isn't "good enough" because your book didn't sell. But they should have an open and frank discussion with you about any patterns in the rejections you're receiving. Perhaps there's a way to revise your book or its concept to make it more marketable, although you shouldn't expect that your agent will undertake a revision process with you. Sometimes, it's better for agents to cut their losses if they can't be confident of a sale worth their time. However, if the agent is genuinely enthusiastic about representing you, they'll likely encourage you to start or finish another, more marketable manuscript they can shop around.

If you feel your agent is failing you, and you want to shop for another, you might not find it easy to secure a new agent. Having had representation in the past won't in itself help you attract another agent. In fact, some agents might wonder if you're a difficult client, especially if they think well of the agency you're leaving. However, if you feel that terminating is your best option, and it might be, then look at the author-agent contract you signed. What are the rules? Some contracts stipulate you have to give the agent at least a year to find a home for your work. Others allow for you to terminate the relationship at will, within 30 days of notice. If you do part ways with an agent before they sell your work, make sure you get a list of all the publishers they've submitted to. That's the first thing your new agent will want to know. If your first agent exhausted every possible outlet, it's not really possible for another agent to approach them a second time. Once a rejection, always a rejection. Even if you reconceptualize the book, or dramatically revise the manuscript, most editors will be unwilling to take a second look at a project they've already considered. They would be doing an agent a major favor to reconsider, and most of the time, the answer would still be no.

If an agent's efforts lead to a dead end, another option is to begin submitting your work to smaller presses or digital publishers that the agent didn't pursue because they didn't represent enough of a financial opportunity. If you get an offer from a small press, it's possible to negotiate your own contract if you know what to look for. (See chapters 11 and 14 and appendix 1, "Contracts 101," for more on small presses and contracts.) Alternatively, you can sometimes find an agent to work on an hourly basis to negotiate the contract for you.

11 : RESEARCHING AGENTS AND PUBLISHERS

Once you're confident about your category or genre of work, and have some idea of how it fits into the literary landscape, you're ready to begin researching specific agents or publishers to approach (known collectively as "markets" for your work). When conducting this research, you need to answer three questions: (1) Is this agent or publisher actively considering new work? (2) Do I think this agent or publisher is a good fit for my work? (3) What materials does the agent or publisher require for my work to be considered?

Some writers wonder if they can hire someone to handle this head-ache for them—to identify the right markets to approach, put together their materials, and track responses. They find the process to be complete drudgery, as well as depressing when the rejections start rolling in. While there are services that will undertake this process for you, I'm not a fan of them. First, I don't think they care about your work as much as you. If it were me, I'd want to know that sufficient time, attention, and research went into selecting the right agents and editors for my work. Why spend years writing and revising your book only to outsource the very important business decision of identifying its best home?

But there's another reason I recommend you do the work yourself, which is perhaps old-fashioned of me: It's good for you. You should do the work that helps you get more familiar with the business side of writing, so you can make better decisions for your career. Plus, by trying to escape it or pay someone else to worry about it, you're ignoring an important lesson of every writer's life: you have to give due attention to both the art and the business.

You should focus on researching agents if you believe your work has significant commercial potential and is a good fit for a major New York publisher, or if you want your work considered by other presses that ac-cept only agented work. You might also want to research competitions, especially for literary work, since it's not uncommon for short story collections, poetry, or essays to be published by university presses as part of a prize package. See chapter 26 for more about competitions.

I recommend you take a methodical approach to the research and submissions process to ensure that you give your work the best possible chance. Here's the big-picture overview:

- Begin with online databases or print market guides that list hundreds, even thousands, of agents and publishers. Develop a broad hit list that includes every potential market you might approach.
- Next, dig deeper into each potential agent or publisher by doing online research. You're looking for any information that might help you understand what submissions they want to see from writers.
- Then start to categorize the agents or publishers according to fit: "my dream," "good fit," "maybe."

You'll be gathering *lots* of information, so use your favorite note-taking tool or software. I like Evernote. Other writers use Microsoft Excel. What's important is that you log the information so that you can easily find it later and refer to it during the query writing and proposal process. You might also use this same document to track your submissions process, to keep track of who hasn't responded and who's sent a rejection.

If you have any interest whatsoever in having an agent, or in pursuing commercial publishers, then try to secure an agent first. Do not pitch your book simultaneously to agents *and* to publishers. Agents prefer to start with a blank slate and be the first to introduce the project to the market. If you collect lots of rejections from publishers, then enlist an agent's help, the agent faces a difficult challenge: to turn a "no" into a "yes." So don't make their job harder than it needs to be. You can always approach publishers on your own (at least those who accept unagented work) if you fail to interest an agent.

If you have a relationship with an editor who has specifically requested to see your work, then it's OK to submit it without an agent. When and if the editor makes an offer, you can seek out an agent through the usual query process, and let them know you already have an editor interested. An agent can hardly object to that, although they may want to strategize with you on whether you should fish around for more or better offers.

Some of the following resources are free. Others require you to pay a subscription fee. As you might expect, the fee-based services typically offer higher-quality information, and your research process would likely be incomplete without investing in at least one of them.

- WritersMarket.com. By far the best place to research book publishers, with thousands of listings. Pay a monthly fee to access its database, or use the annual print edition at a library or bookstore.
- PublishersMarketplace.com. The best place to research literary agents; many agents have member pages with helpful information. A paid subscription is required.
- AgentQuery.com. Free site offering about a thousand agent listings and an excellent community for writers going through the query process.
- QueryTracker.net. Some publisher listings and a lot of agent listings. The basic service is free.
- Duotrope.com. A very useful database if you're shopping around poetry, short stories, essays, or literary novels. Paid subscription is required, but some writing programs have an institutional subscription—be sure to check if you're enrolled in one.

Databases include, among much else, information such as the mission statement or publishing philosophy of an agent or house; what types of work are accepted; what submission materials to send and when; and specific tips from the editors or agents being listed. Publishers may also indicate how many titles they publish per year and how much they pay.

Publishers Marketplace, though expensive, can be particularly insightful since it gives you access to book deals that have been made recently (as well as going back to 2000). For each book deal listed in its database, you'll find the following information:

- the author and title of the book, along with a one-sentence description
- the agent who represented the book
- the editor and publisher who bought the book

You can search the deals database based on your own book's category or genre, and can narrow your search further by using keywords. While it's far from a complete listing of publishing deals, Publishers Marketplace quickly gives you sharp insight into who's buying what, and what agents are actively selling. That said, when you run your search, be careful how far back you go. While it can be instructive to see the history of sales in a category, so much changes over time that only more recent years will give you a strong indicator of what's marketable right now.

All of these market guides and databases have that problem in common: they can go out of date quickly. They also tend to provide only the broadest brushstrokes of a particular market. It takes further digging to understand the tastes of an agent or publisher.

GOING BEYOND DATABASE RESEARCH

Once you're armed with your list of agents or publishers, undertake a more in-depth investigation of each. First, visit their websites, where you'll typically find the most up-to-date information, including whether they're open for submissions. Even if you've found submission guidelines elsewhere, always confirm them on the website. If you uncover discrepancies, follow the instructions that seem to be the most recently updated.

For literary agencies, read the descriptions of all member agents and determine which one is the best match. Usually you should only approach one agent per agency, but check their guidelines to be sure. If an agency offers tips for writers, obviously you should read them and note anything you'll want to remember when you put together your submissions package. Some agents have active blogs or news and events pages, which can be useful to scan. Look for any comment on the types of queries they're receiving (particularly within the last year), what they've recently sold, and what projects they want to see more of.

Publisher websites tend to be far more conservative in their information and advice for potential authors. In fact, you often have to hunt for anything at all related to submissions. If you can't find anything explicitly labeled "Submissions," check the small type at the top and bottom of the homepage for "About Us," "Contact Us," or "Site Map." Worst-case: Google the publisher's name along with "submission guidelines"—that usually turns up something. As with agents, research which editor to approach within the company, look for editor bios to assess the best fit, and approach one. If you can't find any specific editor names, that's OK. Address your submission generally to "the editors."

While you're at the publisher's site, study their recent releases. Usually books are released in two seasons—a fall list and a spring list. Looking at

TIPS FOR RESEARCHING SMALL PRESSES

If you undertake the submissions process without an agent, you'll have to evaluate the qualities of small presses, and look for signs that they will be a good business partner and likely to produce a successful book. Given the extreme ease of publishing and distributing e-books and print-on-demand editions, just about anyone can call themselves a publisher. While working with a newly minted press might suit your needs, you should know it going in and adjust your expectations. Here are some questions to ask when researching small publishers or digital-only presses:

- **Where are their books distributed?** Publishers should clearly state on their website where their books are available or how they can be ordered. Can you find their titles in physical bookstores? The largest publishers—the Big Five—sell direct to bookstores, while smaller publishers work with distributors to reach stores. Very small presses may sell their books only through online retailers such as Amazon.

- **Does the publisher invest in a print run or use print-on-demand only?** This is a back-door approach to the bookstore question. Print-on-demand (POD) is a technology that allows publishers to print their books one at a time, as they are ordered. Your book is unlikely to be stocked on physical store shelves unless the publisher invests in at least a small print run. A print run also represents an investment and indicates some commitment to selling and marketing a book. Ask the publisher what its typical print run is; most publishers will commit to a minimum of 500 or 1,000 copies of any title they publish.

- **For digital-only publishers, what value do they provide that you need?** You'll find many varieties of digital-only publishers—from innovative imprints at the Big Five houses to start-up companies. Most pay higher royalties but no advance—or a very low advance. The digital market remains in flux, with no established standards. So you'll have to study carefully the titles released, who's authoring them, and what level of success they seem to have. Do you want to be part of the family the publisher is building? Do you trust it to provide good editors, marketers, and publicists for your work?

- **What's the publisher's editing process like? Will you be assigned an editor?** Some small presses will take exactly what you give them and publish it, without any copyediting or proofreading. Even if you like the idea of your manuscript remaining pristine, this shows lack of engagement and care. Virtually no manuscript will be ready to publish without considerable editorial work.

- **What marketing and promotion do their titles receive?** Ask what the publisher's baseline marketing plan is for every title. Do they send out advance review copies? Write a press release? Submit the book to specific media outlets for coverage? Find out the bare minimum they commit to, and if it amounts to little more than making the title available for sale, rethink whether you want to publish with them. You can also get a good feel for the sophistication of publishers' overall marketing and promotion by simply studying their online presence and how they present themselves.
- **How can you terminate the deal?** It's less risky to sign with a small press when there's a defined way for you to leave if things don't work out. Some new presses will agree to a limited term that's renewable by mutual agreement. See appendix 1 for more about contract negotiation.
- **Can you speak to recent authors?** This can be the best litmus test of all. Are other authors pleased with the publisher's communication and level of involvement? How much value did the publisher add to the process? Will the authors stay with this publisher for their next books?

---

an entire season gives you an excellent idea of how many titles the publisher handles, the types of authors it looks for, and what topics it publishes on. In the case of nonfiction, you may end up researching some of these titles in depth as part of your book proposal.

Study any formal series or imprints that specifically apply to your work. For instance, Sourcebooks, an independent publisher in Chicago, has an imprint specifically devoted to young adult books, called Sourcebooks Fire. Harlequin, a romance publisher and itself a division of HarperCollins, has more than a dozen different imprints. Most imprints have specific guidelines and market considerations that are distinct from those of the overall company. It's easy to go down the rabbit hole and get confused. If you find you need a map of how all the pieces fit together, check *Writer's Market*, which every year publishes an updated listing of all the major publishers and their imprints.

After studying the website of the agency or publisher, it's time to move on to social media. Twitter is very popular in the publishing community, so you'll likely find a presence there. It's also worthwhile to check for public accounts at Facebook, Pinterest, and Tumblr. Many agents and editors use social media to have conversations with authors, potential authors, and other industry insiders. Studying these communications not only provides insights into the submissions process but helps you ascertain fit. Is this someone you want to do business with? Do you like their demeanor? What gets them enthusiastic?

You'll find that some publishing professionals offer specific information and advice for writers through social media, and some invite questions during specific chat windows. These are good opportunities to ask that market-trend question you've been pondering that maybe only they can answer. Also, a phenomenon has emerged on Twitter whereby agents and editors tell writers what's on their "wish list"—what types of projects they want to sell but haven't been receiving from writers. You can stay informed about wish list requests by following the #MSWL hashtag on Twitter, or by visiting MSWishList.com, which tracks what requests are tweeted.

As a final step in your online research, run a Google search on each of your markets. Put the name of the specific agent or publisher in quotation marks, and see what you get. If you get a lot of results, it can be helpful to add the word "interview," "submissions," or "query." You could also use words connected to your book's genre, category, or theme.

Once you've collected all the information you can find on your target markets, start to prioritize your list. Any agent or publisher who is a weak candidate should not be approached—"Hail Mary" queries will only waste your time. For better candidates, you might further research what conferences or events they attend. Could there be an opportunity to pitch or meet in person?

If you have any doubts about the quality of an agent or publisher on your list, Google their name and add the word "scam." You're probably not the first person to wonder, and that search will help you find the message boards where people discuss their experiences with agents and publishers. You can also check several sites where industry watchdogs actively post warnings. Writer Beware is the best known and most respected.

OTHER METHODS OF RESEARCHING AGENTS AND PUBLISHERS

One of the oldest recommended methods of finding an agent is to look in the acknowledgments section of a book you've read that's similar to your own. Just about every author thanks both their agent and their editor. An added benefit is that you now have an excellent way to open your query letter, which we'll discuss in the next chapter.

Another tried-and-true method is to ask published friends—if you have any—for a referral to their agent. The danger is that your author friend might not believe your book is all that good. If he knowingly sends his agent a dud manuscript, he'll hurt his ability to refer other deserving writers. So it can be a delicate situation. Sometimes it's best to ask your friend if they'd be willing to take a look at your work and offer feedback, which might then lead to a referral. However, many authors have dozens of friends making the same request, and it can be hard to avoid an awkward situation for both of you.

If you're willing to work with a new and "hungry" agent or publisher, then keep a close eye on new market announcements. You can find them reported at Publishers Marketplace, which you can access if you're a subscriber; *Writer's Digest*'s Guide to Literary Agents blog, which posts about new agents; and online writing communities that have dedicated threads for such announcements. Also, every year, *Writer's Digest* publishes a special agent issue in October, highlighting twenty or more agents who are seeking new clients.

12 : BOOK QUERIES AND SYNOPSES

As you research agents and publishers, you'll soon discover that almost no one accepts a full manuscript on first contact. Instead, an author commonly sends a query letter. The query letter is the time-honored tool for writers seeking publication, used by magazine writers and book authors alike. In book publishing, the query functions as a sales letter that attempts to persuade an editor or agent to read your manuscript or proposal.

At its heart, the query is about seduction. In fact, it's so much about charming persuasion that you should be able to write the query without having written a single word of the manuscript. That doesn't mean it's easy. For some writers, the query represents a completely unfamiliar way of thinking about their book and their story. You have to begin seeing your work in terms of a marketable product, which requires having some distance from it.

In addition to the query, you may be asked for a synopsis if you're writing a narrative work. This commonly reviled document (at least among writers, and even some editors) is sometimes requested because an agent or publisher wants to see, from beginning to end, what happens in your book. It helps them determine, without having to read an entire manuscript, if you are able to tell a story, specifically within the conventions of your genre.

As a reminder: Novelists should pitch their work only when the manuscript is final; nonfiction writers can pitch based on an idea alone and some sample material. We'll tackle novel queries first, then nonfiction. I'll be referring to agents throughout, but the same principles apply when approaching editors.

NOVEL QUERIES

I divide the query into five elements:

- some element of personalization, where you customize the letter
- what you're offering: your book's title, word count, and genre/category

- a compelling story premise (the meat of the query)
- biographical note
- closing

Personalization. This isn't required, but it can set your letter apart from the hundreds of others sitting on an agent's desk. A surprising number of writers do little or no research before submitting their work, and blast their materials to any address they can find. Agents, of course, can easily spot blanket submissions, and appreciate writers who are more thoughtful and considerate.

If you consider your query a sales tool, then you're striving to be a good salesperson. And good salespeople develop a rapport with the people they want to sell to, and show that they understand their needs. By personalizing your letter, you can show that you've done your homework and that you're not pushing your work out to everyone indiscriminately.

There are several ways to personalize your letter meaningfully. If you've studied what type of books the agent represents, you can compare your work to that of an existing client. If you've read interviews that mention the agent's interest in what you write, you can cite that as a specific reason for approaching them. Even better, if you've heard the agent speak or met them at a conference, you can reference that. The key here is demonstrating awareness of the marketplace you're trying to enter. It's not that you want to appear chummy, but you should come off as informed and deliberate.

That said, you're not going to be rejected for not personalizing your query—and in some cases, you might find it hard to personalize the letter in a meaningful way. At the very least, address a specific agent (not just "Dear Agent:") and demonstrate some knowledge of the types of work they deal in, based on your research. (A sentence is more than enough, avoid more than two.) This alone will set you apart from the many writers querying, and that's the point.

What you're offering. Even though the title is tentative, even though the genre may be tweaked later due to marketing considerations, even though that word count may change during editing—include all of these details. They signal that you have a fully realized project that's targeted to a particular audience. They could also unwittingly signal some problems with your project. For instance, if your query states that you've written a memoir that runs 250,000 words, that fact alone can lead to a rejection. You're selling a project that doesn't fit well within current market standards.

Sometimes it can be useful to draw comparisons between your book and another title or the work of another author. You can say that your book is written in the same manner or style, or that it has a similar tone or theme. Just be careful not to overdo it. One or two comparisons should be more than enough, and the more thoughtful the comparison, the better. Comparing yourself to a current *New York Times* best-selling author can come across as arrogant or too easy; it's better to demonstrate a nuanced understanding of where your book falls within the literary spectrum.

The story's premise or hook. The most common mistake is to cram in too much detail about the story. Instead, you want to focus on the story's premise. The premise consists of the protagonist(s) and the challenge they face. We need a fairly equal balance of character and plot here—enough to connect with the character and enough to be interested in the problem that will drive the story from beginning to end. We want to avoid anything that might sound or feel like a book report, or an accounting of the plot twists and turns. (If agents want to know that, they will turn to the synopsis, which we'll discuss later.)

When a hook is well-written but boring, it's often because the story lacks anything fresh. It's the same old formula. The protagonist feels one-dimensional, the angle pedestrian, the premise indistinguishable from a hundred others the agent has seen. Your story may be compelling on the page, but your query fails to capture its unique qualities. Figuring out what's truly special about your story, and expressing that in a compelling way—this is the toughest part of writing the query. I recommend you start with one of the following prompts:

- What does your character want, why does he want it, and what keeps him from getting it?
- State your character's name, give a brief description, describe the conflict she faces, and convey the choices she has to make.

Once you have a draft of your hook, work on improving it. You should be able to write an effective hook in 100 to 200 words. Some hooks are just one paragraph, or you might have a few short paragraphs. Usually you only need to mention the protagonist(s), the romantic interest or sidekick, and the antagonist. If you're trying to explain more than three or four characters, you're on the wrong track. If you're getting sidetracked into minor plot points that don't affect the protagonist's choices or the story's outcome, cut them. Finally, don't reveal the ending in your hook. (Again, that belongs in the synopsis.) Your best strategy is brevity. The more you try to explain, the more likely you'll squeeze the life out of your story. Get in, and get out.

Biographical note. This is usually 50 to 100 words. Include any relevant publication credits; if you're unpublished, there's no need to state that. Mention any writing degrees, memberships in major professional writing organizations, and well-known awards or grants you've won. Such things signal your seriousness and intention to develop a career as a writer. But avoid cataloging every single thing you've done in your writing life. If you're unsure whether to include something, skip it. If your book is the product of some intriguing or unusual research—say you spent a year in the Congo, and that informs your characters and plot—mention it. Unique details can catch the attention of an agent. If you have a career outside of writing that informs your work (e.g., you're a former lawyer writing legal thrillers), by all means mention it. But even if there's not a direct connection, agents are often curious about what background you bring to your writing. You are allowed, even encouraged, to be a multifaceted person!

Just about every agent will Google you if they have any interest in your work, and they'll likely find your website or blog whether you mention it in the query or not. If you're proud of your online presence, and very active, you might want to mention it in the query. But it doesn't say anything about your ability to write a great story, and for novelists and memoirists, the art and craft of story come first.

If you've previously self-published your work, the query presents a minor dilemma. Should you mention your track record as a self-published author? That's totally up to you. Lots of people have self-published these days, and while in the past there was a stigma surrounding self-publishing, it no longer affects your chances for traditional publication in the future. If you do mention it, it's best if you're proud of your efforts and ready to discuss your success (or failure). If you consider it a mistake or irrelevant to the project at hand, better to leave it out. Just understand it may come up later, and don't make the mistake of thinking your self-publishing credits make you somehow more desirable as an author. That would require incredible sales success.

Closing. You don't read much advice about how to close a query letter, perhaps because there's not much to it, right? You say thanks and sign your name. But you want to make sure you leave a good final impression and follow good etiquette. You don't have to state that you are simultaneously querying, as everyone assumes this already. However, if the manuscript itself is under consideration by another agent or editor, then mention it if or when someone else requests it.

Resist the temptation to editorialize in the closing, or at any point in the letter. Don't proclaim how much the agent will love the work, or how exciting it is, or how it's destined to be a best seller if only someone will give it a chance. Thank the agent, but don't carry on unnecessarily, be cloyingly subservient, or beg.

Never introduce the idea of an in-person meeting. Don't say you'll be visiting their city soon and suggest you might meet for coffee. The only possible exception is if you know you'll hear them speak at an upcoming event—but don't ask for a meeting. Just say you look forward to hearing them speak. Use the conference's official channels to set up an appointment if it makes sense, perhaps instead of sending the query.

NONFICTION QUERIES

There is tremendous variation across nonfiction queries, because nonfiction spans vastly different types of work. However, it can be roughly divided into two categories, as discussed in chapter 9:

- prescriptive nonfiction (such as business, self-help, and reference)
- narrative nonfiction (including memoir and biography)

For prescriptive nonfiction, rather than relating a story premise, you craft a hook that effectively tells what your book is about and why there's a need in the market for it. You also have to describe your platform: why you're the best person to write the book and in a strong position to promote it. Before querying, you should have a book proposal written and polished (see chapter 13); your query letter will end up being a condensed version of the book proposal's overview—the summary that discusses the most important and salable qualities of your book. (It's OK if your query and proposal include the same or similar language.)

In a prescriptive nonfiction hook, it's very powerful to claim that your book will be the *first and only book to do X*, assuming it's the truth. Such a statement indicates uniqueness sufficient to set your book apart from the competition. You may be entering a crowded field, so you need to nail the concept and make it irresistible. Discuss how your book offers a compelling solution to a problem faced by your target audience. Ask yourself the following questions:

- What special features or content does your book offer?
- What research or investigation does your book include that can be found nowhere else?
- What proven systems, methods, secrets, or lessons do you share?
- How will readers benefit from your book? How will their lives change for the better?

Unless you have platform muscle, it's unlikely that New York publishers will be interested in your prescriptive nonfiction book. Platform basically equates to visibility, or the ability to sell books. You should have visibility among the specific target audience you expect to buy your book. And it's not enough to say you have visibility—you have to be able to point to it, quantify it, and show how you're ready to lift off into the stratosphere of book sales. (For more on platform, see chapter 19.)

For narrative nonfiction, the query looks much the same as it would for a novel. Writing quality and storytelling is usually the primary consideration, and your hook plays an important role in conveying the quality of the story. But the publisher must also be able to envision a sizable audience for the story—so you need to show how the topic is timely, relevant, or otherwise of interest to readers. It's instructive to look at the rejections Rebecca Skloot collected for *The Immortal Life of Henrietta Lacks*, now an award-winning book. Skloot had trouble persuading editors that her story was marketable to a wide audience. Here's what a couple of those rejection letters said:

- "I'm sorry to say that I'm not entirely confident that the approach taken here to tell us the story is the kind of treatment which will reach the broad nonfiction readership that we're looking for."
- "She's a graceful writer with a real talent for presenting scientific material in a lucid and very human way. That said, though, I have to admit I can't quite imagine how a book on this chapter in science might reach more than a very limited audience. To me, the real heart of the story is somehow too short-lived to create a strong sense of narrative tension, and its repercussions, I think, may not spark the interest of a wide enough readership for [our] list."[1]

If you're pitching a memoir, then write the query in first person. Be aware there are a lot of tired story lines out there, as pointed out in chapter 9. From the comments in a 2010 agent roundtable on memoir in *Writer's Digest*, you can get a feel for what makes agents' eyes glaze over:

- "On some days it seems as though every therapist in the country who is dealing with addicts of one kind or another has told them to journal their recovery and then turn it into a book. Quitting booze or drugs is a good thing to do, but it isn't the triumph of the human spirit."
- "I'm sick of dysfunctional family stories, but I'm a big fan of memoirs by people who have lived lives the rest of us only dream of."
- "Though books by cancer and disease survivors are prevalent, I find them very tough to sell to publishers unless the survivor has some kind of name recognition."
- "I try to steer [writers] away from, 'I was born in a big/small town, and I liked listening to punk music, and I hated my mother and blahdee blahda blah blah.'"[2]

PUTTING IT ALL TOGETHER AND SENDING IT OUT

The very first paragraph of your query should put your best foot forward, or lead with your strongest selling point. Some strong ways to start:

- If an existing client or author has vouched for or referred you to the agent or editor, that's your lead.
- If you met the agent or editor at a conference, and especially if your material was requested, put that information right up front.
- Some authors do best to lead with their credentials or prestigious awards. This is especially true for previously published authors, or those with MFA degrees from well-known programs.

If none of these scenarios applies to you, then the default way to begin your query is either with the personalization described in the section on novel queries or with your story hook. As far as polite terms of address, it's best to open formally, such as "Dear John Smith." If an agent writes back using your first name and signs with their first name, you're welcome to match their informality in your response.

Once you have a working draft of your query, it's time to check for a few red flags.

- If your fiction query runs longer than one page, single-spaced, you've said way too much. You need to simplify and trim back your hook or your biographical note. Nonfiction queries may merit a second page, but don't go onto a third.

- Avoid directly commenting on the quality of your work. Your query should show, not tell, what a good writer you are.
- Avoid long explanations of what has inspired the work. It may be OK to reference briefly your inspiration, but this kind of material is best saved for publicity interviews after the work is published. Agents rarely care about your inspiration and can have jaded responses to it.
- When pitching a novel, you don't have to talk about trends in the market or the book's target audience. Your novel's genre already speaks to that, and your publisher will be very familiar with how well that genre sells. What you have to sell is the story. Some writers get confused on this point, because nonfiction queries do need to delve into evidence of marketability. But for fiction, it's the craft that matters at query stage, and little else.

Ask this about every detail in your query: Will it be meaningful, charming, or persuasive to the agent or editor? Ideally, the query should reveal something of your work's voice or personality, rather than being too stiff. While the query isn't the place to divulge too much personal detail, there's something to be said for expressing something about yourself that provides insight into the kind of author you are—that ineffable you.

Once your query is final, I recommend sending it out in batches, to five or six markets at a time, beginning with agents or editors who represent the best fit for your work. See what the response is like. If you're getting no responses or form responses, reevaluate your query and see if you can improve it. If you've been sending the synopsis or first five pages along with the query, you may need to consider if any red flags are hidden there.

You might wonder if it's better to query via email or snail mail. If the submission guidelines allow for either, then email queries can lead to faster response times. However, emails are easier to delete or reject. They usually have to get to the point even more quickly than paper-based queries. When you're ready to email a query, copy and paste it from your word processing document into the email message as plain text, without any special formatting. Make sure it can be read in a glance or two, with minimal scrolling. Don't include your mailing address, special headers or contact information at the beginning of the email—that's wasted time and space. Be captivating and essential with your lead sentence and paragraph; the agent or editor might not reach the end of the message.

When you receive positive responses, they will tend to be something like, "Yes, send the first three chapters," or "Yes, send the full manuscript." If someone asks for an exclusive, that means they want to be the only one considering the project, and you must promise not to send the work to anyone else during the exclusivity period. I would only grant an exclusive if it's for a very short period, maybe two weeks to consider a full proposal or manuscript. When you do receive a manuscript or proposal request, ask specifically when you should expect to hear back, then follow up within one week of that date.

Email replies from agents are typically very short. Don't use a positive response as an opportunity to launch into a lengthy reply talking more about yourself and your work. That's better saved for a phone call if the agent makes an offer of representation.

If you don't hear back at all after an initial query letter, follow up about two to four weeks after the response time stated in the submission guidelines. If no response time is given, wait a couple of months. If you queried via snail mail, include another copy of the query in your follow-up. If you still don't hear back after one follow-up attempt, it's best to assume rejection and move on.

- **See businessofwriting.org for examples of query letters.**

THE DREADED SYNOPSIS

Now that we've tackled the query, we come to what may be the single most despised document that novelists—and some narrative nonfiction writers—are asked to prepare: the synopsis. The synopsis conveys your book's entire narrative arc. It shows what happens and who changes, and it has to reveal the ending.

Don't confuse the synopsis with sales copy, or the kind of material that might appear on your back cover. You're not writing a punchy marketing piece that builds excitement in potential readers. Rather, you're writing for agents, who are looking to see if the characters' actions and motivations make sense. Plus, a synopsis will reveal any big problems in your story. If it turns out the whole book is a dream, or it's an act of god that saves the day, an agent may skip reading the manuscript altogether. A synopsis has an uncanny way of highlighting plot flaws, serious gaps in character motivation, or sweeping failures of story structure.

Because there is no standard method for writing a synopsis—and you'll find different opinions on the appropriate length—this can be confusing territory, for new writers especially. I recommend keeping your synopsis short, or at least starting short. We'll focus on how you can write a one- or two-page, single-spaced synopsis and use that as your default.

You'll need to accomplish at least three things with your synopsis, without exception:

- First, you need to tell us what characters we'll care about, including the protagonist, and convey their story. Generally you'll write the synopsis with your protagonist as the focus, and show what's at stake for them.
- Second, we need a clear idea of the core conflict for the protagonist, what's driving that conflict, and how the protagonist succeeds or fails in dealing with it.
- Finally, we need to understand how the conflict is resolved and how the protagonist's situation, both internally and externally, has changed.

If you cover those three things, that doesn't leave much room for subplots or minor characters. You won't summarize each scene or even every chapter, and some aspects of your story will have to be broadly generalized. If events and interactions don't materially affect the story's outcome, leave them out. While avoiding detail, you can still impress with lean, clean, powerful language. From a mechanics point of view, this means using active voice rather than passive, and third-person, present tense.

Don't make the mistake of thinking the synopsis just outlines the plot. A purely mechanical account suggests no depth or texture—or emotion. Consider what it would sound like if you summarized a football game by saying, "Well, the Patriots scored. And then the Giants scored. Then the Patriots scored twice in a row." That's sterile and doesn't give us the feel of how events unfolded. Instead, you would say something like, "The Patriots scored a touchdown after more than an hour of scoreless play, and the MVP led the play. The crowd went wild."

So you need to share some context and convey the characters' feelings about what's happening. You tell about an incident, which advances the story. The character feels something or reacts to that incident, and makes a decision that further advances the story. As you do this, avoid editorializing—adding phrases such as "In a thrilling turn of events." Transitions between paragraphs should make it clear how events connect, but don't spend any time explicitly deconstructing themes the story may address. It's best to avoid dialogue. If you must include dialogue, be sparing: make sure the lines you include are absolutely iconic of the character or represent a linchpin moment in the book.

While your synopsis will reflect your ability to write, it's not the place to get pretty with your prose. Don't attempt to impress through poetic description. You can't take the time to *show* what happens in the synopsis—you really have to *tell*. Sometimes this is confusing to writers who've been told for years to "show, don't tell." The opposite is true in the synopsis. Here, for example, it's OK to come out and say your main character is a "hopeless romantic" rather than illustrating it.

Finally, your synopsis shouldn't be coy or mysterious. The agent needs to know what happens and how your book delivers. Some writers think "spoilers" in a synopsis will kill the enjoyment of reading the manuscript, but this misses the entire point of why the synopsis is being requested. Assume that an agent has seen it all before. Anyone who asks for a synopsis blatantly does not want their curiosity piqued. They want the goods—and to evaluate whether those goods have money-making potential. Without a clear and accurate synopsis, professionals can't make an informed decision about your project.

Once you have a first draft of your synopsis, set it aside for a week if you can, then return to it. Does your protagonist come to life, and feel interesting? Does the plot effectively build tension? Do we clearly understand what's changed for the protagonist by the end? Does the overall tone or style of the synopsis match that of your novel?

- **See businessofwriting.org for examples of synopses.**

PARTING ADVICE

If you write your query or synopsis and start to get a bad feeling—a feeling that your story has structural flaws—push pause on the submissions process and consider whether you need to revise. Problems with your manuscript won't get resolved by the agent or the publisher—instead you'll get rejected. Since you only get one chance to pitch each work, make sure you resolve any problems that surface during the query and synopsis writing stage.

13 : THE NONFICTION BOOK PROPOSAL

For most types of nonfiction books, the most important document you'll prepare for an agent or publisher is a book proposal. At its heart, a book proposal explains why your book will sell. Rather than writing the manuscript first, as you would with a novel, you instead write a proposal to attract a publisher, who will contract and pay you in advance to produce the book.

Sometimes, a book proposal is not required for memoir if you have a full manuscript, and on rare occasions, you might be able to skip writing the proposal for other nonfiction projects if the manuscript is ready. Only by reading submission guidelines can you determine what an editor or agent prefers to receive, and requirements vary tremendously since each nonfiction category is so unique. But if you're an unpublished writer pitching any kind of narrative, who doesn't have proven journalistic or storytelling skills, agents will likely want to see your full manuscript, in addition to the proposal, to ensure that you can successfully produce a compelling story. Just never assume that having a full manuscript negates the need for a proposal if the submission requirements ask for one.

Securing a contract *before* writing the manuscript can be desirable if your book requires intensive research, travel, or some other commitment; funding can make the difference in whether you're able to devote time and energy to the project. Furthermore, there are a number of advantages to drafting a proposal early on. Crafting a proposal requires that you do market research, which should provide insight into what content your book needs to include, or how it needs to be positioned, to compete on the shelf. Just a little advance legwork can save you considerable time and energy. You don't want to spend a year on research only to find that a competing title has covered the same territory. Be aware, though, that book proposals are complex documents. They can take weeks or months to prepare if properly developed and researched, and it's not uncommon for them to reach fifty pages or more.

As I have emphasized, there are many types of nonfiction, and each category has different market considerations. A sizable platform is typically required to sell a prescriptive nonfiction book to a major publisher, especially in categories such as health, self-help, or parenting, where readers aren't likely to trust your advice without authoritative credentials and the publisher relies on the author's visibility or popularity to drive sales. However, with smaller, more specialized publishers, your platform may have less effect on whether your proposal is accepted. For example, a university press will be more concerned with the quality of your scholarship or ideas than the quality of your platform.

For narrative nonfiction, agents and publishers like to see an established track record of publication related to the book's topic. When the author has established a reputation and hopefully a network of relationships related to the subject matter, there's a greater chance that the book will be successful once it reaches the market. If you're unsure how much your platform will matter to a publisher, ask yourself: Does the book need to succeed based on its artistic excellence and ability to tell a story? If so, the manuscript must prove your strength as a writer, and the proposal may be secondary. If your book instead focuses on sharing information or a compelling idea, then you're selling it based on your expertise, your platform, and your concept—and your proposal must effectively argue why the book will sell and how you'll make the work visible in the market.

There is no "right way" to prepare a book proposal, just as there is no right way to write a book. Proposals vary in length, content, approach, and presentation. Each book requires a unique argument for its existence—or a specific business case—and thus requires a unique proposal. However, all book proposals need to answer three strategic business questions:

- **So what?** Why should your book exist? What unique selling proposition sets it apart from others in the market? Why is this book needed now, and how will readers be enticed to spend twenty dollars or more to buy it? You want to show evidence of need in the marketplace for your work.
- **Who cares?** Who is the target readership or audience for your book? How large is this audience? What do we know about these readers? Knowing your audience or market and having direct and specific ways to reach them gives you a much better chance of success.

- **Who are you?** What are your credentials for writing the book? How visible are you to the target audience? Do not pitch a book expecting that the publisher will bring the audience to you. It's the other way around. You bring *your* audience and *your* platform to the publisher.

These three questions will run through the mind of every publishing professional who considers your project. To be persuasive, you want not only a well-written proposal, but a market-informed proposal. Your proposal should demonstrate a deep knowledge of the community that is concerned with and publications that address your book's topic, and an understanding of the needs of your audience. You'll have a much easier time writing your proposal, and it will be more successful, if you take time beforehand to conduct market research and analyze how you'll reach your target audience.

CONDUCTING MARKET RESEARCH FOR YOUR BOOK PROPOSAL

Your first step in putting together a worthy proposal is surveying the competitive landscape. Visit bookstores in your area—preferably both an independent bookstore and a chain bookstore. Go to the shelf where you would expect your book to appear. What's there? Study the books closely and take notes. Record titles, authors, and publishers, but also pay attention to price, length, and format. Read the back-cover copy: How are the books being positioned? Who do they seem to be targeting? What promises are being made to the reader? Study the authors' credentials. How is each author visible in the market? How do they reach readers? Take note of forewords, introductions, blurbs, or reviews by important people—you may need similar endorsements to establish your credibility.

This initial search will probably give you a list of a dozen or more titles that are at least comparable, if not directly competitive, to your book. If you've come up with absolutely nothing that's comparable, that's not a good thing. It may mean your idea is too weird to have a market, or maybe the market isn't driven by mainstream booksellers. Either way, finding no competitive titles—or just a handful of titles—may rule out pitching your book to agents and large commercial publishers, unless you have another way to prove there's a market for it.

Next, look for publications, websites, and media offerings that are connected to your book idea. Run online searches for keywords and phrases that relate to your book. Where, other than books, does your target audience go for information on the topic? Determine how easy it is to find online information, and whether that information is trustworthy. Is the information free, or do you need to pay for it? How well known are the authors or organizations behind the information? If you're savvy about your subject, you're probably already familiar with the key publications and media surrounding it—and you may even be involved with them. Your goal is to understand how your target audience fulfills its needs for entertainment, education, or resources. As you research relevant online and multimedia sources, as well as books, magazines, and events, think about how they could play a role in your marketing and outreach plan.

Study the authors, experts, and influencers you found as you researched competing titles and complementary media. Dig deeper into the platform and reach of these people. Determine how you can set yourself apart and look for hints for developing your own platform to appeal to a publisher. Ultimately, while these authors or influencers might be competitors, they might also become collaborators. Consider how they might play a role in your marketing plan. Look for opportunities to build relationships with them and include them in your own network of contacts.

You may know from the beginning exactly who your book is for. If not, these research steps should strengthen your understanding of the target audience and what they need or want. If not, go back and look for clues— the language being used in comparable and competing sources, the design aesthetic, and how the material is packaged.

It's a big red flag in your proposal if you say that your book is for "everyone" or a "general readership." Successful books and media, even those with broad appeal, are geared toward some primary audience. Maybe your book *could* interest everyone, but there's a specific audience that will be the most likely to buy it. Who are those people, and how and where can you reach them? Again, this initial research has probably given you some pretty good hints. The more you know about your primary target market, the better you'll able to build a proposal that speaks to that first crucial question: *Who cares?* Plus, a deep understanding of your audience leads to a better book.

Being thorough and thoughtful in this research will help you eliminate the most common problems in book proposals: no clearly defined market, often combined with a concept that lacks freshness or specificity. Your proposal has to show why your idea isn't like a million others.

Once you've completed your market research, you're ready to begin writing. Although every book proposal is different, they all have several key sections. We'll discuss each of these in depth—not in the likely order of their presentation, but in an order that you might find them easiest to write.

Competitive title analysis. This section analyzes similar books, and why yours is different or better. You don't want to skimp or rush here—editors can tell when you haven't done your homework. Gather your research, and determine which titles are the most important to discuss in your proposal. The goal is to pinpoint how your book fits into the landscape of available titles. You might assess as many as ten titles if the category is popular and far-reaching, such as self-help, business, or health. You might be OK discussing just a few titles if your book is on a specialized topic or for a narrow audience.

For each entry in your competitive title analysis, begin by listing the title, subtitle, author, publisher, year of publication, page count, price, format, and ISBN. If it has a specific edition number, include that too. You can leave out things like Amazon ranking, star rating, and reviews. And don't worry about including sales numbers; there's no way for the average author to find out that information, and the agent or editor can look it up for themselves.

Briefly summarize each book's key strengths or approach in relation to your own. This is where you differentiate your title from the competition, and show why there's a need for your book despite the existence of related titles. These summaries usually run 100 to 200 words. You have to play a bit of a game here: you don't want to trash the competition when you might end up pitching the agent or editor who worked on a competing book! On the other hand, you can't describe the book without referencing your own. You need to point out how it's different from your book or if it has limitations. If you haven't read the book, then check out the professional reviews and customer reviews; you'll often find constructive criticism or insightful comments about how the book might be improved or what territory it fails to cover.

Once you've described all of the titles in your list, go back to the beginning and write an introduction that summarizes your book's unique position in the market when compared to the competition. A typical analysis will be three or four double-spaced pages, possibly longer.

Author bio. It can be helpful to begin with a bio you already use on your website, but don't just copy and paste it into the proposal and consider the job done. Instead, tailor your bio and background for the book idea you're proposing. Show how your expertise and experience give you the perfect platform from which to address your target audience. If this is a weak area for you, look for other strengths that might give you credibility with readers or help sell books—such as connections to experts or authorities in the field, a solid online following, and previous success in marketing yourself and your work.

The worst thing you can do here is paste in a résumé or CV and expect someone to pick out what's important or relevant to your book. Instead, focus on telling your story in a way that positions you as an ideal author who's on an inevitable path to success. A typical author bio is between one and two double-spaced pages. Of course, if a résumé or CV is specifically requested in the submission guidelines, as it may be for a university press, you should provide one, but still include a short narrative bio.

Target audience or market. In this section, you identify the readers who will be compelled to spend money on your information or story in book form.

It can be very tempting to make broad statements about who your audience is, to make it sound like anyone and everyone is a potential reader. For instance, let's say you're writing a book that shows readers how to become effective activists and community organizers in their city or region. You might say the audience is "anyone who wants to make a difference." But this broad, vague description is unhelpful and obvious; you need to dig deeper and describe more specifically the interests and characteristics of your potential reader. (You should also avoid describing or detailing the demographic of people who commonly buy books—publishers already know that. They want to know who specifically you're targeting within that known audience of book buyers.)

To help describe your audience, first consider who your ideal reader is. Consider what demographic they belong to, and take into account their behaviors, motivations, and beliefs. Perhaps your community organizing book is primarily for twenty-something female activists who live in urban areas and have likely marched in at least one protest. Now we're starting to go somewhere specific and useful. While your book may end up having broad appeal, be disciplined in your initial assessment of who it should primarily target. After you describe the primary audience for your book, you can also describe potential secondary audiences.

Your target market analysis will be more powerful if you can cite news and trend articles, or any research, that comment on the problem your book addresses or the audience you're trying to reach. Features published by esteemed journalistic outlets, as well as reports from government and nonprofit agencies (such as Pew Research), can help back up your claims. You can also try searching Google Trends to track your topic's popularity over the years and identify significant news stories. Again, be careful to avoid generic statements and meaningless statistics. The number of search results for certain keywords, for instance, tells us nothing about the audience who will buy your book. Instead, try to craft statements like this one, for a cookbook: "There is growing evidence that amateur chefs want to cook more sophisticated dinners at home—such as the success of Blue Apron, founded in 2012. Forbes estimated that its sales crossed $100 million in 2015 and commented, 'It's not a grocery delivery start-up . . . but a cooking company.' Blue Apron now delivers 8 million boxed meals a month to homes in the US."

You won't always find specific, relevant data, but don't assume it's not out there. Many magazines and websites that accept advertising do routine customer research and include extensive data in media kits available at their websites. Businesses of all kinds write press releases that tout their growth and the qualities of the market reached. These can be a rich resource for your market analysis.

A typical market analysis will be two to four double-spaced pages. You know you're finished when it's clear what's at stake for the target audience and how your book speaks to their needs. An agent or editor should have enough information to envision how the book can be successfully positioned and packaged in the market to readers.

Marketing plan. This is where you spell out what you can do to market and promote your own book to readers. Never discuss what you *hope* to do, only what you can and will do, without publisher assistance, given your current resources and platform. Saying that you're "willing" to do something if asked (e.g., "I'm willing to appear on TV") is not helpful. Instead, be confident, firm, and direct about the marketing and promotion efforts you're prepared to undertake. Make it concrete and realistic, and attach numbers where possible (e.g., you'll market to your email newsletter list of 1,000). This section can run anywhere from two to six double-spaced pages, sometimes more.

The marketing plan reflects the strength of your author platform. Platform (discussed in detail in chapter 19) influences the publisher's decision when you're pitching a nonfiction book. A major reason nonfiction books are rejected by agents is "lack of author platform." That naturally leads authors to ask how big their platform must be. This is an unanswerable question, because every publisher is different, every book is different, and every author is different. Still, as a rule, for your nonfiction book to secure a New York publishing deal, you need some kind of publication track record or authority in your field, probably an established online presence, and visibility to thousands of readers.

I think of the marketing plan as having four facets: First, illustrate everything you can do to reach readers directly through channels you control, such as your blog, email newsletter, and social media accounts. These are your resources to capitalize on, and part 4 of this book describes how to develop them, both before you begin pitching your work and as you develop your career. Second, show how you can tap your personal and professional connections and ask them for support. Third, mention how you can connect with influencers who may not yet be part of your network but who reach your target audience. And fourth, discuss opportunities that can put you in front of your target readership in new and hopefully bigger ways. Here are key areas to consider:

- If you have a website or blog that reaches thousands of readers per month, lay out a specific strategy tied to the launch of your book.
- Email newsletters are powerful marketing tools. Discuss how you'll use any existing list to spur sales.
- Describe how you'll use social media to bring awareness to your book. (Don't just state numbers. State your strategy.)
- If you actively speak or teach, indicate how you will ramp up your schedule of engagements and secure more gigs to support the book launch.
- Mention any special contacts or organizational and business relationships that can be tapped to gain coverage or visibility for the book. For example, if you're a former employee of Google, and you're writing a book that would interest the company, would they invite you to speak as part of their Talks at Google program?
- If you can become a regular contributor at a well-known publication in advance of your release date, or if you can place articles or guest posts at influential sites, mention it.
- Who can you tap to be an early supporter of the book—someone who will feature it on their site, blog, or podcast, or otherwise recommend it to their audience?

The secret to a strong marketing plan isn't necessarily the quantity of ideas you present, but how well you deploy the network or advantages you have. Show that your ideas are not just pie in the sky but can be connected to tangible resources or action steps.

Aside from your own network, it's helpful to offer a vision of how and where you think the book might receive media coverage. While you might be tempted to go for the obvious big hitters, like the *New York Times Book Review* or the *New Yorker*, consider outlets your publisher might not already know that reach your target audience. Media-savvy authors may link to interviews or clips of their appearances on TV shows or radio, to prove an ability to effectively market and promote to a national audience. The same goes for any author who frequently speaks or teaches; it helps to show what you're like in front of an audience.

Some marketing strategies shouldn't be discussed, even if you know they're frequently used. Anything related to book giveaways, discounting or price promotions, or advertising may not be within your control. Don't base your marketing plan on initiatives your publisher would need to invest in, or suggest things that could interfere with normal operations with their business partners. For example, suggesting an Amazon-focused book launch, or giving away the book for free, won't be an acceptable strategy for most traditional publishers.

Overview. This is the opening section of your proposal, a compelling summary of your business case. Think of it as an executive summary for the entire document. Because it's the hardest to write, I recommend authors save it for last. Typically one to three double-spaced pages, the overview effectively and holistically answers the three questions: *So what? Who cares?* and *Who are you?* The most compelling and juicy details from your proposal should appear in the overview. Some agents and editors recommend you envision the overview as your book's back cover copy, which should speak directly to readers trying to decide whether or not to purchase your book. That's a good way to start.

OTHER BOOK PROPOSAL ELEMENTS

If you're hitting the average length for most sections, you'll have around fifteen to twenty double-spaced pages once you've completed the above sections. At the end of your proposal, include a table of contents or a chapter outline for the book, followed by one or two sample chapters.

A chapter outline works better for narrative books, while a table of contents makes sense for information-heavy books with a lot of sections. For a chapter outline, write a brief summary of the idea, information, or story presented in each chapter, about 100 to 200 words each. If you want to include both a chapter outline and a table of contents in the proposal, that's acceptable. Just show how your book concept plays out from beginning to end, and strongly convey the scope of material covered. If there are special features or sidebars—or any kind of unique presentation of content—make sure that's conveyed. Any book element that might be used as a selling point to readers should be clearly described and included.

As for the sample chapters, they have to prove that you can deliver on your promise of quality information or storytelling. If the content or writing doesn't measure up to the promise made in the proposal, you won't get a deal. Your best strategy is to include one of the meatiest chapters of the book as your sample. Don't slap together a lightweight chapter that might be easier to write but that doesn't showcase your best material. (Memoirists and others who are telling a story are an exception. For book proposals pitching a long-form narrative, it's best to include the opening chapters, up to twenty-five pages or so. Editors need to see that the story starts strong.)

Before the chapter outline, include a brief statement that conveys the anticipated length of the book (or the actual length if it's finished) and how much time you will need to finish it. Typically, authors are given six to twelve months to complete the book after signing a contract. If you need to conduct any special research, or have any considerations that would affect your ability to complete the project—such as travel costs or the ability to gain access to interview subjects—mention them. This page is usually titled "Manuscript Delivery and Specifications." Note that it's usually not appropriate to discuss what format the publisher should use—such as paperback versus hardcover—or pricing. The publisher decides these matters.

For books that require photography or illustrations, you'll need to include a section that explains how the art will be sourced, obtained, or commissioned. Discuss costs or permissions issues involved with obtaining the art. If you intend to create or source the art yourself, include samples in the proposal so the editor can review the quality and appropriateness for book publication.

If you want to include additional materials in the proposal, agents and editors are generally accepting of anything that contributes to the case for your book's publication. One of the more popular additions is a foreword, introduction, or advance praise from influential people or successful authors. If the author lacks sufficient authority on his own, this can be a useful way to bolster the book's credibility. You might well ask, How do I obtain such materials from important people before I have a book deal? The short answer is, you ask very nicely. Typically you only ask people you have a strong connection to. It's difficult, even impossible, to get endorsements from a completely cold contact.

You'll need to come up with a tentative title and subtitle. For prescriptive nonfiction pitches in particular, it's best to be clear, direct, and benefit-oriented with your titles, rather than vague or overly clever. If you absolutely can't resist getting creative with the main title, then make the subtitle explanatory to eliminate any confusion as to the book's topic. Most publishers like to see your topic keywords somewhere in the title or subtitle, to make sure the book can be easily discovered through an Amazon or Google search. While it's true that the publisher will likely change your title, take time to create something that draws attention and identifies the book's audience and purpose.

ASSEMBLING YOUR PROPOSAL

When all sections are written and ready, create a cover sheet for the proposal that includes your book title, name, and contact information. Center it all on the page. Follow that, on a fresh page, with a table of contents for your proposal, listing all of the proposal sections and what page each starts on.

The sections are usually put in the following order: Overview, Author Bio, Target Market, Competing Titles, Marketing Plan, Manuscript Specification and Delivery, Table of Contents, Chapter Outline, Sample Chapters. The chapter outline and sample chapters traditionally come at the end of the proposal, but other than that, you can organize the information in whatever way makes the best business case for your book.

- **See businessofwriting.org for examples of book proposals.**

14 : WORKING WITH YOUR PUBLISHER

For first-time authors, signing a book contract can be one of the most exhilarating events of their lives. It can also be one of the most terrifying when they realize how much they still don't know.

The first order of business is writing and revision. You'll be assigned an editor responsible for reviewing your work and providing feedback. Sometimes this editor is the same one who bought your book. Other times, the acquiring editor hands you off to another for development. Either way, it's important to understand that your editor serves as your champion for the book inside the publishing house. Treat this relationship as one of the most important factors in the success of your book, because it is. For deep insights into editors' roles, I recommend Peter Ginna's *What Editors Do: The Art, Craft, and Business of Book Editing.*

Depending on the publisher and the type of book, you may be asked to submit partial drafts on the way to the final deadline, to ensure you're making sufficient progress on the manuscript. And even if you have a completed manuscript when you sign the contract, you'll almost always be asked to revise. When you submit your work for review, it may take several months for you to receive any feedback. Try to be patient. You'll be anxious to hear what the editor thinks, but that editor is likely juggling a dozen other authors and projects, if not more, at various stages of development. When you first submit your manuscript, ask when you might expect to hear back so you're not left wondering at the timeline. If you're concerned about how long it's taking, ask your agent for guidance, if you have one. Sometimes the contract specifies how much time the publisher has to review and respond, as well as how much time the author has to revise after receiving feedback.

Writers new to the business sometimes consider an editor's requests for revision a personal affront, when in reality the editor is only trying to produce the best possible manuscript for the intended audience. Editors know what works for the market, and they are eager to help you achieve your best effort—they wouldn't have contracted your book otherwise. Good author-editor relationships are clear and communicative; you deserve to know why an editor is asking for certain revisions, and to receive guidance on how to revise to the publisher's satisfaction. You should be able to compromise if necessary, and say no to specific revisions that you don't agree with. Good editors know that it doesn't help anyone to force an author to revise in a way that makes him lose confidence in the integrity of the work. If there are difficulties or misunderstandings, don't overlook the editor's essential goodwill toward the project. In worst-case scenarios, your agent should step in to handle any disagreements that threaten to jeopardize the contract or publication date.

Whatever deadlines you're given, respect them. While publishers try to build in a cushion—authors are notorious for missing their deadlines!—don't assume there is one. If you think you'll miss a deadline, inform your editor as far in advance as possible, and propose a new deadline. The more transparently you communicate about your situation, the more understanding your editor is likely to be. The worst thing you can do is let a deadline pass by in complete silence or avoid contact with your editor. Be proactive and professional, and work with your editor to ensure the delay doesn't have an adverse impact on your book. Sometimes a deadline is critical if your book is to release on the right date for special marketing and promotion opportunities. You don't want to miss an opportunity that could lead to greater sales because you didn't take a deadline seriously. Of course, manuscript deadlines are included in your contract too, and publishers may have the right to terminate and ask for the advance back if you fail to deliver your work on time.

About nine to twelve months before your book's release date, or sometimes as soon as your contract is signed, the publisher will begin a formal titling process. Your contract may give you the opportunity to consult on this process, but the publisher almost always has the final say. About six to nine months before your book releases, after the title is finalized, the cover and interior design process will begin. As with the title, when a publisher accepts a book, it almost always reserves the right to determine the package design. Publishers work with in-house designers and marketers who typically have a deep understanding of the market, but if you feel the cover design, title, or package conveys the wrong idea or feel for what you've written, raise your concerns with your agent or editor. Be as specific as possible about how or why the title or design misses the mark for the intended readership.

As you've probably heard, not all books are adequately marketed and promoted. This is primarily because publishers don't have sufficient resources—money, time, or staff—to invest in all of the titles they release. Also, while publishers are well schooled in targeting bookstores and trade accounts to make your work as visible as possible, the marketing opportunities related to those channels tend to be limited and competitive. The end result is that publishers sometimes rely largely on hope that a book will find its audience—by simply being in stock at stores and talked about in the mainstream media or by important review outlets.

You may have heard horror stories about authors whose books are "orphaned" during the publishing process—that is, their editor leaves. Some books never seem to recover their momentum and receive lackluster support from sales and marketing because no one inside the publishing house is invested in their success. Let's hope you don't find yourself in that position, because there's not much of a cure; it illustrates the critical role of the editor in ensuring your work gets the sales and marketing attention it deserves. Your editor is responsible for distributing early versions of your work to the in-house sales and marketing staff to drum up enthusiasm and support. The editor will also pitch your work during a season sales meeting, and make suggestions for how the book can be best positioned in the market. Important decisions are made while you are still writing or revising the book.

Publishers are known for putting most of their efforts behind A-list authors or books they're betting will sell big. They'll also better support a book if it receives an encouraging response or commitment from important retail accounts, such as chain bookstores or big box stores. Unfortunately, this leaves the majority of authors behind. You need to find out early in the process—at the time of contract, if possible—if your book will receive the bare minimum support, so you can plan appropriately. If you're one of the rare authors who's received a six-figure advance, you might feel assured of more support because the publisher has a significant investment at risk. But even then, don't assume.

One of the first marketing tasks you'll likely have is the completion of an author questionnaire. The publisher sends you a document that asks about every facet of your network and platform: names and contact information for important relationships or professional connections, information about your local and regional media, and much more. Be thorough in completing this form. The more the publisher knows about your resources and potential networking opportunities, the more they can potentially support your book. They'll want to build on existing assets.

Around the same time, the publisher may nudge you to ask your important connections for advance praise (a blurb) or, for nonfiction, possibly an introduction or foreword. By attaching well-known names to your book, you add credibility and authority to your work, especially if you're a debut author. The publisher, and even your agent, will help in securing these— but they will expect you to reach out to people you know personally, as such appeals are more effective in getting someone to say yes.

Blurbs are always offered without fee—you don't pay for them—while forewords and introductions may involve an honorarium. The size of the honorarium depends on several things: the length of the material required, how well known or in-demand the person is, the complexity of the material to be written, and how "big" or important your own book is. Rates range from a couple hundred dollars to thousands. If the author is personally interested in your book and you are well connected to them, you may pay little or nothing. In some cases, the publisher will pay the honorarium, or offer to split the cost.

If your publisher is serious about your book gaining traction, they will produce what's known as an advance reading copy, or ARC (also known as a galley), about four to six months before your book releases. ARCs are sent to trade review outlets such as *Publishers Weekly*, *Kirkus Reviews*, and *Library Journal*. These publications are read by booksellers and librarians to help them decide what to read or order. ARCs are also sent to publications and media outlets to solicit additional mainstream reviews and coverage.

As for book tours, the costs often outweigh the benefits. Only A-list authors who can be sure of drawing crowds typically receive book tour support. If you're a new or midlist author, don't expect it—and you should hesitate before planning one on your own. (For more on this, see chapter 22.)

Roughly four to six months before your book is released, once your book has a relatively final cover and title, the publisher's sales process will begin. This tends to coincide with the release of the publisher's seasonal catalog. Ask your editor for a copy of this catalog. Turn to the page that lists your title. How is it positioned? If it has a full-page listing near the beginning, that indicates A-list treatment and support. If it's buried, not so much. What does the catalog say about the publisher's marketing plan for your book? If you've been communicating well with your editor or publisher, nothing you see in the catalog will come as a surprise.

The biggest traditional publishers send out sales reps to call on key

WHAT'S THE PUBLISHER FOR THEN?

When I first started working in publishing, no one questioned the value of a publisher. Now they do. When I tell nonfiction writers they'll need to demonstrate to an agent or editor that they have a big enough platform—enough visibility—to sell books without the help of a publisher, they ask, "What's the publisher for then?" When I tell fiction writers that their work needs to be compelling, polished, and ready for publication before they query, they too ask, "What's the publisher for then?"

For first-time authors who have no readership, the answer is easy. Quality considerations aside, a publisher raises your profile and makes you look bigger than you've ever looked before. Someone is taking a financial risk to launch your work into the world and make your name recognizable, and the risk can be taken only for a finite number of authors, so readers make quite logical assumptions about quality that are in your favor.

Of course, publishers fail at launching authors every day. But authors promoting themselves tend to fail at it more dramatically. It's not that publishing is hard. It's the ability to spread the word about your work's existence at the right time to the right people that's crazy difficult. So far, most publishers are still better at doing that.

If you're an author who can make influencers jump when you ask, or have a siren call that lures readers to your door, then all bets are off on what the publisher is for. You'll have to decide. But these are just a few of the reasons some authors prefer working with publishers.

They want the security of an advance. For nonfiction authors who require money up front to research and write a book, this can be a significant motivation. Novelists may secure multibook deals with the promise of a paycheck over a span of years, allowing them to focus on producing the next work.

They trust the editor they work with. It's one of the romantic fantasies of every author: to have a nurturing editorial relationship that makes every book better. It does still happen, and once authors find an editor they trust, they tend to be invested in staying with them.

They don't want to fuss with the details. Publishers take care of many administrative tasks related to publication that are time-consuming or confusing for an author to handle—everything from registering for ISBNs to filling out book metadata to filing for library CIP data to managing distribution across multiple formats.

National print distribution is important to their goals. An author working alone will rarely see their book distributed widely to stores or to libraries without the help of a publisher, plus getting on the *New York Times* best-seller list requires nationwide print sales.

They seek credibility or attention from industry media and mainstream media. Publishers have established relationships and connections that open doors. Without their backing, authors are more likely to be brushed aside by reviewers and the media, as well as teachers, librarians, booksellers, and other gatekeepers.

They hope to see their work widely licensed. The Big Five houses, as well as midsize publishers and literary agents, attend international book fairs and are better able to secure licensing or subrights deals that may lead to increased income and visibility. (Think: translations, audiobooks, book club editions, and more.) Publishers and agents also have relationships inside Hollywood and can shop book projects to producers and studios. It's nearly impossible for an author—especially a new or unknown one—to tackle these kinds of deals on their own.

Having a publisher can give you more power and visibility, even if the publisher isn't particularly engaged in marketing, promoting, and selling your book. Plus, authors often take pride in the fact they've been vetted, selected, and anointed as someone deserving of investment and publication. This isn't an invalid reason to want a publisher, but getting a publisher's stamp of approval doesn't guarantee success or sales. Rather, it's just the first step in a long journey; every author must then make the most of the business partnership—and any prestige it brings—by marketing and promoting their work to the best of their ability.

---

accounts, which include chain and independent bookstores, wholesalers, distributors, and specialty retailers. They will suggest order quantities based on sales of comparable titles, as well as the enthusiasm and support coming from inside the publishing house. (Remember: it's your editor's job to stoke this support, and hopefully they'll have done so effectively.) Because a major publisher releases dozens, if not hundreds, of titles per year, not a lot of time can be spent on each. A-list titles tend to get the most attention, and the sales person will emphasize those titles over the others. By the end of the sales meeting, there's usually a rough indication or informal agreement as to how many copies the account will take, but this isn't a sure thing until the order actually comes through.

Sometimes, accounts will ask for changes to a book before they will place an order. For example, it's not uncommon for a buyer at Barnes & Noble to ask for a cover to be changed. An account may also push for a better marketing plan or support from the publisher. In most cases, the publisher tries to please the account if a large sale is at stake.

By the time the sales call is made, the publisher has already determined and budgeted for the most important marketing initiatives for each book. Advance praise should be secured, large-scale advertising campaigns will be on the calendar, and forthcoming media commitments—such as an excerpt set to run in a magazine or online outlet—will be touted as a reason to commit to a strong sales number. This is why it's so important that you communicate what you'll be doing to support your book many months before its release—I'll offer some tips on that in a moment. If your efforts are to contribute significantly to the prepublication sales push, the publisher should have that in its plan before making sales calls.

There are a few good signs that your publisher is extra invested in your book. One of the best is securing display space at a major retailer—because every display is paid for, displays are limited to the most marketable and sales-worthy titles. It's a significant coup for both the publisher and the author to get display placement, so celebrate if that happens. You may also be invited to appear with the publisher at an industry event, such as BookExpo or an independent bookseller show. Such an invitation means you're considered worthy of personally meeting booksellers, librarians, and other opinion makers who have the power to hand-sell or place your book in prominent display positions. Finally, there's a chance you'll be invited to the publisher's offices to talk to the sales and marketing team personally, to help build a better relationship, support, and understanding for your work.

HOW TO BE A PROACTIVE MARKETING PARTNER

Most authors work from afar with their publisher, and may never meet the sales and marketing team. Here's what you can do at any point after signing the contract to help ensure you get the best possible results from them.

First, come up with a marketing plan that you can execute on your own. If you have already developed such a plan—for example, as part of the proposal for your nonfiction book—now's the time to follow through on it, as well as update it with new resources and ideas. Tell the publisher what you will be doing, and identify areas where the publisher could be of assistance to you. Publishers are much more likely to be helpful if you proactively show them your plan and ask for what you want—as opposed to calling up and demanding to know what they'll be doing to support your book.

If you have a really early start—let's say you sign a contract two years before the book is due to be released—then you're in an even better position. You can begin to establish your online presence (see part 4) and develop relationships with your target readership as well as influencers who recommend books. Make a dream list of online and offline publications where you'd want your book reviewed or mentioned; then start cultivating relationships with the people related to them. Identify groups or organizations that would be most interested in your book, and start compiling a spreadsheet of email and snail mail addresses. As you write and revise your work, think of ancillary materials or products that would complement the work. Consider competitions or giveaways that would be interesting to someone who enjoys the book.

All of these things can contribute to a strong marketing plan you send to your publisher, which then goes into their sales pitch to the accounts. You should also inform your publisher if you plan to hire an independent publicist or firm to assist you. They will see it as a wise investment—and certainly not be offended. But they need to know early on, so their own team can either collaborate effectively with your publicist or focus on areas that your publicist isn't covering. Look at it as a partnership that will work best if the right hand knows what the left hand is doing. (More on this in chapter 22.)

Around the time the sales calls begin—again, about four to six months before your book's release—you'll be introduced to the publicist who'll be working on your book. This person will likely schedule a phone call with you to talk about the game plan, or otherwise send you information on what their process looks like, what media outlets they'll be pitching or targeting, and how to direct your own requests or needs for assistance. Unfortunately, publicists at most publishers are stretched to the limit. They might do a great job with the time they have, but they probably won't have time for an in-depth approach, which is why it's often a good idea to hire your own publicist. People need to hear about a book many times and in several ways before they really notice it.

PARTING ADVICE

Very few books succeed without any marketing and publicity—somehow, the book needs to gain visibility among potential readers. Most publishers rely heavily on retailer placement and visibility, as well as the serendipitous word of mouth that may occur among reviewers or other influential figures in the bookselling community. Once your book releases, most of that work is already finished. Much of the media coverage you'll receive will have been seeded weeks or months earlier. If nothing happens to help the book gain sales momentum in its first three months or so, the publisher will turn its attention to the next season of books. But it's not until their book's release date that some authors have this horrifying realization: that some of the critical elements of their book's success played out many months before the book reached the market. If the book doesn't sell in sufficient quantities in its first six months on the shelf, it will be returned and not restocked, to make way for next season's titles.

If your launch ends up being a disappointment, and it was a hardcover release, there is still hope. It may find new life as a paperback, with a second shot at best-seller lists and editorial coverage. Or if your book scores a major award or media attention after its release, that may give the publisher a way to resell or repitch the book to accounts, to argue for a bigger buy. It's rare, but it happens. However, to avoid disappointment in the first place, start with the assumption that your publisher will do nothing but act as a packager and distributor for your book, and that you'll need to take responsibility for the marketing.

15 : SELF-PUBLISHING

Until the late 1990s, only one viable option existed for 99 percent of authors seeking publication: to gain acceptance from a traditional publisher. While it's popular to say that authors have been self-publishing since the time of Walt Whitman (if not earlier), the chances of gaining visibility without a publisher's stamp of approval were slim to none until distribution and formats began shifting in the digital era. The predominance of online retail and e-book formats for adult fiction in particular have leveled the playing field and made it possible for authors to effectively compete against books published by the Big Five.

Especially in the United States and United Kingdom, an outspoken class of successful self-published authors now promotes the tenets of "indie" authorship. They're likely to portray traditional publishers in a negative light, as dinosaurs about to go extinct, especially given the growing power of Amazon. Because it's common for authors to feel underserved and unsupported by their publishers, the freedom, control, and potential earnings offered by self-publishing is very real and potent. However, even if thousands of authors abandoned traditional publishing tomorrow, more than enough people would take their place and accept a book deal. Most writers need and prefer guidance from industry professionals, and particularly in the literary publishing community, it's difficult if not impossible to gain acceptance, critical acknowledgment, or a teaching position through self-publishing.

Still, what's happening today in the publishing industry—the emergence of self-publishing and indie authorship as a viable and sustainable career—remains a confusing and divisive issue. With so many divergent voices and opinions, it's not surprising that new authors struggle to understand their choices. Not only have dozens of new publishing services entered the market, but there are now "hybrid" publishers that don't fit any known model, either traditional or indie. Whether these new publishing options are right for you will depend on your goals, your personality as a writer, and the qualities of your work.

A BRIEF HISTORY OF SELF-PUBLISHING

For most of publishing's history, if an author wanted to self-publish, she had to pay thousands of dollars to a so-called vanity press (as opposed to being paid at least a nominal royalty by a traditional publisher)—or otherwise study up on how to be an independent publishing entrepreneur. That all changed with the advent of print-on-demand (POD) technology in the 1990s, which allows books to be printed one at a time. POD publishing services arose that focused on providing low-cost self-publishing packages. Without print runs, inventory, and warehousing, the only expense left was creating the product itself: the book. Outfits like iUniverse, Xlibris, and AuthorHouse (which have since merged and been consolidated as AuthorSolutions) offered a range of affordable packages to help authors get their books into print, though most books never reached a bookstore shelf and sold a few dozen copies at best.

If the low cost of POD weren't enough to change the game, two other developments made it possible for authors to hit a best-seller list and sell thousands of copies at a significant profit without a publisher. First, Amazon not only became the number-one retailer of both print books and e-books, but also began offering easy self-publishing services that authors could use for free (CreateSpace for POD books, Kindle Direct Publishing for e-books). Ingram also began offering services to authors at a nominal cost (via IngramSpark), giving self-published titles the advantage of its distribution muscle around the globe. Second, e-books took off as the preferred consumer format for popular fiction. Every online retailer offers a portal for authors to upload their e-books directly for sale. Amazon and its competitors now attribute some 25 to 30 percent of their overall e-book sales to self-published work.

Bottom line: anyone can make their book available for sale, in print or e-book format, at the most important retailers, without significant up-front costs, aside from creating book production files. Every time a self-published book is sold—either print or digital—the retailer takes a cut, and delivers the author's cut after the close of the month.

SHOULD YOU SELF-PUBLISH?

As late as the mid-2000s, a significant stigma surrounded both self-published books and self-published authors. I recall speaking at the

Chicago chapter of the Romance Writers of America during that time, and running a workshop on how to self-publish. Three people showed up, and two of them were already self-published; it was by far the worst-attended session I've ever run at a major writing event. At the time, self-publishing was not a well-regarded path to success, but was seen to indicate some kind of author failing or eccentricity. Today, romance authors are the most successful indie authors and lead the charge in innovative marketing and promotion of self-published titles.

Even though it's become straightforward and more attractive to self-publish, every author needs to carefully evaluate their goals in doing so. Here are the key factors to consider:

Do you expect or want to see your book physically stocked in bookstores across the country? It's next to impossible for a new, self-published author to achieve on-shelf placement at bricks-and-mortar stores. You may be able to get your book stocked locally or regionally, especially if you have the right connections or are a well-known person in your community. But for the most part, self-published books sell primarily through online retail. That's not the drawback it used to be, given that's where most books sell today, regardless of who the publisher is.

Do you want to hit the *New York Times* best-seller list? If so, you'll probably need a traditional publisher's muscle behind you. That said, self-published authors are not uncommon on Amazon best-seller lists or the *USA Today* list.

Do you want major media attention? Self-published authors, at least those who are unknown, struggle to secure major media attention. (Traditionally published authors struggle as well—just not as terrifically hard.) It's difficult to score traditional book reviews or media coverage, or even hire a traditional publicist. New indie authors find it exceptionally frustrating how much they're ignored by traditional media. Traditional publishers have a much easier time getting those doors to open. However, if your book appeals to a niche audience, the media outlets that serve that audience are probably open to coverage.

Does your book appeal to a specific audience that you can (or already) reach on your own? It makes little sense to partner with a traditional publisher if you can reach the audience easily and comprehensively on your own—whether through your own business, website/blog, speaking engagements, or anything else that brings you in touch with your readership or fan base. If you're looking for a book to increase your readership in some way—or to help you pivot—then a publisher can be useful in setting the stage, helping secure traditional media, or extending distribution in a way that supports those goals. For example, best-selling indie author CJ Lyons partnered with Sourcebooks when she started a new young adult series, since it was a departure from her previous work that focused on adults.

What are the qualities of the market you are targeting? Some genres or categories of work are ideal for self-publishing efforts because the audience is already primed to consume things digitally and to discover their next read through online channels. Romance and erotica are prime examples. But in other markets, you may find it difficult to gain traction because either they haven't moved predominantly to digital consumption, or the traditional publishers still perform a valued gatekeeping role. Literary work is one such market: you'll find it hard to gain acceptance within a certain community unless your work has been editorially selected, plus the literary audience still prefers print. Children's books—especially books for young readers—is another area where it's challenging to gain acceptance without a traditional publisher. Educators, librarians, and others who are in a position to introduce books to children still use trade publications, reviews, and other traditional methods to guide their selections.

How much of an entrepreneur are you? Becoming a self-published author means you are fully responsible for your book's success. If you're a first-time author, you may have little or no knowledge of what a professionally published book looks like. You may not understand the editing or design process, or how sales and distribution work. Some authors outsource as much of the work as possible, and that's not a bad thing—as a self-published author you can hire whomever you want to assist you—but some authors' personalities are a really poor fit for the demands of a professional self-publishing operation. You need an entrepreneurial mindset to undertake a serious and successful effort.

If you would rather work with a team of people, or feel like you have a business partner, you may be better suited to traditional publishing. Some authors have always dreamed of working with a traditional publisher, and nothing other than that experience will satisfy them. The Catch-22, however, is that once you experience what traditional publishing has to offer, you may end up disappointed by it. Or maybe not. Authors' experiences vary so widely (even within the same publishing house) that it is difficult to generalize.

Finally, successful self-publishers must have some level of proficiency and comfort with being active online. Because most of your sales will happen through online retail, you need to show up and be familiar with how books get marketed and promoted in online environments, plus be willing to experiment with new digital tools and tactics to gain visibility and readers.

WHAT ABOUT AGENTS WHO OFFER SELF-PUBLISHING SERVICES?

Increasingly, agents are helping their clients self-publish. Help might consist of fee-based services, royalty-based services, and hybrid models. Such practices are controversial because agents' traditional role is to serve as advocates for their clients' interests and negotiate the best possible deals. When agents start publishing their clients' work and taking their 15 percent cut of sales, a conflict of interest develops. In their defense, agents are changing their roles in response to industry change, as well as client demand. Regardless of how you proceed, look for flexibility in any agreements you sign. Given the pace of change in the market, it's not a good idea to enter into an exclusive, long-term contract that locks you into a low royalty rate or into a distribution deal that may fall behind in best practices.

BEFORE YOU DECIDE TO SELF-PUBLISH

One of the worst possible reasons to self-publish is the belief that it will help you score a traditional publishing deal for the book. Such efforts rarely succeed. Even though there is no longer a stigma associated with self-publishing (at least for most genres), it will be exceedingly difficult to garner agent or publisher interest for a book you've already published. Of course, you can find exceptions. For example, *The Martian* was self-published and then picked up by a traditional publisher. But such cases are outliers, far from typical of the average author experience.

Don't worry, though, that self-publishing will hurt your chances at traditional publishing on some future project. You'll more or less start with a clean slate when pitching a new and different project to agents and editors. One caveat, however: Don't self-publish a *series* unless you're committed to self-publishing the entire series. A traditional publisher will almost never pick up book two in a series when the first book is self-published.

I see some writers self-publishing mainly because they lack patience with the querying and submissions process of traditional publishing. Or they want the instant gratification of seeing their work on the market. But if you have any interest whatsoever in traditional publishing, exhaust all your agent and publisher options first. Get thoroughly rejected (as much as that may hurt), and then self-publish. It's very, very hard to go in the other direction successfully.

Perhaps the best argument offered in support of self-publishing—at least within the self-publishing community itself—is that you will earn a lot more money than you would with a traditional publisher. That may be true. It's possible to sell far fewer copies as a self-published author and still earn more than a traditional deal would pay you. But it's also possible to sell more copies as a self-published author and not earn as much as you would with a publisher's advance and royalties. It all depends on the book and the type of deal or contract you're offered.

The success rate is not that different for self-publishing and traditional publishing. A few authors end up as best-selling superstars. Some do very well. And the majority do not make a living from it. Self-published authors may find that marketing and promoting their book is much tougher than they imagined. Self-publishing careers typically take years—and four or five books—to gain traction and produce earnings that are meaningful. Are you committed to producing more work, and marketing that work, month after month and year after year?

As I've continually stated, each author is different, and each book is different. If you know your target market, and have a clear set of goals for your book, you should be able to figure out the right publishing strategy for you.

16 : PUBLISHING SHORT STORIES, PERSONAL ESSAYS, OR POETRY

Rather than pitching or publishing a book, most writers' first experience with the business of publishing comes in the form of submitting to a literary journal—or working for one as a creative writing student. My publishing career started at an undergraduate literary journal, the *Evansville Review*. When I became editor in 1996, it was the first paid editing job I'd held. What I found most astonishing about the position was the volume of submissions we received, as a virtually unknown publication, from all types of writers around the country, both skilled and beginner. It was a tremendous education in what it means to read a "fresh" piece of writing. I began to realize the slush pile is accurately named; it is a shapeless mass of submissions often lacking distinction.

The slush pile can hardly be avoided if you wish to build a reputation as a short story writer or poet, since literary journals and magazines are the most likely and appropriate outlet for such work. Creative nonfiction writers and essayists have a bit more flexibility: it's possible to make a name for oneself by focusing on online publications alone. The world of online media is highly driven by nonfiction, and hardly at all by fiction and poetry, although there are exceptions in genre fiction and fan fiction.

Agents almost never pitch and sell short work unless it's for existing clients who are also book authors, or for very high-profile clients (think: US poet laureate). That's because the payment for short work, particularly in literary magazines and online markets, is low and sometimes nonexistent, except for exclusive or high-end markets such as the *New Yorker*. So publishing short work is a process the emerging writer must undertake for himself.

It is practically impossible to make a living based on publishing short literary work. Such pursuits must be supplemented by other sources of revenue—such as teaching, grant or prize money, freelance editing, or any combination of the options outlined in part 5. The most common *business* reason to seek publication of short pieces is to build up a track record of publication that can lead to other milestones. It may also be important to your creative process or to your identity as a writer, and it may advance your reputation in the publishing community. It may even attract an agent and book deal, as it did for Yiyun Li, discussed in chapter 3. But it will rarely make you a living all by itself, unless you start writing for consumer magazines (see chapter 17) or move into more journalistic forms of writing. Even then, as any freelance writer would tell you, it's far from a lucrative living except for an elite few.

PUBLISHING IN PRINT LITERARY JOURNALS

Publishing short stories, poetry, and personal essays is a much more straightforward process than pitching book projects or even magazine articles. You're not selling your work so much as submitting it for consideration—it has to be *read* (a few sentences, anyway) before an editor can know if they want to publish it.

Whereas you're likely to send a query letter to book publishers, literary agents, and most commercial magazines—and hope you're invited to send more, or given a contract—you typically send a cover letter to literary journals *along with the manuscript.* The cover letter literally "covers" the work and introduces you; it mainly consists of a biographical statement. You should include the following:

- past publication credits (if these are numerous, be selective; mention those that would carry the most significance to the staff of the publication you're submitting to)
- awards, fellowships, or grants received—the more recognizable, the better, of course
- any writing degrees or credentials

Mainly, the cover letter gives the publication a sense of where you're at in your career. If your track record looks intriguing or impressive, it may favorably influence editors or staff readers, and make them slow down and consider your work more carefully. It can also do the opposite, if you portray yourself as a type of writer the publication avoids. It's easy to figure out a publication's "type": look at the last few issues and read the biographical notes of the writers it's published. Do you feel like you fit in?

If you're unpublished, there's no reason to belabor that status in your cover letter, but it does raise a question: What do you say if you have absolutely zero writing experience or credentials? You'll have to exercise your creative writing muscles, but your letter will likely remain brief regardless. You can mention specific pieces or contributors you've enjoyed in the journal (it's always best to peruse some recent issues before submitting), and maybe discuss what influences your writing—but don't get carried away. It's better to keep your cover letter to a few brief sentences than to write paragraphs of material that may turn off the editors. The more you go on, the more you may get yourself in trouble, unless you're particularly charming. The good news is that because you're sending the work along with the query, readers may only glance at the cover letter before turning to the submission itself.

Almost every publication has specific submission guidelines you should follow when submitting work. They cover the rules and etiquette for sending unsolicited work (that is, work that the publication did not ask you to send). The guidelines will tell you

- what categories of work are accepted (poetry, short fiction, essays, reviews, etc.)
- what length of work is accepted (minimum and maximum word counts)
- how many pieces will be accepted as part of a single submission
- when it's possible to submit (some journals read submissions only a few months of the year)
- if they accept paper submissions or electronic submissions
- where to send your submission
- how long it takes them to respond (or if they'll respond at all if they don't accept your work)

In addition to stipulating what the publication will consider, the guidelines may spell out what you should put in the cover letter, as well as what kind of work they're most looking for. For example, the *Gettysburg Review* explicitly states that it's interested in stories that are "off-beat, penetrating, and surprising" and does not publish genre fiction.[1] Some magazines run themed issues, and submissions must conform to that theme to be considered.

Most literary publications demand that writers send only *unpublished* work for consideration, which sometimes leads to confusion. Does your work remain unpublished if it has appeared at your blog or website? What if it appeared briefly on your blog but was then taken down? What if you posted portions of the work on Facebook? What if it appeared in a private writing community or forum? Generally speaking, literary journals consider your work published even if you self-published it or put it on your website (or social media account) for a short time. It is generally considered unpublished if it was shared in a private forum or community for critique purposes and not meant for reading by the general public.

In the past, it was common for journals to prohibit simultaneous submissions. This is when writers submit the same work to many different publications at once. However, because of very long response times (and because writers began ignoring the prohibition, which is very hard to enforce), simultaneous submissions are now generally accepted. Still, it's polite and expected that you'll mention in your cover letter that you're making a simultaneous submission.

If your piece is accepted for publication at Journal A while it's still being considered by Journals B and C, then you should send a respectful notification to B and C that says you're withdrawing the work. If you submitted your work using the popular service Submittable (see below), then it takes only a click or two to withdraw your submission. If you *don't* withdraw your submission, and you're then contacted with a second offer of publication, you'll be in an awkward position, and the second journal's editors are likely to remember your name for a long time, and not in a good way.

READING FEES

When I began my publishing career, there was one ethical guideline that reputable journals, magazines, publishers, and agents all agreed on: no reading fee, ever. Writers should never be charged for the opportunity to submit their work, nor should publications make a profit off writers hoping to get their work published. This was a rule of thumb I repeated often at conferences and workshops. It helped writers avoid scams and target their efforts to the most reputable outlets.

In 2010 a start-up entered the scene that has forever changed that rule: Submittable. Submittable has two standout benefits: (1) it allows publications to streamline and automate their submissions review process, and (2) it gives writers a single portal through which they can submit to many publications at once, track what's been submitted, and see the status of those submissions at a glance.

This efficiency and frictionless submissions process has come at a cost: submissions can be made with little effort by the writer, which increases the volume of submissions journals receive. Publications pay to use Submittable based on that volume of submissions: fees start around $150 a year and go up to more than $1,000 per year for nonprofits, which generally have to pass along this cost to writers using the service.

Writers often feel ill-used by reading fees. But it's important to look at what the fees would really add up to if you were submitting to the most popular literary journals. At the time of this writing, I checked on the policies of twenty well-known publications. About 75 percent charge no reading fee at all, although some require writers to mail in submissions and thus pay postage. The remaining journals that do charge waive reading fees when writers are also subscribers, and only two journals charge nonsubscribers to submit while *not* offering a free mail-in option. So despite complaints, it's still easy to submit your work widely without paying reading fees.

When reading fees are instituted, they roughly equate to what a writer would pay for postage and handling—two to four dollars—which helps the publication cover the cost to use Submittable, and possibly pay staff or readers to go through the increased number of submissions they're receiving. Keep in mind that Submittable takes a percentage of reading fees, in addition to charging journals to use its service—that, after all, is its business model.

INCREASING YOUR CHANCES OF ACCEPTANCE

The number-one way to increase your success rate with literary journals is to be selective and purposeful in how you submit, and make sure you're submitting only the most appropriate work. While it may not be feasible to read multiple issues of each journal you submit to, you should become familiar with the publication. At the very least, study its website, look at recent contributors, and look for interviews with the editors. If you can get your hands on a couple of recent issues through a library or newsstand—or by buying digital issues from the website—not only do you increase your knowledge of what kind of work is being accepted and published, but you're supporting the literary community in doing so.

If you have an opportunity to attend the Association of Writers and Writing Programs (AWP) conference, then reserve at least a couple of hours (if not much more) to walk the AWP Bookfair, where you can look at hundreds of publications firsthand, talk with editors, and immediately get a sense of which publications are a good fit for you. It also helps editors put a face with a name when they see your submission come through. You may even be personally invited to submit if you hit it off with the staff. (That said, I recommend you do *not* walk the AWP Bookfair asking editors why they rejected your work. No editor wants to have that conversation with you.)

You can also supercharge your writerly intelligence by becoming a volunteer, reader, or editor at any type of publication where you're exposed to the slush pile. By reading a high volume of submissions yourself, you'll begin to notice patterns in the work that's submitted: how writers tend to start off stories in the same way (making them boring and easy to skip over); what styles and voices have become tired, cliched, or overdone; what it means to write work that's "surprising," "unique," or "interesting." Those descriptive words are vague and cliches in themselves, but once you've tunneled through a stack of submissions at a journal, you begin to understand the recurring problems that pervade writing—particularly work by writers who haven't yet found their voice or uncovered stories really worth telling.

While it's more common in book publishing, some writers look for an "in" at a publication—such as a recommendation or referral by a contributor—in hopes of receiving priority consideration from the editors (rather than, say, the interns, editorial assistants, or other readers who may go through unsolicited submissions first). This won't necessarily improve your success rate. And in asking for such a favor, you may be putting the contributor in an awkward position—not just with you, but with the editor. This also raises the question of how you should submit your work if you do have an "in" with the staff. Unless you're *directly invited to submit* your work to an editor, or you've been previously published by the journal, it's typically best to use the normal channels of submission (and follow the guidelines) rather than consider yourself the exception and go straight to your contact. Mention your connection or referral in your cover letter—that's usually the best way to help your work get priority. If you try to bypass the standard process, you may be told to go ahead and use it anyway—meaning that rather than gaining an advantage, you've wasted the editor's time.

YOU'RE ACCEPTED! NOW WHAT?

Every acceptance, no matter how small, deserves recognition. Consider having a ritual to celebrate each publishing victory (and possibly a ritual for each rejection—but make it a brief ritual that aids you in moving on).

Just about every publication will have some editing suggestions, even if they are minor copyediting changes, that require your review and approval prior to publication. If you're asked to make a significant revision, then you have a decision to make. Do you think the editor's suggestions will improve the work? Do they make sense to you? It's best to sit on suggestions for at least a day or two before making a decision or sending a response—unless your response is undeniably positive and you feel happy about making the changes. Most editors consider this process a series of compromises and negotiations. You may not be expected to agree with all the changes, but you may be asked to send your reasoning or justification for *not* revising certain areas. If you hit a major roadblock during the editorial process, and see no way to productively revise in a way you're comfortable with, then you may have to withdraw your submission. Unfortunately, it's not unusual to end up in a cycle of confusing revision suggestions, especially if a lower-level editor loves your work just the way it is but a higher-level editor wants changes made.

At some point prior to publication, you'll be sent a contract or letter of agreement that stipulates payment, rights, and other terms. Read this carefully and make sure you understand it. (See appendix 1, "Contracts 101," for a breakdown of common contract language.) Typically, a print journal will demand rights to be the first to publish your work in print, and also to make it part of its digital edition, if one exists. Thereafter, rights should revert to you, although the publication may reserve the right to reprint your work, anthologize it, or make the work indefinitely available on its website. Payment for short stories, poems, and essays are typically in the hundreds of dollars, or you may be paid only in copies of the journal.

SIDE-STEPPING LITERARY JOURNALS

Publishing in journals is only one way to crack the nut; it's entirely feasible to build a respectable reputation and publication record (and a writing career) without placing a single piece in a traditional print literary journal. Take the example of Ashley C. Ford, whom I first met while she was a Ball State creative writing student. Her first pieces appeared in well-known online publications—such as *PANK* and *The Rumpus*—and she later became a staff writer at BuzzFeed. She's now a full-time freelancer, writes for *Elle* online, and has a book deal.

Still, there's an overriding bias in the literary community in favor of print-based publication, even though it demands waiting for years, receiving little or no pay, and being seen by few readers. Entrepreneurial-minded writers should direct their efforts more widely—consider print but also publish, experiment, and distribute through digital media to build a readership directly. We'll discuss these strategies in parts 4 and 5.

17 : TRADITIONAL FREELANCE WRITING

Freelance writing is typically associated with the big glossy magazines on the newsstand. But, as discussed in chapter 6, it's an increasingly complex market. While a writer might've got their start freelancing for mainstream magazines thirty years ago, that's less and less likely today. It now takes considerable experience and expertise to land paying work at a traditional print publication, and I don't recommend it as a first line of attack. New writers will do better to look to online-only publication. Fortunately, the art of pitching and understanding how editors think is more or less the same no matter what type of publication you're dealing with. Thus the following advice applies equally to traditional print magazines and to online-only publications (e.g., *Slate, Salon, The Awl*, LitHub, and so on, as discussed in chapter 7). Later, in chapter 23, I'll discuss the big picture of what it means to establish a full-time freelance career, whether that involves writing, editing, or other types of work done on a temporary, by-contract basis.

THE MOST COMMON TYPES OF ARTICLES

While every publication has its quirks, across the business you'll find consistent types of pieces that get assigned and come with certain expectations from editors. A feature article is the most visible and important part of a print magazine's content, usually mentioned on the cover; the "feature package" refers to the collection of features a magazine offers in a particular issue, which may be built around a theme. (For instance, the *New Yorker* does an annual feature package focused on food.) Features may be written by full-time staff writers or freelancers, or even by the editors. Departments and columns are recurring pieces written by a mix of staffers and freelancers. By studying a publication carefully across two to three issues—or the span of a few weeks online—you can get a sense of what material is written by editors and what's regularly assigned to freelancers. Here are the most common article types you'll find across all publications:

- **Front-of-book items.** It's common wisdom that if a writer wants to break into a print magazine, the easiest place to do so is in the "front of book"—those first pages, where the magazine offers quick-to-read, browsable items that ease the reader into longer articles and features. A front-of-book item might be as short as 50–100 words; rarely does it run longer than 500 words.
- **Profiles and interviews.** Interviews may run Q&A style—always with editing for length and clarity—or as profiles, which present a bigger challenge for the writer and require a narrative structure to retain reader interest. Q&As work well with people who are well known, where readers ostensibly prefer unfiltered, direct answers. Profiles may work better for lesser-known people, and for figures where there's as much of a story to be uncovered or told through the people who surround them. Both are staples of all print and online publications.
- **How-to.** A how-to article teaches readers to do something, step-by-step. It's almost always written in second person. Both print and online publications do well with how-to content, and it's a favorite of advertising-driven sites such as wikiHow.
- **Roundups.** A perennial favorite, roundups may be annual features and, if successful, can attract significant advertising. Think of "Women We Love" in *Esquire* or the annual debut poets roundup in *Poets & Writers* magazine. Annual roundups tend to be written and curated by the magazine's staff.
- **Listicles.** Consider this a fluffy version of the roundup: same principle, just less formal, and a staple of high-traffic, pop-culture websites such as BuzzFeed. Think: "10 Cute Kittens Caught Asleep in Odd Places." Listicles are ubiquitous online—people just can't resist clicking and browsing.
- **Service pieces.** A service piece offers information that promises to better the reader's life: to lose weight, to invest money more wisely, to improve relations with their spouse. While it may sound straightforward, the challenge is to offer advice that's both fresh and written in a style and voice that appeals to the target audience. A service piece on spicing up a romantic relationship may work for *Cosmopolitan* but not the readers of *Woman's Day*. Service pieces can be written by experts or by journalists who conduct sufficient research. For online publications, service pieces can drive

consistent traffic over a long period of time, assuming the content is "evergreen" (meaning it doesn't go out of date).

- **Reporting.** A reported piece requires interviews and research, usually out in the field. Magazines like the *New Yorker* or the *Atlantic* will expect key interviews and research to be conducted in person. Other magazines—especially those that are service oriented—may be OK with "armchair" reporting: research conducted from home, phone interviews, and possibly email interviews, depending on the topic. Because reporting is expensive, you won't find many online-only publications focused on hard reporting, except for the very largest and best funded, such as ProPublica.

- **Essays and criticism.** This can be a hard area to define but typically involves a writer researching and writing about a topic on which they have some expertise or authority. The piece may not involve original reporting, but offers insight, analysis, and—if successful—a new way of understanding an issue. One characteristic of such pieces is that the writer leaves the boundaries of objective reporting and argues a position. A recent, already classic example is "The Case for Reparations" by Ta-Nehisi Coates, which appeared in the *Atlantic*. Essays and criticism are an affordable way for online publications to feature serious content that may not require expensive reporting.

- **Columns and commentary.** The nature of recurring columns depends on the publication and the background of the columnists, but usually they're opinion pieces that focus on current events and trends. This category includes book, movie, and TV criticism and reviews, as well as news opinion and commentary. There's no expectation of reporting or objectivity. One of the most successful online columns of all time is an advice column published by *The Rumpus*, "Dear Sugar," written by Cheryl Strayed.

- **Personal essay.** One of the most difficult pieces to get paid for is the personal essay—because such writing can be found in abundance, and everyone has a story to tell. Most publications have a recurring department that features personal essays of a specific length; it's always best to read a half dozen or more before pitching your own, to understand the taste of the editors. Today, the *New York Times*' "Modern Love" column is among the most popular and sought-after venues for placing a personal essay.

Online publications tend to feature *lots* of personal essays because they're cheap to source, edit, and produce. In recent years, as more writers have written about intensely personal topics, such as sexual abuse, critics have suggested that writers are allowing themselves to be exploited by publications interested mainly in sensational headlines that attract lots of traffic.

- **Humor.** This is yet another difficult area in which to sell work, whether humorous columns or personal essays (think Erma Bombeck or David Sedaris). If writing is subjective, humor is even more so, and it requires an incredibly astute understanding of what will be considered funny by a magazine's readership. One of the most important (and only) online venues for literary humor is *McSweeney's Internet Tendency*.

- **Inspirational.** Think of the stories you'd find in the Chicken Soup for the Soul books, or in a typical issue of *Reader's Digest*—they're uplifting and leave you feeling good inside. Note: Sometimes in publishing (especially book publishing), the term "inspirational" is used to denote content with an explicit spiritual or religious message.

- **Quizzes.** Quizzes have always been popular in magazines, and in online publications they're highly valued as traffic generators. They're also used frequently as content marketing for movies, TV shows, and brands seeking frequent sharing on social media. (Think: Which *Game of Thrones* character are you?)

If you've encountered even the smallest bit of advice about freelance writing, you've probably heard how important it is to study a publication before you submit your work. The audience for each is incredibly distinct, with shared experiences, backgrounds, and belief systems implied by the voice and positioning of each piece. That, of course, makes it easier to pitch a publication you avidly read, but a writer who's a quick study can pick up on the personality of any publication by studying a recent issue or a week's worth of online articles—as well as reviewing the media kit. (The media kit is essentially a fancy brief prepared to help potential advertisers or sponsors understand the readership they'll be reaching. To find it, Google the publication's name plus the phrase "media kit.") You can also use directories such as *Writer's Market* to learn more about markets to pitch and what they're looking for.

If you remember nothing else about freelance writing, remember this:

Readerships are not interchangeable, which means publications' content is not interchangeable. If a publication's content is not distinctive and customized for its core demographic, it will not stay in business long.

A WORD ABOUT TRADE PUBLICATIONS

One of the most-ignored sectors of publishing (both print and online) is trade publications. These serve people working in a particular trade—from plumbers to daycare providers to costume designers to coffee growers. Because of their specificity, trade magazines—and their related digital media offerings—rarely appear in the public eye, but they tend to be well read by the target demographic, since they may be the only reliable source of news, trends, and information. In the 1990s it was estimated that trade magazines represented one-sixth of the leading, revenue-producing periodicals in the United States.[1] *Writer's Market* frequently recommends that writers consider pitching trade publications because they're often easier to break into, pay reasonably well, and can represent a reliable income stream once you learn to produce the kind of material they're looking for. In other words, you needn't be a specialist in a trade to write informatively for it. Aside from *Writer's Market*, here are resources for identifying trade markets:

- Trade Pub (www.tradepub.com)
- WebWire (www.webwire.com/IndustryList.asp)
- All You Can Read (www.allyoucanread.com)

THE SCIENCE OF PITCHING

We discussed pitching in broad strokes in chapter 2. Here we'll get more into the nitty-gritty of sending a pitch letter. First, know that certain pieces rarely or never get formally pitched for publication. Poetry and short stories are almost always submitted on spec, which means that you write and submit the full piece for consideration; you aren't assigned it or contracted to write it. This is often the case as well for personal essays and short pieces by freelance writers. For example, *Runner's World* has a recurring column, "Life & Times," that features first-person essays about running; these are submitted strictly on spec, and you may not even hear a response unless the magazine is interested.

Professional freelancers, especially journalists, are accustomed to pitching their ideas and working on assignment. This means sending a brief query or pitch letter to the publication's editor that essentially sells the piece before it is written. If the editor likes the pitch, she'll send a contract or letter of agreement that outlines the terms, deadline, and payment; payment is typically made only when the piece is accepted for publication, or sometimes after it is published.

In addition to studying a publication before pitching, look up the official submission guidelines. They should detail what sections of the publication are open to freelancers, state the average pay rate and standard terms, and perhaps offer other advice for writers. (Some even list the biggest mistakes writers make when pitching, so pay attention!) Assuming you have no personal invitation to pitch from an editor, follow the guidelines and never assume you're an exception to any stated rules.

The difficulty is that every editor and publication looks for something different in a pitch, and you may not figure out what that is unless you gather some intelligence. Whenever possible, speak to other freelancers who have written for the publication, search out interviews with the editors themselves (or go hear them speak at an event), and study any editorial calendars the publication makes available. An editorial calendar outlines upcoming feature packages or special issues, which can help you time your pitch more appropriately and for a specific month. Monthly print magazines work far in advance of their publication dates; you'll need to think four to six months out. (For example, winter holiday pitches should be sent in July, and summer-themed pitches in December.)

A typical pitch shouldn't be longer than a few hundred words, although a complex piece that requires funding may merit more. Experienced freelance writers know that quality pitching is a time-consuming practice, and a lot of their time and energy is devoted to the search for interesting people, ideas, and stories that can be successfully pitched.

Here are the key qualities of a successful pitch:

- Speak the same language as the publication. Some writers begin their pitch in the same way they might lead into their story, which demonstrates how well they understand the style and voice of the publication—and therefore the readership.
- Hook the reader quickly. If you can't deliver the hook in twenty-five words or less, then you may not have an appealing pitch. Reading the kicker, or subtitle, under dozens or hundreds of headlines can help train you in the art of the hook.
- Show the legwork or research you've already done. For example,

A GOOD MAGAZINE PITCH

At the time freelancer Grace Dobush sent the following pitch letter (published here with her permission), she had already done about three months of research. Although Grace had never before worked with *Cincinnati Magazine*, she sold the article to them within a week of sending the letter. You can read the final piece in the April 2014 issue.

> Hi, [editor's name],
>
> I'm a freelancer here in Cincinnati, and [mutual acquaintance] suggested I get in touch with you about this story I'm working on.
>
> A man trained as a kosher butcher emigrated from Lithuania in 1886 to serve an orthodox Jewish congregation in Cincinnati. Behr Manischewitz eventually became the patriarch of a mechanized matzo empire that led the world in matzo production—and ruffled rabbinical feathers. The family's history illustrates the story of Jewish life in Cincinnati: Like many Jews, they settled in the West End in the late 1880s and moved to Avondale as they became more affluent in the 20th century. Eventually, the Manischewitz headquarters moved to New Jersey in 1930, and Cincinnati's matzo fame waned. But Behr and his wife remain buried in Covedale.
>
> I've done extensive research on the family in local archives and would love to tell the Manischewitz story for *Cincinnati Magazine*. There's a wealth of interesting historical imagery and maps to go with the story, and I have a few ideas for interview subjects.
>
> My writing credits include *Wired*, *HOW*, *Family Tree Magazine* and other national publications. This story could be great for April 2014 to coincide with Passover. What do you think?

if you've already secured or conducted interviews, use the most compelling details to your benefit. (If you've done no legwork, and have never published on the subject matter, the editor may not have confidence in your ability to pull off the article.)

• Demonstrate your credentials as a writer or authority on the topic. If the publication has never worked with you before, describe your experience and point to work published elsewhere. If you have no previously published work, you may be asked to submit on spec.

HOOK EXAMPLES

Why more women seeking abortions are ending up at anti-abortion pregnancy centers[a]

If it killed politicians instead of prisoners, this illness would be national enemy number one.[b]

What it's like to be gay in Putin's Russia on the eve of the Sochi Olympics: a report on life in the Russian underground[c]

From the dawn of history to dusk last night, fire is mankind's oldest and most useful tool. Learn how to harness its strength to cook, survive, and connect to a primal force as old and powerful as time itself.[d]

Yemen's Hidden War: A journey into one of the most remote and dangerous countries in the world[e]

Looking after an elderly parent is a challenge, but hiding from the inevitable won't make it any easier. Our guide will help you face the future head-on so you can give the best possible care.[f]

On August 13, 1986, Michael Morton came home from work to discover that his wife had been brutally murdered in their bed. His nightmare had only begun.[g]

a. Meaghan Winter, "'I Felt Set Up': Why More Women Seeking Abortions Are Ending Up at Anti-Abortion Pregnancy Centers," *Cosmopolitan*, December 17, 2015, http://www.cosmopolitan.com/politics/news/a50961/medical-crisis-pregnancy-centers/.

b. David Ferry, "How the Government Put Tens of Thousands of People at Risk of a Deadly Disease," *Mother Jones*, January/February 2015, http://www.motherjones.com/environment/2015/01/valley-fever-california-central-valley-prison.

c. Jeff Sharlet, "Inside the Iron Closet: What It's Like to Be Gay in Putin's Russia," *GQ*, February 4, 2014, http://www.gq.com/story/being-gay-in-russia.

d. Casey Lyons, "The Complete Guide to Fire," Backpacker, October 2014, http://www.backpacker.com/survival/survival-skills/starting-fire/the-complete-guide-to-campfires/.

e. Matthieu Aikins, "Yemen's Hidden War," *Rolling Stone*, July 30, 2015, http://www.rollingstone.com/politics/news/yemens-hidden-war-20150730.

f. Jane Gross et al., "Ready or Not: What It's Like to Care for Aging Parents," *OPRAH*, November 2014, http://www.oprah.com/spirit/How-to-Care-for-Elderly-Parents-Elder-Care.

g. Pamela Colloff, "The Innocent Man, Part One," *Texas Monthly*, November 2012, http://www.texasmonthly.com/politics/the-innocent-man-part-one/.

- Describe any expenses you need covered, especially if the submission guidelines require it. Some publications pay for writers' expenses, and a pitch should outline your expectations if it affects your ability to accept the assignment.

A pitch is the editor's first look at the writer—can this person write and express themselves effectively? If the pitch is well done, it increases the chance that even if the story's rejected, the editor will invite the writer to pitch again, or send feedback on how to revise the story idea to make it work for the publication. Rejections are far more common than acceptances, even for experienced writers, especially before they've established working relationships with an editor or publication. Here are some of the most common reasons for rejection.

- Your angle is too narrow (or broad). A publication can be a bit like Goldilocks—you need to offer it an idea that's specific enough to distinguish your article from others that cover the same subject matter, but not so unique that the editor doesn't think it merits an entire article.
- The publication ran something too similar, too recently (or has it on assignment already). This is common, and there's nothing you can do about it. A lot of pitching is about timing. Your intuition and timing improves as you gain experience.
- You don't have the writing or reporting chops. This can be something of a Catch-22 when you're just starting out. How do you collect experience or clips when you're inexperienced? Lots of ways: submit on spec; write very short pieces; write for local or regional publications that may be willing to take a chance on you to build your portfolio.
- Your idea is too boring, too cliched, too overdone, or some combination of these. Usually this is a result of not reading the target publication carefully enough to realize that your idea isn't a good fit. Every publication has a list of story ideas they're pitched so frequently as to elicit eye rolls and instant rejection. For example, *Runner's World* says right in the submission guidelines that you shouldn't pitch them on the health benefits of running.[2]

Once you have your foot in the door and successfully pitch and publish a few pieces, there's a good chance you can shift to a more organic and informal process for pitching and discussing ideas—such as having a phone conversation with the editor or sending a pitch with several ideas outlined. (Never do this if you don't have an established relationship!) If you become especially trusted and valuable, the editor may even contact you with assignment ideas.

18 : ONLINE WRITING AND BLOGGING

It may seem arbitrary to discuss online writing as if it were separate from other freelance writing—just as it would to distinguish "print book writing" from "e-book writing." But we shouldn't pretend that writing for online publication can be approached in exactly the same manner as writing for print. First, there can be differences in reader intent and engagement. The reader who clicks on a Twitter or Facebook link to read an article is often less motivated, and has a shorter attention span, than a subscriber sitting down with the latest issue of a favorite magazine. Second, profit-driven corporate media companies can quantify the success of online content, in terms of its contribution to their bottom line, and ultimately base publishing decisions on these numbers. (This is not to say that print is immune from number-focused decisions; seeing what readers gravitate toward online can affect what happens in print as well.) And, let's not forget that online writing generally doesn't pay as well as writing for print, as explained in chapter 7, although you can find many exceptions.

It's common for online writers to produce a large volume of content very quickly, without much time to research, interview, and fact-check. While this is changing—releasing a flood of low-quality content can backfire for a publication—online writers are typically valued less than print-focused writers, justly or not. Journalist Felix Salmon sums up the challenge best: "Online writing isn't really about writing any more—not in the manner that freelance print journalists understand it, anyway. Instead, it's more about reading, and aggregating, and working in teams, doing all the work that used to happen in old print-magazine offices, but doing it on a vastly compressed timescale."[1]

Today's emerging writer will typically begin by writing for online venues, then over time gain enough credibility and visibility to start securing better-paying gigs with more established publications. Still, though, the *Atlantic Online* got in trouble in 2013 for offering established freelancer Nate Thayer no payment at all to rerun a previously published article. There was a loud outcry, and *Atlantic* editor Alexis Madrigal wrote a long response explaining how and why freelancers were offered so little payment for online-only pieces.[2] The magazine, he wrote, uses in-house writers and editors to generate the majority of online content, because it's a more reliable way of getting quality content and higher traffic. Non-staff work often contributes very little to the bigger picture—thus the lower investment. This is a frustrating reality for writers, but it is possible to find a compromise. Some valued freelancers are able to negotiate an ongoing or long-term contract to contribute regularly, or even land a spot on the publication masthead, thus ensuring greater security and better pay.

THE CHALLENGES OF ONLINE WRITING

The online reader—unless a loyal subscriber or follower of a publication—is almost always skimming. A 2008 study found that a typical user reads no more than 28 percent of the text on the page, if not far less.[3] A more recent study looked at the percentage of people who reach the end of online articles, with similar results.[4] Attention spans are shockingly short, regardless of the device used, for the majority of the audience consuming online content. However, high-quality content produces higher levels of engagement, and a highly engaged reader who reaches the end of an article is very valuable, if the site knows how to funnel their attention appropriately. (For more on funnels, see chapter 21.)

Aside from the skimming challenge, there's incredible competition to get clicks or visits to an online article in the first place. In mid-2015, a Pew Research study showed that more than 60 percent of Facebook and Twitter users get their news from those social media sites.[5] Rather than going first to the *New York Times*, or the *Atlantic*, or some other mainstream media outlet, social media users are likely to let the news be curated for them by a feed or stream they've customized over time, or by following the links posted by friends, family, and the brands they like. This puts pressure on a writer or media company to ensure an article is shared or spread via social media, starting with crafting a headline and description that will compel users to click. A headline that works well in print will not typically work as well in an online environment, where the piece may be seen or distributed out of context, especially if clever or imaginative wordplay depends on a reader's ability to skim the article or see accompanying images. Furthermore, online headlines need to make strategic use of keywords to ensure that search engines and other aggregators can identify the content and surface the article during searches.

It's helpful to categorize online articles in terms of their performance:

- **High traffic, low engagement.** Writers and publishers of "clickbait" use provocative or sensational headlines and content of indifferent quality, with no other goal than gathering clicks and ensuring high traffic, commonly to support advertising.
- **High traffic, high engagement.** This is the holy grail for quality publications: lots of visits to content that creates substantial engagement. Engagement can be measured in many ways, including overall time spent on the site, number of social shares, number of comments, subscription conversion rate, email newsletter sign-ups, donations, and more.
- **Low traffic, high engagement.** This is the sad situation of much online content: a story draws little traffic (or not the desired traffic), but when people do visit, there is high engagement. It's particularly common with new publications, "quiet" or literary sites, and others that haven't found an effective way to spread the word about their content.

Much time and energy is spent by publications trying to improve the lot of articles that fall into the third category—it's not game over if the article doesn't gain traction in its first days or weeks online. There are many ways to revisit and remarket or repromote. If engagement is high, that indicates there's something to gain through additional tweaking or promoting of the article.

Headline Writing

While headlines are typically written by editors, you'll almost always be asked for suggestions, plus you'll need to craft suitable headlines for pitches. Headlines or titles for online pieces must be literal, specific, and clear. If it's a piece that also appears in print, the headline almost always needs to be adjusted for online publication. For example, the *Virginia Quarterly Review* published a piece in Fall 2012 with the print and online headline "Dreaming of El Dorado." It's a lyrical and artful headline, but it tells you nothing of the nature of the content, which is the story of a girl's struggle to get an education in a Peruvian gold mining town. Without more context or explanation, the headline can't be expected to generate much interest or attract meaningful organic search traffic. And that exactly was the outcome: after a social media push, during which it enjoyed high engagement with readers who did click through and read, the article fell off the map and had very low discoverability when compared to articles on the same topic in other publications. However, *VQR*'s policy is to use the same headlines online as it does in print.

For a better strategy, study the *New Yorker*. The print headline "College Calculus" becomes "What Is College Worth?" online. "The Weight of the World" becomes "The Woman Who Could Stop Climate Change." An important technical note: these headline changes are not always made to the *display* title (the title the average reader sees at the top of the article), but to the search engine optimization (SEO) title—which affects how the article is "seen" by search engines. It's also the title that appears in a search result or when the article is shared via social media.

Search Engine Optimization

SEO—search engine optimization—has many ingredients (discussed further in chapter 20), but among the most pertinent is keyword use. Using appropriate and relevant keywords and keyword phrases in the article title, description, and subheads helps the content surface in online searches; over time, if the content is engaging (if people spend a lot of time with it), or gains other positive SEO marks (such as links from high-quality sources), it may enjoy another wave of traffic that can span months—even years—without active marketing and promotion. This is what's known as organic search traffic, or search traffic you don't pay for.

In other words, even if an article fails to gain much attention when it is first published, it can gain visits over time if search engines rank it as an important piece related to specific topics. For example, as a user search (at Google), "What is college worth?" grew exponentially between 2009 and 2015. It's not an accident that a *New Yorker* editor used a title that matches that search query; as of this writing, the "College Calculus" article appears on the first page of results when someone asks Google "What is college worth?"

Along with headlines, your editor will likely be responsible for handling SEO concerns, but a valued and successful online contributor considers SEO when pitching, and can use such knowledge to craft and publish better trafficked articles over time.

Social Media and Distribution Savvy

Sharing and distributing online work through social media is a given, but much of the sharing (by both professionals and amateurs) is done without much thought or effort. Most users post a link, add a sentence quoting the piece or asking a question, and call it a day. The best publications and writers create multiple customized graphics to market the same story, with specific social media or distribution outlets in mind. Sometimes a story is even recast, redesigned, or repurposed to gain traction on a specific platform, such as Snapchat. If the piece has photos or illustrations, writers may post one (or more) with an extended caption or self-contained story, on Instagram or Pinterest. If it involves statistics or data, publications may create an infographic or image that can be shared. If there's a specific quote that's hard-hitting or inspiring, it's common to turn it into a graphic that will stand out on social media. You'll notice a theme here of creating visuals, which is no accident. Just about every trend, study, and report on social media use indicates the growing importance of strong visuals.[6]

Every online publication also has a content repurposing or distribution plan to use birthdays, holidays, anniversaries, and other current events as opportunities to pull content from the archives and give it a new life. Sometimes the content can be shared as-is; other times, it's lightly updated. The ever-popular listicle is a well-known method of reviving older content. For example, the *New Yorker* publishes roundups of its own pieces at the end of each calendar year, such as "Six Bits of Good News from 2015" and "Our Fifteen Most-Read Blog Posts of 2015." Its staff writers also write blog posts with fresh analyses or updates whenever people or events from their articles show up again in the news cycle.

BLOGGING

Blogging, as a form of online writing, is its own art form. As most commonly defined, a blog is an informal, often personal type of writing by a single individual (although you'll find many types of group blogs and organizational blogs with multiple contributors). The posts appear in reverse chronological order; while some may remain relevant over many years, most blog posts are ephemeral and gradually become buried under newer posts. For our purposes here, blogging refers to writing you do on your own turf, meaning you don't need permission to publish and, for the most part, are publishing only your own content. Although most blogs are available to readers for free, with enough traffic or attention, you may find ways to monetize your blog through advertising, donations, subscriptions, or other methods described in part 5.

Since its emergence in the early 2000s, blogging has often been declared dead or dying, mainly due to the rise of social media, as well as community publishing sites such as Medium. The argument goes that people who read online no longer visit scattered blogs, but instead head to their favorite social media site. Don't be fooled. Blogging isn't dead, any more than journal writing, opinion writing, or current events writing is dead.

Writers who ask, Can I blog to get a book deal? probably think of the blog as a lesser form of writing, a vehicle to something bigger and better. But for a blog to be successful, it should have its own unique reason for being—blogs truly written as blogs do not aspire to becoming books. Never use a blog as a dumping ground for material written for the print medium—or for book publication—without considering the art of the blog. As with all types of online writing, blog posts should be optimized for online reading. That means being aware of keywords, SEO, and popular bloggers in your subject area, plus including visual and interactive content (comments, images, multimedia, links).

For authors who excel at blogging, it can become their number-one marketing tool for books or other projects that put money in their pocket. But it requires patience and persistence, and it's not quite the same as writing for paid publication. It may take a very long time before you see a direct connection between your blogging and your monthly or annual income.

Blogging is often straightforward for nonfiction writers, less so for novelists. How-to authors have it the easiest of all, because their subject matter often lends itself to blogging, especially if they're teaching workshops or regularly interacting with their target readership. Such authors probably know off the top of their heads the questions they're asked most frequently, and the problems that surface again and again for their audience. This is invaluable fodder for a blog. However, with a little creativity and imagination, fiction writers can have successful blogs as well, for instance, by focusing on literary citizenship activities, as discussed in chapter 2.

For an effective blog, think through how can you bring your own voice or perspective to a topic, theme, or subject matter without repeating what's already out there. (This is easier said than done. It took me eighteen months to find the right angle—to realize I do best when I focus on publishing industry trends and business topics for authors.) The most successful blogs have a focused angle and appeal to a specific audience. This makes it easier to attract attention and build a community around common interests or perspectives.

For new bloggers, consistency is critical—you need to make a commitment to see a payoff. And there are two types of consistency:

- **Frequency.** To gain momentum initially, commit to at least two posts a week. Some people may get by on one a week, but you'll struggle to gain traction. Ideally, starting out, you should post three to five times per week. Once your blog becomes established, and you build up an audience, you can ease back on the frequency.
- **Subject matter.** If you look at a month's worth of titles for your blog posts, they should convey a strong message about what you cover on your blog and who it's for. A potential reader should be able to tell easily if they will benefit from reading your posts on an ongoing basis. Authors can have trouble staying focused and disciplined in this way, often because they get bored or they think readers will get bored. But again, it's hard to gain traction if you're switching it up all the time and not consistent in your coverage.

If you're interested in blogging but worry about the time commitment, then consider creating a multicontributor blog, where several authors in the same genre (or targeting similar audiences) band together. That can reduce the burden as well as increase the size of your audience starting out—since more people will be marketing and promoting the blog.

The best platform to use for blogging is whatever you use for your author website. Having everything under the same umbrella is good for both long-term marketing strategy and search engine visibility. So, for example, if you have an author website on SquareSpace, start your blog there too, not over at Wordpress or Blogspot. If your website platform does not support blogging, then it may be time to switch platforms.

BUILDING A BLOG READERSHIP
People may have to see links to your blog posts for months before they actually click through to read one—or even become aware that your blog exists. This isn't necessarily through any fault of your own; there's an incredible amount of noise online, and enormous demands on everybody's attention. But if you make a steady series of impressions over a long period of time on the same topic, it should start to click: Oh, this person is blogging, and they're regularly covering this topic. Some writers assume everybody knows they're blogging because they've posted about it. But no, that's not the case, and that's why consistency is so important.

The more time you spend blogging, the more value you build for readers and the more readers will find you. Your efforts snowball. Even if it seems no one is reading, commenting, or sharing, assume that they are.

Only about 10 percent of your readers (or even fewer) will make themselves known to you or engage, so it takes a while to spot concrete indications of growing activity or interest.

Before you start a blog, it's wise to identify the key people already blogging in your area—the influencers. Start reading and sharing their content, and comment at their blogs. Eventually, if possible, you might guest-blog for them. See the other bloggers not as competitors but as community members who may become supporters of your work. If your blog is of high quality, and generates conversation, they'll be likely to recommend you or send you traffic by linking to your posts. So identify the notable community players, or the people who you'll want to build relationships with over time.

Whether your site is self-hosted or on another platform, make sure Google Analytics is installed. It's a free service and easy to set up. After Google Analytics has collected at least a month of data, take a look at the following:

- How do people find your blog? Through searches? Through your social media presence? Through other websites that link to you?
- What search words bring people to your site?
- What pages or posts are most popular on your site?

Knowing the answers to these questions, you can better decide which social media networks are worth your investment of time and energy, who else on the web might be a good partner for you (who is sending you traffic and why?), and what content on your site is worth your time to continue developing (what will bring you visitors over the long run?).

Create Guides on Popular Topics

If you're a nonfiction writer, then this probably comes naturally: Put together a 101 guide, FAQ, or tutorial related to your topic or expertise— something people often ask you about. If you're a novelist, this strategy may take some creative thinking. Consider a few examples:

- If your book is strongly regional, create an insider's guide or travel guide to the region. Or think about other themes in your work that could inspire something fun: a collection of recipes; a character's favorite books, movies, or music; or research and resources that were essential for completing your work.
- Create a list of favorite reads by genre/category, by mood, or by occasion. Tie into current events or "look-alike" media whenever

you can; for example, if you write romance and you know your readers love *The Bachelor*, create a list of books that fans of the show might enjoy reading.

- If you have a strong avocational pursuit (or past profession) that influences your novels, create FAQs or guides for the curious.

Create Regular Lists or Roundups

A popular way to make people aware of your blog is to link to others' blogs. If you can do this in a helpful way, it's a win for you, for your readers, and for the sites you send traffic to. You can create lists or roundups on any theme or category that interests you enough to remain dedicated, enthusiastic, and consistent for the long haul—at least six months to a year, if you want to see a tangible benefit.

Run Regular Interviews

Believe it or not, it's rare to come across an informed, thoughtful, and careful interviewer and interview series. Think about themes, hooks, or angles for a series of interviews, and run them on a regular basis—bearing in mind that a well-researched, quality interview requires an investment of time. Such series also offer you an excellent way to build your network and community relationships, which has a way of paying off in the long run.

Be a Guest on Other Sites

Whenever you guest-blog or appear on another website, it's an opportunity to have multiple links back to your own site and social network accounts. Arranging a meaningful guest post involves pitching sites that have bigger audiences than yours, but whose readership is a good match for your work. For a strong introduction, visit Copyblogger and read the excellent post "The Essentials of Guest-Blogging Strategy for SEO, Traffic, and Audience-Building." If you're not the type to write guest posts, then consider proactively offering yourself up to be interviewed as part of other bloggers' interview series. Any time you make an appearance on another site, promote the interview on your own social networks and create a permanent link to it from your own website.

A FINAL WORD ON ONLINE WRITING

Some writers feel discouraged and put off by the attention spans of online readers. To the extent you're able, don't work *against* the behavior of online readers, or assume your work will magically receive people's full attention.

Be up for the challenge and see how you can artfully entice and persuade people to spend more time with your pieces. Some writers add irreverent humor and visuals (such as animated GIFs) to retain interest and emphasize key points; others include plenty of paragraph breaks, headings, and lists to make the article easier to skim. When you read an online article in full, from beginning to end, ask yourself: Why did I stick with this? What can I learn from the writer or publication? Learning to write well and effectively online can and does translate into writing well for print or traditional outlets.

Part Four
THE WRITER AS ENTREPRENEUR
LAYING THE FOUNDATION

The next four chapters dig deep into the foundations of creative entrepreneurship, offering a roadmap on how to succeed in the market, particularly in a crowded online environment. They address the most important facets of author platform—building readership and visibility within a community—and varying strategies for marketing and promoting your work in online environments. Part 4 ends with an in-depth discussion of how to have a successful book launch—a complex endeavor that will draw on every business skill and resource in your arsenal.

In the literary world in particular, there's a persistent fear that directly engaging or cultivating a readership may distract from producing the best art, or prevent a writer from being taken seriously by his peers—as illustrated by the statements from Will Self in chapter 8. Another example of this mindset is the celebration of Elena Ferrante, the pseudonym for an Italian novelist. She remains beloved by the literary community for not marketing or promoting herself, for—as they say—letting the work speak for itself. When she was unmasked in 2016, the literary establishment was outraged on her behalf: the majority believed her work was stronger without having any brand or identity associated with it.

If this is how you feel, you are not going to enjoy the discussions ahead. But even if you disagree about how much time or energy you should devote to such activities, you should understand that writers are often guilty of putting the burden on publishers, agents, editors, or other gatekeepers to help them achieve career goals that are really their own responsibility. It's understandable why writers unschooled in the business of authorship might want to shift this burden onto someone else. After all, shouldn't people trained in marketing take care of the marketing, and writers the writing? But if you wait for someone else to make things happen for you, or rely on others to discover your great art, the most likely outcome will be disappointment, followed by a frantic scramble to remedy the situation.

You will find endless, conflicting advice about how writers should approach marketing and promotion activities, but that should be reassuring. As I've emphasized throughout this book, we're not discussing questions with firm or static answers. Successful authorship isn't a formula. It requires individuality, thoughtfulness, and critical thinking.

Given that there can be no formula, this section approaches the topic of entrepreneurship with the hope of establishing principles, best practices, and helpful guidelines for a writer who doesn't see a conflict in attending to the business aspects of their writing career. While there's no reason not to seek counsel and advice from agents, publishers, and others who play a role in that career, always remember that *you* must take the initiative on activities that don't have an immediate payoff but are important for future success. Agents will focus primarily on work that can be sold in book form, publishers on short-term returns on their investment. That means the writer must manage the long-term, strategic picture.

19 : AUTHOR PLATFORM

Platform is a challenging concept to discuss, partly because everyone defines it a little differently. My definition is this: an ability to secure paid writing opportunities—or sell books, products, and services—because of who you are or who you reach. As such, platform plays a role in every writer's business model.

Platform as a writing and publishing concept first arose in connection with nonfiction book authors. Sometime during the 1990s, agents and publishers began rejecting nonfiction projects when the author lacked a "platform." At the time—before the advent of the internet or social media—publishers wanted authors to be in the public eye in some way (usually through mainstream media appearances) with the ability to easily spread the word to sell books. They weren't interested in the average Joe who had an idea for a nonfiction book but had no particular professional network or public presence. Sometimes "platform" is used as shorthand for a writer's celebrity factor, especially online. Because of that, platform sometimes gets conflated with a social media following. But that's not really what platform is; impressive online followings tend to be the *result* of having a platform.

Platform does not develop overnight. You aren't going to finish reading this book, follow a three-step formula, and—*presto!*—have a platform and be done. No two writers' platforms are developed in the same way or have exactly the same components. Think of your platform as a fingerprint; your background, education, and network affect what your platform looks like in the beginning. Luck also plays a role. For most writers, platform is an organic result of building visibility in their community and developing readership for their work.

Unless you're experiencing unusual, serendipitous fame (of the fifteen-minute variety), platform can't be built separate from your creative work. Your work is the fabric of how you get noticed and known. Platform grows out of writing and publishing in outlets you want to be identified with and that your target audience reads, as well as producing a body of work that brings followers to your own turf, such as a website and blog, email newsletter, podcast, or video series. Your platform also grows as a result of online and offline relationships: engaging with others on social media; speaking at, attending, or organizing events important to your target audience or community; and partnering with peers or influencers to produce creative projects or extend your visibility.

The concept of platform applies to all types of creative professionals, not just writers. Kevin Kelly, the founding executive editor of *Wired* magazine, is well known for a theory called "1,000 True Fans." He postulated that the ability of any person to directly connect with a thousand people who would buy anything they produced would amount to a sustainable living.[1] This idea continues to be debated. Whether you believe it takes a thousand or a hundred thousand fans, Kelly is making an argument about the power of platform in the digital age. Every person now has the tools to directly reach an audience, which can lead to a great deal of creative freedom if that audience is willing to support their work.

Nonprofits and arts organizations often talk about "audience development" as critical to their survival, and if you prefer to think of platform in that way, that's fine. It's the same theory, just a different label for paying attention to how you can develop a dependable and supportive (often financially supportive) audience for your work over time.

HOW PLATFORM AFFECTS YOUR ABILITY TO LAND A BOOK DEAL

If you're an unknown, unpublished writer hoping to land a nonfiction book deal with a Big Five publisher, that will require some amount of platform building. However, small presses, and especially university presses, have more interest in the quality of your work than in your platform. It's not uncommon for writers to begin their careers with quieter publishers, then sign with a New York house once they've built visibility and a strong track record—that is, a platform.

Memoirists and narrative nonfiction writers can sometimes find themselves off the hook when it comes to platform. With narratives, the focus tends to be more on the art and craft of the storytelling—or the quality of the writing. A lot depends on your credibility as a good writer; a track record of newspaper or magazine publication can be sufficient to get yourself a book deal. However, one look at the current best-seller list will often betray publishing's continued interest in platform: you'll find books by celebrities, pundits, and well-established writers occupying a fair share of it. To help overcome the platform hurdle, it helps to be writing a narrative that is timely and taps into current events.

Fiction writers should focus on crafting the best work possible, since agents and publishers will make a decision based primarily on the quality of the manuscript and its suitability for the current marketplace. That's not to say, however, that platform plays no role in what fiction gets published. For instance, if you have a MFA in creative writing from Iowa or Columbia, you've already been vetted and selected by one of the most competitive degree programs in the United States. Agents and editors are more likely to extend their time and consideration because you've already jumped a difficult hurdle. A publication credit in a top-tier publication can likewise ease the path to a book deal. And if you're a huge celebrity or internet star, it's possible you'll get a book deal based on that alone, and be paired up with a ghostwriter or publishing team to help you produce a best-selling book that takes advantage of your stardom.

HOW MUCH SHOULD WRITERS FOCUS ON PLATFORM BUILDING?

New writers often express confusion about how to build a platform when they have not a single book or credit to their name. The bigger obstacle, however, may be that they don't yet know who they are as writers. Remember, platform grows out of a body of work—or from producing great work. It's difficult to build a platform for work that does not yet exist (unless, again, you're some kind of celebrity).

Participating in literary citizenship activities, as described in chapter 2, plays a role in building platform and is an ideal focus for a new writer—and it's more likely to contribute to or inspire new work rather than to distract from it. While you're focused on your writing and creative process, it can be helpful to find a new mentor, connect with an important influencer, or apply to a writing retreat. Relationship building directly contributes to platform and can lead to publishing opportunities.

Unfortunately, building platform is often identified with social media and portrayed as a waste of time, or with marketing and promotion, which some see as undesirable activities. While platform gives you the power to market effectively, it's not something you develop solely by engaging in marketing activities. It is not about self-promotion or hard selling, or being an extrovert, or yelling "Look at me!" at everyone you meet online or offline. Platform isn't about who yells the loudest or who markets the best. It's about putting in consistent effort over the course of a career, and making incremental improvements in how you reach readers and extend your network. It's about making waves that attract other people to you—not begging them to pay attention. Ultimately, your platform-building process will become as much a creative exercise as the work you produce.

If you're a writer pursuing a freelance career and trying to piece together a living through the various methods described in part 5, the size of your platform will affect how easy it is for you to earn money or bring opportunities to your door. Editors, businesses, organizations, and other potential benefactors will be more likely to consider you if they've heard of you, seen evidence of your work in the market, or otherwise become familiar with you through online or offline interactions.

Some people have an easier time building platform than others. If you hold a high-profile position or have a powerful network; if you have friends in high places or are associated with powerful communities; if you have prestigious degrees or posts, then you play the field at an advantage. This is why it's so easy for celebrities to get book deals. They have built-in platform.

SIX COMPONENTS OF PLATFORM

Platform equates to visibility in the market. Consistent visibility develops name recognition among readers or a target audience, including influencers or gatekeepers. I often discuss author platform as having six components:

- **Writing or content that's publicly available.** This includes all of your traditionally published work, self-published work, and online writing.
- **Social media activity.** Often overlooked as a publishing tool, social media can provide a micro-publishing outlet for writers—a way to play with ideas and gather leads for work, as discussed in chapter 3. Most people immediately think of Twitter and Facebook, but online groups and message boards also constitute social media activity. Sometimes these spaces are even more valuable than the usual social media sites.
- **Website.** As the hub for all of your efforts on social media and offline, your website is critical to platform building.
- **Relationships.** These include people you know either online or offline, as well as devoted members of your readership. Relationships tend to start (and sometimes stay) within a

particular community; the more your relationships stretch across communities—the more diverse they are—the more powerful your platform will be.

- **Influence.** This is your ability to get people you don't know— especially influencers—to help you out, listen, or pay attention.
- **Actual reach.** This is the number of people you can reliably reach with a message at any given moment.

When writers conflate platform building with social media, they can suffer burnout and question whether it's really a useful practice. For long-term sustainability, it's best focus on cultivating stronger relationships and connections to existing fans, and partnering with other organizations, businesses, and other individuals to extend your visibility. Sometimes it's about creating and pushing out more work—being prolific—which may be preferable for writers who don't feel like their strength is in building relationships. Other times, by experimenting with new mediums or distribution channels, you can reach an audience you weren't able to find before. As an example, Seth Harwood is a crime novelist with an MFA in fiction from Iowa, who built his readership by distributing work in podcast form. He bought recording equipment, read his work chapter by chapter, and distributed each installment via iTunes and his website. Before long, he had enough of a following to attract the attention of a traditional publisher, who released his book in other formats but allowed him to continue producing the free podcast. He now actively publishes with an imprint of Amazon Publishing.

When writers ask me if they can't just hire someone to build their platform or engage with readers, they're often missing the point. Building a readership, or networking in the community, usually requires just one thing: you. You have to be present and authentic. Furthermore, if a third party pretends to be you, then you'll miss important insights into how people engage with your work—which can provide inspiration for new work, as well as improve your long-term marketing and promotion efforts.

However you decide to build platform, it's important that you enjoy the activities, so you can stick with them for the long haul. This is too often discounted. Platform-building activities take time to gather momentum, and just about every author has abandoned an approach too soon, before it was really clear if it would work out.

Also, it's best to have some consistency with your voice and style. This isn't about being predictable so much as having a message or approach that people begin to associate with you over time. Avoid adopting a "marketing voice" that's different from that of your work; you can get pegged as a boring shill.

Participate in platform-building activities that reflect your interest in the world, and in other people. Find ways to publish, post, and share about things that fascinate you or puzzle you. Post questions for other people to answer. Ask people to share something with you. You may not get it right at first, but that's OK. A spirit of playfulness helps.

HOW TO PRIORITIZE YOUR TIME AND FOCUS YOUR EFFORTS

Working on an author platform can feel overwhelming. How can you explore the universe of possibilities without going a little insane? Here's my rule-of-thumb list for platform-building priorities, specifically for new and midcareer writers:

- Identify new publishing opportunities or partnerships to spread your work to the right audience, or at least to a bigger audience than the one you currently reach.
- Look at new mediums in which to present your content or stories. If you've focused solely on written work, is there an opportunity to also try audio, video, or visuals?
- Establish or improve your website. Sometimes this means investing a little money in design or development.
- Improve the cohesiveness of your writer identity or brand. This might be as simple as printing a business card that matches your website, or having a Facebook cover photo that reflects your brand. Again, it may involve hiring design help.
- Add an email newsletter to your activities if you don't have one. (More on this in chapter 20.)
- Identify the social media outlet(s) you want to use creatively and focus on for growth, or those where you might simply experiment and play.

Full disclosure: I rarely set such specific platform goals for myself. Instead, I mainly work off of signals. I pay close attention to how people are engaging with me and my work (and sometimes I measure it, using a tool like Google Analytics), and what themes show up in the comments, questions, or conversations in the community, then I adjust. I also pay attention to people I admire, and sometimes I imitate them if I see a better way of doing things. While I read trend articles and stay current on how the industry is unfolding, such things don't influence me on a day-to-day basis; it's more about understanding how best practices evolve and only acting when I feel compelled to do so—because that's where the energy of the moment directs me. For example, at the time of this writing, podcasting and digital audio is one of the most overwhelmingly popular areas in writing and publishing, but I personally consume very little audio content and don't feel that's where my talent lies. Even though several people have suggested I should get into audio, I've resisted because no appropriate opportunity has presented itself—but maybe it will in the future.

I favor experimentation and letting my enjoyment drive platform building. Whether you're a goal setter or not, it's important to pay attention to what gives you energy and what takes it away. Avoid pursuing a platform-building activity if it doesn't feel like a good match for the rest of what you're doing. Put another way: Don't make your life difficult by forcing something that's not really you. There are so many ways to develop a strong platform that you have the freedom to focus on the activities you like, which in turn will lead to the satisfaction and growth you want.

So set some goals. Or don't. But get started on the process of building. It takes time, and you won't get far if you wait for some magical moment. The magic happens as you make a writing life—piece by piece.

20 : YOUR ONLINE PRESENCE

WEBSITES, SOCIAL MEDIA, AND MORE

In the previous chapter, and elsewhere throughout the book, I have discussed various elements of author platform, which include author websites, social media activity, and other forms of online communication that help create and sustain relationships. It is difficult, if not impossible, to be a writer in the digital era without maintaining some level of involvement in the online world—starting with a strong website.

This chapter covers the key components of author websites, as well as the basics of an online presence that will sustain your business as a writer.

AUTHOR WEBSITES

All serious writers, even those not yet published, should create and maintain a website as part of their career development. A website serves as your online home and a hub for everything you do, whether in real life or in the digital realm. You own and control it, and can use it to tell your own story and connect directly with interested readers or influencers. It's hard to overstate its importance over the long term. Consider it a cost of doing business in the digital era, a necessary business card and networking tool. In some cases, it can also be a creative outlet and community area, especially for writers who blog. (To be clear, having an author website does not require blogging. Blogging is a separate issue addressed in chapter 18.)

Your website will improve over time—in search ranking, in appearance, and in content—assuming you tend to it and don't abandon it. And why would you, if you're still writing and publishing? If you start the process early, before you "need" a site, you can enjoy a gentler learning curve, as well as the power of incremental progress. You don't have to launch and perfect everything at once. Start small, and build your skills and presence over time. You want something you can manage. Sustainability is key.

This is not an exhaustive list, only a starting point. For very new writers, a website might consist of only one or two pages, mainly focused on your bio and portfolio of work.

About page. Your full-length bio (discussed in chapter 2) goes here. Include a professional headshot if you have one; if not, a casual photo will do fine.

Published work. For books you've written or contributed to, always show the cover image. Offer a brief description of the book; include a couple of blurbs, quotes, or words of praise that indicate its value; and add buy links for major retailers. If you want, include or link to an excerpt—usually the introduction or chapter 1. For published essays, articles, stories, or poems, always link to where a piece can be found or read, assuming it's online. It's usual to group publications by genre and to list them in reverse chronological order. If a piece appeared with illustrations or was otherwise highly visual, it's helpful to add an image showing the opening or an interior spread, assuming you have permission.

Prolific or multigenre authors should consider building a separate page for each genre, series, or type of work (for example, pages labeled "Poetry", "Fiction" and "Personal Essay").

Contact page. Always make it clear how you can be reached, even if not directly (especially if you're a freelancer or journalist). Published authors can include their agent's or publicist's contact info if they don't want to field media or publicity requests. If you are open to being contacted directly, then add a proper contact form to your site rather than just giving your email address.

Links to social media profiles. If you're active elsewhere and invite interaction, make it clear, either with social media buttons in the header, footer, or sidebar, or by using widgets and badges that reflect your activity.

Email newsletter sign-up. Every author should consider having an email newsletter, as discussed later in this chapter, to keep readers updated, at minimum, on new releases and events. Many authors place the sign-up very prominently in the middle of their homepage.

Pay special attention to headers, footers, sidebars, or other elements that repeat from page to page throughout your site. These are typically where you want critical information or calls to action. For example, many authors put an image of their most recent book cover in a prominent, recurring area on their site.

TECHNICAL STUFF

If you don't yet have a website, I recommend building one with WordPress. It's a robust, free, open-source system with good search engine optimization (SEO) right out of the box. Perhaps more important, it now powers more than 20 percent of the world's websites, so it's easier to find help and ready-to-go functionality when you need it. Enough people use WordPress that it's unlikely to fail or disappear any time soon, and it's continually updated to keep pace with changes in web technology. Customized versions of Wordpress underpin many sites you frequent—the *New York Times*, the *New Yorker*, Tech-Crunch, CNN, and more.

There are two ways to use WordPress: you can use WordPress.com, a full-service website hosting platform, which is free to start but may incur costs for customized design or functionality; or you can install the WordPress system for free on your account at most website hosting providers. (A hosting provider is a company that stores your website on its servers and keeps it up and running; basic hosting costs $5–$10 month but can easily cost thousands of dollars per year for high-traffic sites.)

When you pay a hosting provider to keep your site up, this is generally known as "self-hosting." In the long run, you will probably want to self-host. Self-hosting is like owning, as opposed to renting, your site; you have full control over what appears there with no "landlord" to interfere. If you're technically challenged, or a new or unpublished author, you can ease into site building and management with a free account at WordPress.com. When you're ready to move, the company offers inexpensive "relocation" services to a hosting provider, but you will still be using the WordPress technology, so the transition will be seamless. After relocation, your site will be stored on a different set of servers but will look and function the same—and you'll have responsibility for keeping it up and running (with your host's help).

Some writers find WordPress too intimidating or difficult to use. If that de-scribes you, a decent alternative—and a fully hosted solution—is Squarespace, which charges monthly fees. Just know that if you ever leave Squarespace, you'll essentially be back at square one in building your website. Because Squarespace is a proprietary platform, you can't really "take" your website design or code anywhere else. Be extremely wary of site-building services and platforms, including those sponsored by major writing organizations, as some may be here today and gone tomorrow.

While it's not necessary to buy your own domain name in order to have a website, it's best to do so even if you don't use it right away. A domain is your website's URL, and in most cases it should be based on the name you intend to publish under—not a book title. Your author name is your brand. It will span decades and appear on every book you publish. If you can't get yourname .com, try for yournameauthor.com, yournamebooks.com, or yournamewriter .com. If that fails, consider an extension other than .com (like .net or .me). That's not to say you can't also buy domains based on your book titles, but that's second priority (especially since your publisher may change a book title at any time up to its printing and release).

If even this technical conversation is causing you headaches, you may prefer to hire a web designer or developer. Costs dramatically vary, but expect to spend $1,500–$3,000 for a bare-bones website, and considerably more for custom design and functionality.

How to Craft Your Homepage

A homepage typically includes the following elements:

- A header with your name and, ideally, a tagline that characterizes your work (one thriller novelist uses the tagline "thrillers with heart"). Commercial authors often include a headshot somewhere on the page, to make the site feel more welcoming. Some authors, though, feel this suggests they're self-absorbed. Do what feels comfortable.
- The cover of your most recent book, if you have one. Authors with multiple books may even want to show the cover of every published book on their homepage. Regardless of your decision, if you have many books, include a menu tab labeled "Books" so visitors can jump to a complete listing.
- If you're a freelancer, mentions of or links to recently published work.
- If you're unpublished, a brief description of who you are or what you do, somewhere around 50 to 200 words. Published authors should usually skip any long, introductory welcome message, focus on their books instead, and have a clearly labeled "About" page.
- A call to action, such as an email newsletter sign-up or a link to where you're active on social media. Writers with new books will often include links to an excerpt, to sites where visitors can buy the book, or to related news or event announcements.
- Social proof. We're all susceptible to signaling that says, "This

person is liked and trusted by others." Some authors include logos of the publications they've appeared in or mention grants or awards received. Others mention important communities they belong to. And published authors can include brief blurbs about their work.

Homepage design is incredibly subjective, but the most important criterion is that the type of writer you are—and the work you produce or services you offer—should be recognizable quickly. You have about three seconds to convey the message, and you don't want visitors guessing. Some authors can get away with a fair amount of intrigue or cleverness, but try to be honest about whether you're actually intriguing people or frustrating them.

Make the homepage navigation or menu system plain and clear. This usually means providing an obvious path for people to learn more about who you are ("About"), how to contact you ("Contact"), and what you've written ("Books" or "Publications").

You might not have the resources to do it right away, but in the long run, it's helpful to hire a designer to create a custom header image, or a custom look that fits your personality and work. If you're using WordPress or a blog-centric system, be careful that your homepage doesn't default to showing blog posts—especially if you're not going to blog!

The good *and* bad news is that your website is never finished. It is always a work in progress. You'll improve it, tweak it, experiment with it, and hopefully take pride in how it showcases your work. It's better to get your site established while you're unpublished, so you own your domain early on, learn how to use the tools, and begin the journey of expressing who you are within a digital media environment.

SEO FOR WRITERS

Search engine optimization is the practice of improving the ranking of one's website or content in organic searches (e.g., through Google) in order to boost traffic and visibility—to gain new leads or readership, in other words. SEO is one of the most overlooked areas when writers consider what it means to sell and effectively grow an audience.

You may have heard about unsavory tricks that were used in the early days of SEO, such as keyword stuffing. Over the years, search engines have become much better at detecting such ploys and identifying good-quality websites, authoritative writers, and helpful content. Optimizing your site or your content for search is the process of ensuring that you're increasing the number of good signals and decreasing the bad.

Generally, SEO is divided into "on the page" and "off the page" factors. On-the-page factors are things more under your control, such as the content itself, the HTML coding, and the site architecture. Off-the-page factors are things over which you have less control, such as what websites link to yours and social media shares. Here are some of the most common ways to improve your site's or your content's SEO:

- **Inbound links.** When Google debuted in the late 1990s, it was seen as delivering superior search results because it used a novel method: considering what types of sites, and how many sites, were linking to each other. How many links point to your website ("inbound links") is still one of the strongest SEO signals. Both quality (authoritativeness of the linking site) and quantity (number of inbound links) play a role. You can increase your number of inbound links by writing for other websites (and making sure your bio links to your site), being interviewed at other sites, and commenting on other sites.
- **Site speed.** The faster your site loads, the higher it will rank.
- **Mobile usability.** If your site isn't optimized for mobile devices, it will be penalized in search results.
- **Quality content.** Google evaluates quality using a range of factors, such as the length or comprehensiveness of the content, its timeliness, and keyword use that matches a user's search intent.
- **Time spent on site.** If visitors spend a long time on your site, that indicates engagement and quality content, which helps your ranking. This is why comments sections can be a good thing.
- **History.** The longer your site's been around, the more authority it will likely have, and the better it will rank.

You can improve your visibility online and in searches by being consistent in how you present your name and your work. This helps search engines like Google connect the dots and show the most appropriate result when people look for you or your work. When it comes to your name, try to use the same convention whenever you create a profile name, display name, or profile URL on a social media account and whenever you publish online. For example, no matter where you find me, I'm always "Jane Friedman"— not "Jane E. Friedman," "Jane Ellen Friedman," or "J. E. Friedman." In your bios across the online universe, be specific about the type of work you produce, and be consistent in the keywords you use to describe it. You can use book titles, but also consider genres, categories, or other descriptors that readers might use in relation to your work. This helps when people run a search looking for the "John Smith" who writes formal poetry and not plumbing instruction manuals.

SEO in relation to your writing or online content is discussed further in chapter 18. For more on the topic, I recommend "The Beginner's Guide to SEO," freely available at Moz.com. It's written in language anyone can understand.

SOCIAL MEDIA AND WRITERS' CAREERS

At writers' conferences, I'm sometimes asked, Why start an author website? Why not just use Facebook, Tumblr, or some other social media network? Isn't that where everyone is spending their time? Why would people visit my site? Why bother establishing a website that, if it becomes dusty or out of date, could be more damaging than no site at all?

In focusing on social media instead of an author website, you favor the short-term over the long-term. You invest your time and energy in a platform that may lose its effectiveness or disappear in several years. It may benefit you today, in your current business project, but you can never be sure it will help with your next one. In the meantime, your author website will remain unfinished, and people who don't use that particular social network will be difficult to identify and reach.

Perhaps most important, you can never control what any social media platform does or how it evolves—in terms of design and functionality, user interface, or your likes/followers/relationships. You're limited in what you can control, and your insights into your readership are limited to what that network measures and decides to pass on to you. And make no mistake, the companies that run these platforms are concerned about their own needs, not yours. While a site with millions of users is undeniably attractive to anyone trying to reach readers, it will become increasingly frustrating over time that you don't call the shots.

Still, most new authors, upon securing a book contract, are advised to establish a Facebook page and perhaps a Twitter or Instagram account. Why? To market their book, of course. This presents an immediate dilemma: If you're not already active on these channels, through your own interest and volition, you now have the mindset of using them as marketing tools—and worse, you may have no idea what that means beyond telling people to like your page or follow you. To translate social media activity into book sales requires showing up consistently within your community for long periods of time, communicating in an organic way that's relationship-driven rather than sales-driven, and (eventually) sharing news about your publishing accomplishment, in a way that aligns with your previous activity and messaging.

You'll hear tons of conflicting advice about how to use such-and-such social media tool, perhaps more than for any other aspect of author business practice. That's because social media best practices differ depending on your unique career situation, how you behave online, what you're using these tools for at any particular time, and how that makes you feel. There is no one-size-fits-all advice; the best strategy, frankly, is whatever works for you personally and is sustainable over a long period of time. Well-meaning authors (and experts) can give bad advice to writers, ignoring where they are in their careers, their disparate goals, and their differing attitudes to online engagement. You can trust yourself to make many decisions, even if you're not so experienced. Pay attention to how you feel about your actions and the results.

The Facebook Dilemma

Facebook is, hands down, the most important social media network as of this writing—not just for writers, but anyone building an online presence. This is due almost entirely to its size and prevalence in daily life, with two billion users worldwide. One of the initial questions facing writers: Should you start an official page (to garner likes) that's separate from your personal profile (with friends)?

An official page takes work to become meaningful. It may double the time you spend on Facebook, assuming you engage on a personal profile as well. It takes a long time to collect likes, and I find authors get better results if those likes build organically out of a growing readership (rather than through advertising). Your Facebook page should be linked to from your author website and mentioned in your books and other places you publish. Over time, the page will gain momentum, although Facebook will limit your page's reach to 5 or 10 percent of those who like your page. You usually have to pay Facebook to reach more.

If your first step in developing your Facebook page is to blast your Facebook friends with "Go LIKE my page!" there may be no real divide—yet—between your Facebook friends and your target audience. That's not unusual; your friends are often your first circle of readers, people who are eager to know what you're doing and to be supportive. But that's also a reason to avoid pleading with them to like your page: they're already in your corner. The additional page is primarily for readers you don't personally know.

Here are some common scenarios in which an official Facebook page may be helpful and merited:

- You have significant privacy concerns and need to keep your personal profile personal.
- You need to keep your personal life and author persona strictly separate (e.g., you're a K-12 teacher who's writing erotica).
- You write under a pseudonym.
- You already have thousands of friends on your personal profile, and you're constantly filtering requests and messages.
- You're an established author with a fan base already in place.
- You want (and know you'll use) the marketing functionality and metrics that go with official pages.
- You're interested in Facebook advertising.
- You hire help with social media strategy and posting.

If you're not crazy about Facebook in the first place, and don't have time for the additional work, then you can allow the public (your readers and fans) to follow your personal profile. Any of your Facebook posts can be marked as public, so your followers can see them without being your friends. (This is what Mark Zuckerberg does with his Facebook profile; he has no official page.) Here are scenarios where you might want to stick with your personal profile with the "follow" function turned on:

- You're an unpublished author or have very little work available.
- You're new to social media.
- You hardly know what to do with your personal profile, much less a fan page.
- You don't like Facebook.
- You have no privacy issues, and your following probably won't be (soon) in the five figures.

The choice between Facebook profile and fan page is a personal decision. Do what you're comfortable with and what makes sense for your needs. It's hard to offer general advice because everyone's situation differs, but one thing's for sure: maintaining two pages on Facebook will increase your workload.

Meaningful Engagement on Facebook

Facebook is one of the easiest ways to stay engaged and visible in your community, whether you're using your personal profile or a professional page. It's a place to be informal, fun, and casual with people who have already expressed some level of interest or affinity for what you're doing. When people friend, follow, or "like" you, they've given you permission to be in touch and offer updates—and they may see or hear nothing else from or about you except what appears in their Facebook newsfeed. You're creating an impression (even a brand) each time you post. Consider: What do those impressions add up to after a week, a month, a year? Are you conveying a personality, voice, or image you're comfortable with?

If you make helpful, interesting, or valuable posts on Facebook, targeted to a particular sensibility, you will attract an audience that responds in kind, and engages you through likes, comments, and shares. If you're argumentative or frequently complain, you'll attract the same. This is true for just about all online activity, but particularly on Facebook, which people tend to treat like their living room—they're comfortable saying or doing anything. If you don't like the activity or conversation surrounding you, look first at what you're putting out.

Studies show that one of the biggest annoyances for Facebook users is people or companies that post too often. But rather than unfriend or unlike these nuisances, we typically mute them. Thus, I'm a strong advocate of the "less is more" philosophy when it comes to content and social sharing. We all have too much to read anyway, so why share anything except the best and most essential stuff? That said, there is no "right" frequency for posting. It depends what you're posting about and your audience's appetite for your point of view or personality. For some people, frequent posting (to the point of TMI) is their shtick, and if you want to ride that personality wave, go ahead. Just accept its limitations in terms of who you'll attract.

When something special happens, such as a Kickstarter campaign or a book launch, people's tolerance for your posts will often increase, because they know—eventually—the campaign will end. When you undertake such campaigns, keep the tone humorous and entertaining—don't hesitate to poke fun at yourself for yet another post about your new book. (But try to find creative ways or angles for talking about it.)

It's best to avoid automated posting—allowing a third-party service or tool to post to Facebook for you based on specific triggers, without your customizing what gets posted. People don't like engaging with bots. Plus, you're missing an opportunity to say something geared toward your audience on Facebook—perhaps asking a compelling question to spark a discussion, or otherwise conveying your perspective and personality. Usually a more intimate approach is more successful (that living room phenomenon). Scheduling your posts in advance, to go live at a specific time, isn't a problem, but if you don't show up to interact with people who comment, it's another missed opportunity. The first hour or so of engagement on a post can affect its overall success—when Facebook's algorithms detect more response than usual to a post, it pops up in more newsfeeds.

When you share links on Facebook (or elsewhere), offer context, whether it's your own content or someone else's. Explain why you're posting, share an interesting quote from it, or otherwise introduce the content so people understand why it deserves their time. Be a thoughtful curator, not a blaster. It takes practice and skill to get people to read and possibly click or respond to whatever you're posting. When you write a post, consider your reader's perspective—they'll be thinking, What's in it for me?

Social media activity can draw on the same creativity and imagination as your "serious" work. Ideally, whatever you post connects back to the motivations and themes that drive your writing. The most important thing you can do on any social network is to share things you care about—to express something meaningful rather than dutiful. Never throw up a link or a photo without giving the story behind it, or explaining why it matters to you. People crave meaning. Facebook is an excellent tool for delivering that.

THE EMAIL NEWSLETTER

Early in actor Bryan Cranston's career, when his gigs were primarily guest spots on TV shows like *Matlock* and *Murder, She Wrote*, he sent postcards to casting directors about his upcoming appearances. "I knew 99 percent of them wouldn't watch," he told the *New Yorker*, "but my face and name would get in front of them, and it would plant the subliminal message 'He works a lot, this guy!'" Later on, when he received three Emmy nominations for his role as the dad in *Malcolm in the Middle*, he took out "for your consideration" ads promoting his work. He said, "The whole idea is to put yourself in a position to be recognized for your work so opportunities increase. False humility or even laziness could prevent that."[1]

If Cranston's career had begun in the internet era, his postcards might instead have been emails. While email lists have many uses, their most immediate use for freelance writers and authors is to keep readers and professional connections informed about what you're doing. A regular email newsletter sent to your readers creates a long string of impressions, keeping your name at the forefront of their mind. When an opportunity arises—a book club needs a new book to read, a publication is searching for a freelancer, a journalist is looking for an interview subject, or a conference needs speakers—people are far more likely to think of you if they've frequently seen your name.

When most people are overwhelmed with unwanted email, it may seem counterintuitive to categorize the email newsletter as one of the more effective, even intimate, forms of digital communication. However, email has a longer, more stable history than social media, which is constantly shifting. Emails can't be missed like a social media post that disappears in readers' feeds as more posts follow it. You truly own your email list, unlike Facebook or Twitter accounts. And if you use people's email addresses with respect (more on that in a minute), those addresses can become resources that grow more valuable over time.

Developing a Strategy

Getting started with an email newsletter is simple, as well as free, but let's review a few principles before getting to the technical aspects.

Decide on your frequency and stick to it. Your efforts will be more successful if you're consistent. For example, freelance journalist Ann Friedman sends an email newsletter that reliably arrives on Friday afternoons. Weekly is a common frequency, as is monthly, but the most important criterion is what you can commit to. If you choose a low frequency (bimonthly or quarterly), you run the risk of people forgetting they signed up, which then leads to unsubscribes. The more familiar with your work your subscribers are (or the bigger fans they are), the less likely you'll encounter this problem. High frequency is associated with list fatigue, when people unsubscribe or stop opening your messages. Daily sends can be too much, except for news- or trend-driven content.

Keep it short, sweet, and structured. Hardly anyone will complain that your emails are too short, and the more frequently you send, the shorter they should probably be. It can also help if the structure is the same every time. Every newsletter Ann Friedman sends has links to what she's recently published and what she's been reading, plus an animated GIF of the week.

Be specific and honest about what people are signing up for. Your newsletter sign-up form should tell people what they'll get and how often. It's also helpful to link to your newsletter archives or to an example of a past issue.

So what should you put in this newsletter? The only limit is your imagination, and while the intent is to keep your name and work in front of

THE POWER OF VISUALS AND DESIGN

A robust online presence, and advanced online literacy, increasingly requires finding, modifying, and posting compelling images and employing strong visual design. Many images can stand alone and be enjoyed for what they are, while also bringing attention to written content or helping build a brand. Memes, infographics, Instagram, Pinterest, Snapchat, Facebook videos with subtitles—these all attest to the evolution of digital media and how strongly our attention is captured by visuals. Writers who recognize this and find ways to incorporate visuals and strong design into their work or marketing stand to gain an advantage over those who don't.

Fortunately, nondesigners now have more tools and resources than ever to help them find and produce decent visuals:

- High-quality photographs and illustrations with Creative Commons licenses don't require payment or permission for most noncommercial uses. (In most cases, you need only credit the source.) Flickr Creative Commons is one of the largest repositories of permission-free images. Aggregators such as VisualHunt.com will also help you search for images for noncommercial use.
- Canva.com offers cloud-based design software that helps nondesigners create good-looking images using a variety of templates for specific use scenarios. It's mostly free, with fees for premium images or designs from their library.
- Video captured on a smartphone is of sufficient quality for YouTube. Windows Movie Maker comes free with most PCs, and iMovie with Macs, and both are simple to learn.

When creating and distributing an image or video online, remember that people often share visuals without much, if any, attribution. For that reason, you may want to include an attribution or watermark on the visual itself that references your name, website, or brand.

Writers seeking a competitive advantage should consider the following:

- A professional headshot or illustrated portrait that looks good on social media and an author website. Like it or not, professional images convey seriousness of intent and success.
- A brief video clip of you giving a reading or speaking at an event. This is valuable in securing more gigs—assuming you're good on camera. You don't have to hire a videographer, but if you want to attract paying events, it's a wise investment.

- A customized website header or overall design that evokes your style or personality.
- A professional business card that echoes other elements of your brand (consider using design elements from your website, your professional head shot, or a book cover image).
- Professional note cards to use for thank-yous and notes of admiration—again, incorporating design elements you use consistently.

In marketing speak, all of these things represent touch points, or opportunities to make an impression on someone, whether a reader or influencer. It's very powerful when your touch points repeat the same theme or design—it reinforces the message you want to send about who you are and what type of work you produce.

---

people, you also want to keep things interesting—which means trying to provide value or otherwise focus on other people or quality content. Ask yourself: What do you love sharing with other people? What are you already curating or collecting? What do people ask you about all the time? What do you have special insight or expertise on? Assume subscribers won't open every message and will often just skim your content. Then keep these suggestions in mind:

- Have a unique subject line for each send to differentiate the issues.
- Subheads, lists, bolded text, and other visual cues make your content easy to scan and can help readers quickly find what interests them.
- A table of contents is essential for lengthy newsletters, and sometimes even short ones.
- Include important links at least twice, if not three times.
- For items that call for action, use a high-impact visual: a high-contrast box, an accompanying image, or a button.

Starting and Growing Your List

To begin, the only tool you need is a formal email newsletter service that will automate the subscription process, store subscriber email addresses, and archive newsletter issues. One of the most popular services is MailChimp because it's free until you reach two thousand names.

TinyLetter is also popular because it's free with no such limit, but it offers minimal functionality.

While it is possible to add names manually to your newsletter list (without opt-in or confirmation), never do so without the recipient's permission. The number-one reason email newsletters get a bad reputation or are marked as spam is because people break this rule. Just because you've connected with someone on LinkedIn or emailed them once two years ago doesn't mean you have permission to add them to your email newsletter list. The best practice for building a "healthy" newsletter list is collecting voluntary sign-ups at your own website or blog. You can also put out calls on social media.

If you've already experimented with email newsletters, then you know the toughest part is long-term engagement and list growth. You can feel it when your list begins to stall, when even you aren't that excited about putting out another issue. Don't hesitate to shift strategy when your content starts to feel stale and your metrics flatten or decline; your readers are likely suffering from the same boredom you are.

It's easy to pigeonhole email as a practical (even boring) mode of communication, but it can be a creative publishing medium that's easy to read, share, save, and later repurpose into something else. What if you had a limited-time email newsletter that delivered a specific story series? What if you changed the theme of your newsletter every month? What if a reader had to search for clues in·each newsletter? Expand your idea of what email can do.

A FINAL WORD

I've offered a lot of prescriptive advice in this chapter. Nonetheless, I don't believe in hard-and-fast rules when it comes to writers' online presence. Good principles or best practices, yes. But what you create will be as distinctive as your fingerprints. It's hard to copy someone else's strategy, tactics, design, or approach, and doing so is unlikely to yield the same results. To some extent, everyone must find their own way—what fits their personality, their work, and the audience they hope to find or engage. I recommend you loosen up (especially if you need to find your voice), not take it all too seriously, and experiment to find what works. If you need a place to start, then focus on talking about or posting about others you admire. When done well, your online presence isn't about focusing on yourself; it's about focusing outward.

21 : TURNING ATTENTION INTO SALES

To establish a full-time living from your writing, it's essential to learn basic marketing principles. There is something of a formula, and it looks like this:

The right message + the right words + the right audience = success!

Typically, the biggest missing piece for writers (and publishers too) is the right audience. That's partly because of the continuing belief that good art means not thinking about audience. While you may tune out market concerns during the creative process, once that process is over and it comes to the business of writing and publishing, there's no way around the discussion of audience. If you can't reach an audience, your career will stall. And to reach an audience, you first have to develop some idea of who they are.

While "word of mouth" plays a powerful role in making anyone's work more visible, a strong marketing plan can be integral to sparking that word of mouth in the first place. Such a plan cannot depend on artistic excellence, or the belief that great work eventually gets noticed. Nearly all great work has to be thoughtfully marketed to gain visibility, and thoughtful marketing starts with an understanding of audience.

UNDERSTANDING YOUR AUDIENCE

At my first publishing job, while still an intern, I was asked to research specific communities of hobbyists. Everyone else was so busy producing new books they didn't have time to study the audience the books were serving. I developed two in-depth reports: one looked at the comics industry, and the other focused on a popular craft trend at the time, rubber stamp art. To put together the reports—this was before the internet really took off— I pursued a variety of information sources:

- **Print publications.** One of the most useful ways to understand an audience is to read what they read. In their magazines, newsletters, and books, the hobbyists' challenges and concerns clearly came through, and I could pick out the voices who were important to the field. The advertisements were often as helpful as the content.

- **Retail environments.** I visited small comics stores and rubber stamp stores, as well as large retailers such as Walmart and Michaels. The indie stores were invaluable because clubs and organizations met there, and the proprietors were usually experts in understanding their audience.
- **Websites and online communities.** Though few and far between at the time, these were as useful as print publications in showing the size and impact of a particular interest area.
- **Real-life events.** At regional conferences and chapter meetings, I talked one-on-one with members of the target audience, asking questions and developing a clearer picture of what they cared about.

While the average fiction writer would not conduct this level of market research to understand their readership—after all, they probably belong to their target audience—it doesn't hurt to step back, analyze the different facets of your work, and think through who it most appeals to. The wealth of online information and social media means it's easier than ever to develop a portrait of your audience: where they hang out, what types of media they consume, where they shop. To better understand your readers and how to reach them, here are some starting points:

- Come up with at least two or three established writers who produce work similar to your own. (If you can't come up with any, you aren't trying very hard, or you're not reading enough.) Study reader reviews of their work on Amazon or Goodreads. When you find a stellar review by a person who uses their real name and is active online, dig deeper—take a look at their Amazon or Goodreads profile and their website if they have one, and develop a portrait of someone who could be your "ideal reader." (This works best if you don't choose a mega-selling author guaranteed to hit the best-seller list just by releasing a new title.)
- Again, think of a writer similar to you or one you wish to emulate. Which publications have interviewed or reviewed that writer? Do those publications serve your target audience? What can you learn about the audience from the publications?
- Where do writers similar to you appear—both in real life and online? What events do they attend? Look at their social media

activity: what does it say about who their readership is? As you follow the digital breadcrumbs, a picture will start to emerge of the community the writer is engaging, and how you can reach them too.

- If you consider yourself part of the target audience you're trying to reach, study your own habits and how you discover new work. Is it by reading mainstream publications? Through social media? From a literary blog? From podcasts?

These questions focus on writers reaching readers, but the same process applies if you're a freelancer thinking about potential clients. Study freelancers similar to you, see what behaviors they engage in, and research the behavior of your target clientele.

As you conduct this research, soak in the language and concerns of the audience or community. Take note of specific keywords or phrases that come up frequently, and note what gets people most engaged or enthusiastic. Thoughtful marketing requires engaging your audience in a way that will resonate—which means speaking their language. For writers who have studied the concept of a "discourse community" in classes on pedagogy, that's a good way to think of what you're researching.

COMMUNICATING WITH YOUR AUDIENCE

Once you know *who* you're approaching and where you can reach them, that's half the battle. The other half is communicating well: the right message and the right words. Your marketing communications will usually have one of two objectives:

- to drive a sale
- to build a relationship

Platform building (see chapter 19) is directed toward the second goal and is what most of your marketing communications consist of. It's an ongoing effort to develop your audience and reach new readers or clients. Big corporations participate in this type of communication as well, and it's typically called brand building. When Coke runs an advertisement that says, "Open happiness," that's not a sales-driven message; that's a brand-building message. Conversely, when McDonald's advertises a $1.99 McRib sandwich available only for the next two weeks, that's a sales-driven message meant to directly affect the bottom line.

Sales-driven communications are typically tied to specific marketing campaigns, product launches, or short-term initiatives. This is where you would be most likely to measure your effectiveness, and look at cause-and-effect outcomes. For example: Did my promotional posts on such-and-such social media network affect my email newsletter sign-ups? Did my appearance on blog X or podcast Y lead to more paying clients? Did this discount or free offer affect book sales? And so on. By paying attention to what moves the needle, you can improve your efforts next time. But when you're building relationships (or building platform), you typically do *not* measure cause and effect, because making a sale or landing a new client isn't the point. Building a conducive environment or making a connection that will lead to a sale *later* is the point. Be aware that if you emphasize sales-driven messages across all of your marketing communications for extended periods, your community will tire of you (and you'll likely tire of yourself).

However and whenever you communicate with members of your audience, it should be with their permission: don't contact them unless they have indicated they want to hear from you—by liking you, following you, signing up for emails from you, and so on. And your behavior should be in keeping with the level of interest expressed. For instance, how you behave and communicate with Twitter followers will be different than how you communicate with longtime subscribers of your email newsletter. This brings us to the concept of a funnel.

THE FUNNEL

In the film *Glengarry Glen Ross*, in a scene made famous by Alec Baldwin's performance, a group of underperforming salesmen is lectured on how to become "closers." On the chalkboard—aside from "Always Be Closing"—is written the following breakdown of sale stages:

A—Attention
I—Interest
D—Decision
A—Action

This is an example of a sales funnel. While most writers don't like to think of themselves as salespeople, anytime we're active on social media, or doing something to market and promote our work, we're attracting attention or building interest. Decision and action (to spend money or time) are much more likely once people have heard of you. While it sounds obvious, it bears stating: a prior relationship makes a sale more likely. This is one of the reasons social media is so valuable—it's a relationship builder.

At the top of the funnel—the widest part—is where you find the largest number of potential customers, people who have been "qualified" in some way, but it's also where the weakest relationships are. For writers, this might describe a large number of their Twitter followers, or someone who has read one of their pieces for free but hasn't purchased a book or paid them for a story. At later stages of the funnel, the number of customers decreases (some lose interest or lack commitment), until there's just a handful who take the desired action—customers who make a purchase. Getting people to act almost always requires a specific "call to action," which writers sometimes feel uncomfortable issuing because it puts them in the role of salesperson. While a call to action may sometimes be a sales-driven message—"Buy my book at 20% off!"—other times it's offering something for free. As soon as you do that, you're starting to develop a content strategy, which we'll discuss further in a moment.

There are entire professions focused on improving the effectiveness of sales and marketing funnels—particularly improving online conversion rates. "Conversion" refers to the percentage of people who ultimately take a specific, desired action. Most conversion rates are very low—in the single digits. But improving a conversion rate by even a tiny amount can mean a lot more sales and profit. Here's an example of one of my funnels:

- **Attention.** A writer searches online for how to get a book published and finds my blog post on the topic.
- **Interest.** The writer reads the post and perhaps a few related posts at my site.
- **Decision.** The writer sees my book referenced and decides he should read it.
- **Action.** The writer makes a purchase on Amazon.

In this particular funnel, I use free content (my blog posts) to attract attention through search engine results—to reach people who search online for answers to questions about publishing. Here's another funnel:

- **Attention.** Someone subscribes to my free email newsletter for writers.
- **Interest.** They learn from the newsletter that I'm offering a class on social media.
- **Decision.** They read testimonials from past students at my website and decide to take the class.
- **Action.** They register at my site.

In this funnel, I again use free content (an email newsletter) to attract attention, which this time requires having someone's email address. This is a highly qualified type of lead, more so than a social media contact. This person is sufficiently interested in hearing from me that they've given me their email address. My conversion rate on email is much higher than my conversion rate on social media.

What about funnels for writers of fiction, poetry, or narrative writing? The same principles apply. Say you're a poet with a newly published collection of love poems:

- **Attention.** A potential reader notices people in the literary community tweeting about your article.
- **Interest.** They click and read your piece about the history of love poetry at a literary website; your bio mentions your latest collection.
- **Decision.** The potential reader checks out your book on Amazon or at your website and notices positive reviews or sees that it's recommended by other poets she likes.
- **Action.** The reader makes a purchase online or at a local bookstore.

For a novelist (who may or may not have a new novel out):

- **Attention.** A potential reader hears from a friend about a great podcast episode on Asian-Americans in the media and downloads it to their phone.
- **Interest.** They listen to your conversation with another novelist on the portrayal of Asian-Americans in the media. They research your work further at your website or through social media.
- **Decision.** They see on social media that you actively share and discuss issues related to the Asian-American community and literature.
- **Action.** They follow your activity on one or more social media sites, or sign up for your email newsletter.

CONTENT STRATEGY AND MARKETING

Let's back up and pay closer attention to the start of the funnel: attention and interest. How successful you are in attracting attention depends on where or how you're spreading your message and how appealing that message is to the audience. Reaching the right people is all about being active in the places where you know your audience lives. If you're not reaching the right people, you'll need to conduct reader research to understand where best to find them, as described earlier in this chapter. Whether the message is appealing will depend on your depth of understanding of your audience, along with your copywriting skills, one of the most undervalued skills in the writing community.

Many writers wonder how they can get more people to visit their site, or to buy their books or services, but have spent no time or effort considering how to get people's attention in the first place. Content is the number-one way to attract attention, especially online. Content is the currency of the web—it's what gets shared, talked about, and acted upon. "Content" in-cludes writing (articles and blog posts), but also anything else that can be liked, shared, or engaged with, such as social media posts, images, pod-casts, videos, slideshares, and more. My earlier funnel examples are ex-amples of a content strategy in action.

Content strategy—as a way to gain visibility and market yourself—is not about giving away your stuff for free. Rather, it's an approach to creating and distributing work so that it reaches and develops a paying readership. It requires having specific goals and clear answers to questions such as, What type of readership are you trying to build or attract? Where does your ideal reader or client go online, or who do they listen to? Who should be publishing your work if you want to attract more opportunities? Here are examples of clear goals with specific content strategies:

- I want to become a regular contributor to Brevity's blog, to gain attention and awareness in the creative nonfiction community and help build an audience for the essay collection I'm working on.
- I want to create a weekly email newsletter focused on new poetry book releases, to extend my network within the community of poets and influencers and increase opportunities to review and write about poetry.
- I want to target an essay to the *Sun* magazine, to generate interest in my nonfiction book proposal on my yearlong dating experiment.
- I want to produce a podcast series for Audible Channels on hard-boiled detective stories, to increase my visibility as a freelance editor in the genre.

In the 2000s, a blog was considered the linchpin of any content strategy. Blogs have somewhat fallen out of favor, but content that's available for free online still remains the focal point of many strategies, whether that

WHAT IS COPYWRITING?

Copywriting is anything you write to help market or promote something—or to get someone to take action. Pitching is a form of copywriting, as is (at least in some respects) writing your bio. Copywriting isn't about convincing *everyone* to do what you ask, but convincing those who are a great match for what you're selling. Fortunately, if you work with a traditional publisher or publication of any kind, they normally have people trained to write good marketing copy, which will give you a baseline to work from. But you'll find that good copywriting skills benefit you at every level of your career, since great copy is needed for your website, grant and fellowship applications, promoting events, selling your services, and more. To begin learning copywriting skills, I recommend reading the classic guides and posts available for free from Copyblogger.

---

content is available at your own site or not. That's because free online content is highly discoverable and not limited to paying subscribers or those investing in print.

Content strategies are most effective when they mix free and paid content. In the examples above, the first two are directed toward producing free content, the last two toward paid content. Free content is the opening of a funnel—at the end of which some people will become paying readers or clients. Paid content usually means the writer is getting paid as well (when readers pay, you should expect to benefit), and may offer prestige that builds your platform, but the audience is more limited. Making use of online opportunities is by far the easiest, least time-consuming, and most expedient way to reach new people who don't know your work. Focusing on "real-life" activities or print-based activities will take longer and require more effort to reach the same number of people.

Roxane Gay is a classic example of a very active online writer, someone who may have appeared to be an overnight success when she started appearing everywhere in print, but it was only after working hard for many years, in smaller venues, that she broke out onto the national stage. In 2013–2014, you could see her hit the tipping point, aided not only by her prolific output as a writer but by conversations and engagement with a growing community through Twitter and Tumblr. (As mentioned earlier, her memoir, *Hunger*, began on her Tumblr.) With her books *Bad Feminism* and *An*

Untamed State, released within months of each other in 2014, everything fell into place: the right work published at the right time for an audience she'd long cultivated online.

Or take Jeanne Bowerman, who had little working to her advantage as an aspiring screenwriter in upstate New York. She had no industry connections and no prior experience in publishing—only a long-distance writing partner. In an effort to build a network for herself, she started #scriptchat, a Sunday evening conversation with an experienced screenwriter that she moderated. She began attending script conferences, blogging about her journey, and within several years became editor of an industry magazine, *Script,* and a working screenwriter.

METRICS AND ANALYTICS

The moment you decide that you want your online activity to have a measurable payoff—or the moment you decide to invest money in marketing, promotion, or publicity—that's the moment you should start caring about the numbers and metrics associated with your activity. To measure your efforts in a quantifiable way, you need a few tools and the discipline to use them consistently.

Google Analytics

Your own website, with Google Analytics installed, is one of the best tools you have. And it's a free tool. You can analyze how people find you, how they behave on your site, and what links they click. Even better, you can tell where the most valuable traffic comes from. For instance, you may notice that people spend more time on the site and are more likely to make purchases when they come by way of the website of a fellow author, and have worse engagement when visiting from Facebook. You'll also notice that some pages or posts have a very high average session duration, which indicates the highest level of engagement—the content that people are most interested in. Here are a few of the most important areas to explore in the analytics:

- **How do people end up at your site?** Go to Traffic > Channels. Traffic sources fall into about half a dozen categories, including traffic from search engines, social media, and referrals from other websites. Blog posts generally start with a high level of social media traffic, and if successful over the long term, transition to a high level of organic search and referral traffic. There isn't a right mix here, but if (for example) you're seeing very little traffic to your blog posts from social media—despite repeated social media promotion— then you need to rethink your approach.

- **What search queries bring people to your site?** Go to Search Engine Optimization > Queries. As an author, you want your name and book titles to be reflected here. You might also discover some interesting queries you wouldn't have suspected. For example, maybe you're getting a lot of traffic from people searching for a bog myrtle beer recipe, which you posted about in connection to your novel set in Ireland that features a character who brews the beer. (In such a scenario, you'd want to make sure you clearly point readers to more information on that novel and how to buy it!) For in-depth information about search traffic to your site over time, you should also register for Google Search Console (free).
- **What content is most popular at your site?** Go to Behavior > Site Content. For a basic site without a blog, the homepage is usually the most popular page, followed by the About page.
- **What pages do well at conversion (getting people to complete a call to action)?** This requires that you to set up Goals in Google Analytics. For example, you might set up a goal that tracks how many people visit your site from Facebook and then sign up for your email newsletter—or how many people click on a link to your book on Amazon. Google Analytics will then measure the conversion rate for that goal, e.g., 3 percent of Facebook visitors sign up for your email newsletter or click on a specific link. There's no limit to what types of goals you can set, or how many.

This just scratches the surface of what Google Analytics can do, and the longer you have it installed, the more powerful it can be. It stores data going back to the first day it began monitoring site visits, so you can compare your numbers month-to-month, year-to-year, or for any time period you like. It tells a powerful story about how your traffic has changed or been shaped over time by social media activity, referrals from other sites where your writing has appeared, or sites where you've been interviewed. For serious online entrepreneurs or publishers, it's possible to acquire even higher-powered analysis and analytics through third-party services, particularly when it comes to optimizing site content for organic search. Moz is one of the most respected and valued providers.

Social Media Analytics

If you're on Twitter, Facebook, or nearly any other social media site, you should have access to a dashboard that tells you how many people you're reaching with each post, and what the engagement is like. If not, third-party tools can help fill in the gaps (search "[social media tool] + analytics").

Of all the social media analytics, Facebook's Insights for official pages are the most powerful and advanced—not a surprise given how long Facebook has been around and its focus on persuading businesses to pay for advertising. Facebook's ability to target specific audiences is powerful if you're investing money in a marketing campaign. You can target a Facebook advertisement based on many criteria, including people who've visited your site within a specific period of time, people who are on your email newsletter list, or people who like other Facebook pages. If your advertisement is configured correctly, you can track how effective it is in meeting your sales goals and see which types of audiences are most receptive, which can improve your campaigns elsewhere. But fair warning: knowing how to create and manage an effective advertising campaign on social media is a specialized skill. You'll need proper training or a consultant to help you get started, to avoid wasting time and money.

Link Shorteners

Link shorteners create unique links that you can track indefinitely; they tell you how many times your links are clicked and from where. It's ideal to get in the habit of using link shorteners with social media and promotional efforts, even if you aren't actively measuring your success, to build up a repository of statistics on how well your links perform over time. One of the most popular link-shortening services is Bit.ly, which offers free accounts; if you upgrade to a paid plan, you can add a + sign to the end of any Bit.ly link (yours or someone else's) and see the list of people who shared that link. This can provide useful insights when you are putting together a list of people who could be influential in spreading the word about something you've written.

Bookstore Affiliate Marketing Account

With an affiliate marketing account (see chapter 29) you can see how many people actually make a purchase after clicking a link you share, and thus determine how successful each link or placement ultimately was. For example, an Amazon affiliate link posted on Facebook that sends people to Amazon to make a purchase may get a hundred clicks but only three purchases—a 3 percent conversion rate. You may find that a link shared on your blog, sending people to Amazon to make the same purchase, gets thirty clicks and six sales—a 20 percent conversion rate. This kind of data is invaluable when identifying what marketing messages are successful, and how you can craft the most appropriate and successful messages—and put them in just the right place—over the long term.

WHAT THE NUMBERS CAN AND CAN'T DO FOR YOU

Once you're active on Twitter or Facebook, or have Google Analytics installed on your website, you have actionable information about who you're reaching, where you're reaching them, and how to reach them better. Having this data is just as important—sometimes more important—than the quantity of followers you have. It's like having a personalized marketing research database that allows for more strategic efforts in the future: you'll be able to build and place better ads, run more effective promotions, and identify the most important influencers based on past performance. Some of the easiest ways to start:

- Use website, Facebook, or Twitter analytics to pinpoint geographic locations that would make the most sense for events or retail initiatives.
- Use tracking and affiliate links to identify where you reach people who are most likely to buy. Is it Twitter? Facebook? people who end up at your website through a search?
- Use website, Facebook, or Twitter analytics to identify important qualities about your readership—e.g., what other books, movies, or TV shows they love. Can you create content or advertise in such a way to reach others in the audiences of those books, movies, or TV shows?

When social media was still relatively new, there was a lot of focus and attention on raw numbers. How many followers do you have? How many likes? How many shares? While numbers are still a surface-level indicator of your platform strength, it's too easy to boost social media activity in an artificial way, leading to numbers that are fairly meaningless. This is why there's been increasing attention and focus on engagement. A strategic writer should be evaluating their ability on three levels:

- ability to reach a new audience
- ability to engage an existing audience
- ability to mobilize a loyal audience

Social media can be disappointing when it comes to reaching new people if you aren't spending ad dollars (or offering something for free or at discount), but it does a great job at engaging people who are already aware of you and speeding word-of-mouth throughout a community. Social media makes it easier to reach the required threshold of three, four, five, or more impressions that you need to make on someone—solidifying their awareness that you exist, then compelling them to take action when they feel like they see you "everywhere." (Remember the old advertising cliche says that your brand needs to appear in front of your customer seven times to be remembered? Same principle.)

Writers who have multiple ways to make an impression are by default in a stronger position—they're both better protected from future changes in social media and have more touch points out there. This doesn't mean you have to be active on every social media channel, but you do want to build as many impressions in as many places as possible, to break through the noise. Because more people are playing the game than ever, you'll need to be more creative, experimental, and diverse with the types of moves you can make.

Established, full-time writers know that a large online following doesn't equate to a sustainable business model. Instead, an engaged audience that helps spread word of mouth leads to success. Use analytics to identify how and where you get the best engagement, and what tools help you find the right audience, rather than the biggest audience. Ultimately, this is the most powerful feature of digital media: its ability to find and reach just the right person, who enjoys your work or who can benefit from your services.

22 : THE BASICS OF BOOK LAUNCHES

There are more than thirty-two million books in print, and some industry observers believe that fifty thousand new e-books are released for Kindle every month.[1] Given the ease of book publishing today, the biggest challenge facing authors is rarely how to get published, but how to make their book visible and discoverable in a market with so much choice and competition. With or without a publisher, every author must give some thought as to how to build a network to assist in the varied marketing and promotional efforts it takes to produce one sale. Given the pace of change, a responsible author also has to keep an eye on digital and technical advancements that affect how a book gets on the radar of interested readers. Be careful when you encounter marketing advice from authors who became established before e-books entered the market: their brands and readership developed during a different era. Anyone starting a career now has a different set of considerations in play. You can't push the same buttons that were pushed in 2007 and expect the sales or success you might have achieved then.

The entrepreneurial foundations we've covered so far in part 4 will be indispensable in planning a book launch (or the launch of any other product or service you wish to market). Before you embark on any plan, find out what your publisher is doing, and avoid duplicating efforts. If your publisher has little or nothing planned, you'll need to launch your own book-marketing campaign. It's not desirable, but it is possible. Mainly, it requires time and energy. It may also require some financial investment to hire a publicist or marketing consultant. It's not unusual for authors to invest a good portion, or all, of their advance in hiring professional help for the book launch. (More on that in a moment.) If you commit to putting in a strong effort from the very beginning, by the time your second, third, or fourth book comes out, you should have a solid base of readers, a base developed from marketing activities associated with previous launches.

A comprehensive book-marketing campaign uses a combination of tactics to reach readers. As you think about the components of a book launch, keep in mind these definitions:

- **Marketing** refers to efforts that require an expenditure of your own time or financial resources. Running an advertising campaign, for example, is a classic marketing strategy. In the digital age, you'll hear about *inbound* versus *outbound* marketing. Inbound marketing is marketing to people who end up at your website, social media, or some other owned territory. Outbound marketing means going out in search of potential readers, such as through paid advertisements.
- **Publicity** refers to media attention and editorial coverage that's not paid for. You've probably heard the cliche "There's no such thing a bad publicity." You can decide for yourself if that's true, but if you or your book score media coverage, you don't have control over the story or message, as you do with marketing efforts. Sometimes publicity can be a happy accident, but more often than not, it requires having a good pitch and good connections with the media.

Marketing and publicity campaigns almost always work better when they combine online and offline efforts. If done right, each amplifies and strengthens the other. Real-life events may require high investment and sometimes be disappointing in turnout, but they are more likely to be talked about and shared online with those who didn't attend—and lead to more media attention overall than online activity. On the flip side, having high levels of engagement through an online channel, such as a Facebook group, can help you with planning the right events at the right locations—with satisfying turnout and word of mouth.

HIRING MARKETING AND PUBLICITY HELP

There's no shortage of services that promise authors they can secure media coverage, reviews, and better sales. For the unschooled, however, it's hard to know whom to hire, how much to invest, and what type of marketing and publicity will make a difference.

I've heard stories from disappointed authors who worked with a book publicist and didn't get what they wanted out of the investment. Sometimes that happens because of misaligned expectations, or even a misunderstanding of what a book publicist can accomplish. When it comes to book marketing and sales, it's not always easy to say "effort A led to outcome B," especially if book sales gain momentum from word of mouth, and authors don't have access to sales analytics. You can't always figure out how or why someone decided to visit Amazon or their local bookstore to buy your book, especially if you're traditionally published.

You cannot realistically expect to see each publicity dollar come back to you in the form of book sales. Nor can any publicist guarantee you specific coverage or sales. To complicate matters, authors get very focused on things they know and understand, regardless of their effectiveness—like being on the *Today* show or running an ad in the *New York Times Book Review*—which don't always lead to the sales you might expect. Consider your investment in marketing or PR as an investment in your long-term career as an author—something that increases your visibility in a way that will benefit all of your future books and projects, and might lead to future paying work. Publicity is often more about getting people to recognize who you are in a world of oversaturation than sparking immediate sales; it elevates you above the rest of the noise and focuses on the long runway of promotion. Sales or publicity hits may happen in the first ninety days of the campaign, but no one knows when your visibility will pop—effects can trickle out over years and years.

Publicists are often seen as key to mainstream media coverage, but they have tremendous value beyond that. Some of the marketing and promotion activities they cover you could do yourself, but they can often do them better, more efficiently, or more knowledgeably. Their professional finesse may create a better impression and more sales over the long term, and leave you time to focus on other high-value activities. They can also help you avoid marketing tactics or campaigns that they know are problematic, or point you toward new, useful tools they've discovered. While "I just want to sell books" might be your initial motivation for hiring a publicist, you're hiring someone who can see the entire strategic landscape, everything that needs to happen.

Before you hire a publicist, make a list, in writing, of the specific outcomes you want them to achieve, and how those goals connect to what you are doing and what your publisher is doing. Share this with each publicist you interview and ask for a proposal (along with their fees). As you consider which publicist to hire, research other campaigns they've worked on. Have they achieved the kind of results you're looking for? Talk to past clients if at all possible. Once the publicity campaign starts, it's helpful to establish check-in dates to meet with your publicist and talk over which aspects of the campaign are working and which are not. It's common that some refocusing is necessary.

Even when they hire publicists, all authors should be willing to learn how to market their books. Good marketing and publicity is a team effort, and the author is part of that team. Publicists look for clients who are willing to do some things on their own, and they also look for authors to be realistic. For example, most publicists will not be able to meet the expectations of first-time authors with no platform who want their books to become *New York Times* best sellers. Publicists seek clients who understand that marketing and publicity is a process and that it will take time to see the effects of their efforts.

Publicity seeks to locate, identify, or target the right audience to make them aware of your book. If you're focused and clear about your target audience and your objectives in reaching them when you start your campaign, you have a better chance of reaching a national market. While one of the big things a publicist does is help you figure out your audience, if you are already familiar with your audience and have aspects of your online presence in place, you hold an advantage and your publicist has assets to work with from the start: social media, websites, and other tools that connect with the book's target reader. To build momentum before you hire a publicist, consider learning the social platforms that your target audience uses. Being well versed in the relevant languages of social media helps set the stage for a strong campaign.

Another part of understanding your audience is knowing which authors are your competition, those who reach the audience you should also reach. Even though you probably feel your book is truly special, for marketing purposes you want it to be like other books. Therefore, one way to prepare for marketing your book—which is probably part of your routine anyway—is to read anything and everything in your genre. When you find books you like, befriend the authors if possible, talk about their books on social media, and try to do events with them, as discussed in chapter 2. They will be part of your supportive community when it comes time for your book launch.

How Publicists Work and What They Cost

Every publicist works differently, and cost greatly varies. Brief consultations or assistance may cost hundreds of dollars; intensive, months-long campaigns can cost tens of thousands. Most publicists prefer to work with authors as early in the process as possible—up to a year before the publication date. They certainly need to be involved at least three to four months before publication to be effective. That doesn't mean that's when you, as an author, should start thinking about publicity. That should begin as soon as the book is signed with a publisher, and sometimes even at the conception of the idea, or while you're writing the book.

Traditional publishers concentrate their publicity around a book's launch date, within a three-month or six-month window, which fits with the bookstore retail model. Publishers are focused on selling as many copies as possible right after the book goes on sale to avoid returns from bookstores. This publicity works for the publisher, not you, and while you may have all kinds of great ideas about your marketing and publicity campaign, they'll give their goals priority over yours. As stated earlier, it's important to communicate early with the in-house publicity team and understand what they have planned. If you decide to hire an outside publicist to augment the work of the in-house team, you'll need to coordinate their efforts so they're not reaching out to the same people.

It's common for authors to wait and seek a publicist or marketing help after a book has already launched and not done well. Panicked authors belatedly realize they should've developed a plan months earlier, and end up on social media blasting self-promotional pleas: "Buy my book!" Try to avoid that panic. Your audience will grow as you write and produce many things over the course of your career, and your social media efforts should be about building community. No matter what type of author you are, the hard truth is that marketing and publicity never really ends—it's ongoing for as long as you seek a writing life that pays.

AUTHOR EVENTS

While you still find *New York Times* best-selling authors doing tours for their new releases, the days of the traditional author tour are over. Still, events can play an important role in marketing, mainly because they help create a footprint. When you visit any city, it's not just about the books sold, but the people you speak with—about making connections and building a network that will persist long afterward. Touring also makes it much easier to get local and regional media coverage, which can boost sales even if event turnout is low.

Thus, the primary reason to schedule an author event today may be less to boost book sales than to gain media coverage. Unfortunately, the number of media outlets available to pitch has dramatically shrunk. That makes the field competitive and all media outlets very selective—across radio, TV, and print. However, when you do get a hit in the media, it tends to stick with people and make an impact.

Another challenge is that bookstores aren't always the best place for events, at least if the author wants a good turnout. Many authors and publicists—and even bookstores themselves—have caught on to this and now plan events in alternative venues, such as bars or clubs. They may even sell tickets to author lunches held at restaurants, where the ticket price includes a copy of the book. Such events feel more social, and they avoid the lower perceived value and less compelling nature of the reading-signing format.

Chicago-based publicist Dana Kaye has often written and spoken about ways to bring authors together for events and tours, since that generally leads to better turnout and a stronger pitch for media coverage. For example, Kaye's firm organized and promoted the Young Authors Give Back Tour, in which four YA authors, all of whom had published before age twenty-five, toured the country and taught writing workshops for teens. That angle garnered two TV appearances and a feature in the *Chicago Sun-Times*.[2]

Because of the expense of author touring, some authors organize virtual book launches or participate in virtual book festivals with other authors. Such events can sell books, but to see a direct effect on sales, you have to encourage sales in some specific way, usually by providing a discount code or other incentive for attendees to make a purchase within a limited timeframe during or after the event. When I contributed to the anthology *Every Father's Daughter*, edited by Margaret McMullan, she and the publisher, McPherson & Co., organized about a dozen author events, all at the same date and time, at independent bookstores around the country. Each contributor gave a customized talk and signed books at their hometown location, then the entire group linked up via Skype for a Q&A broadcast to all of the stores.

Some authors go out of their way to support their independent bookstore as part of their book launch or overall marketing campaign. For example, they might "adopt" an indie bookstore to be their fulfillment center for anyone who wants a signed copy. When authors do that, it gives the bookstore something to offer that their competitors can't. And that means the bookstore is likely to put the promotion on its Facebook page, or tweet about it, or help the book generate more buzz. More broadly, independent bookstores can play a role in turning a book into a best seller through the power of hand-selling. This is where staff members make personal recommendations to their customers and get behind a book in a focused way; they might put a book on prominent display because they believe it

TIPS FOR A GOOD READING OR BOOK EVENT

Unless you're a household name as an author, you need to think carefully about how you'll structure your reading or event. What will be instructive, entertaining, or delightful for those who turn out? Readings have a tendency to be dreadfully boring, with audience members wondering when they will end. To avoid that kind of reaction, consider the following:

- Don't read in one long stretch. Choose several short passages, and break the reading up with personal stories or a bit of background.
- Choose passages that will be engaging when read aloud. Snappy dialogue or funny scenes are good candidates for a reading, while long, descriptive passages can be dull.
- Writing that's meant to be read doesn't always sound great when spoken. Read your selections out loud at least once before your event, and listen to how they sound. It's OK to edit them to improve the experience for your audience.
- If your work was inspired by travel, people, music, or objects, can you share some of those during the reading? Sometimes having visuals or props that complement your talking points can help engage the audience.

Above all, prepare. Don't try to wing it, and do whatever you can to bring energy and enthusiasm to your reading. The worst possible thing is to read in a monotone that makes your audience feel like even you are bored by what you're doing. Often the problem is that authors are nervous or anxious, which leads to an understated delivery. You'll be more easily forgiven for nerves than for being a bore.

---

deserves to be read. That kind of support is more likely when an author has built a relationship with their local or regional independent bookseller over many years prior to their book's release—by being a loyal customer and involved community member.

SECURING REVIEWS

Reviews are one of the key ways books gain traction and attention in the market, so every author should understand the different types of reviews, how each works, and what role the author plays in securing them.

Trade reviews. Trade review publications are read by booksellers, librarians, and others in the book industry (as opposed to consumers). Two of the best known are *Publishers Weekly* and *Library Journal*. Such publications primarily provide prepublication reviews of traditionally published books. A prepublication review appears several months before a book's publication date; bookstores and libraries use such reviews to help decide what to order for their customers or patrons. Most trade publications have been operating for a long time and have a history of serving publishing professionals. However, with the rise of self-publishing, some trade review outlets have begun separate review programs especially for self-published authors.

The publisher is almost always responsible for securing trade reviews and will send advance review copies four to six months in advance of publication. If authors are unsure of their publishers' plans, they should ask. Unfortunately, even with a publisher's support, only a small percentage of books receive trade reviews.

Reviews in mainstream publications. Reviewers for the *New York Times*, *New Yorker*, literary journals, and other mainstream publications are flooded with books for potential review. As with trade reviews, the publisher is typically responsible for sending an advance copy for consideration, early enough that the review can appear close to the book's release date. The review package sent by the marketing and publicity department almost always includes a print copy of the book, along with a letter and possibly other ancillary materials to convince editors that the book is worthy of coverage. With the biggest and most important outlets, review copies need to be sent well in advance of the publication date; other types of outlets are more flexible and might not be as concerned with timing. Publishers typically ask authors if there are smaller outlets, particularly local or regional publications, or niche websites or blogs, that would be likely to offer a review or coverage if contacted. If the publisher is unable to invest the time or energy to approach those smaller outlets, the author should take it upon herself to do so, usually with digital copies to avoid expense.

Fee-based book review services. Because of the increased demand for professional reviews, especially for self-published work, you can now find publications that specialize in providing fee-based services. They may have some reach and visibility to industry insiders, or may be reader-facing, or a mix of both. Examples include the *Indie Reader*, *Blue Ink Review*, and *Self-Publishing Review*. Paying for professional book reviews remains a controversial topic. It's not widely known even within the author community that paid book reviews exist, and even less is known about their value.

Reader (nonprofessional) reviews. Reader reviews and star ratings are as important as professional reviews; books with more such reviews and higher star ratings often receive greater visibility at online retailers. Thus, publishers commonly urge authors to drum up as many reader reviews as possible in the days and weeks following release. However, Amazon and other sites sometimes take down reader reviews if they believe there's too close a connection between author and reader. (Also, it's considered unethical and violates terms of service to pay for reader reviews posted at Amazon or other sites.)

The best way to sell more books on Amazon, or through online retail, is to generate as many *reader* reviews as possible. Authors tend to be more interested in professional reviews because of the prestige associated with them, and some might argue that having such a review as part of the book's description on Amazon (or elsewhere) adds a sheen of professionalism and encourages readers to take a chance on the book. But I don't believe one professional review makes up for a lack of reader reviews or a low star rating. Like it or not, purchasing behavior online is generally driven by quantity of reviews, assuming no prior exposure to the author.

However, if your marketing or outreach plan involves approaching independent bookstores and libraries to consider your book, then having a positive review from a source they know can help you overcome an initial hurdle or two. It does not guarantee they will carry or buy your book, but it contributes to a favorable impression.

PITCHING TRADITIONAL MEDIA

For the purposes of this section, we're talking about pitches for editorial coverage—not review coverage. It's tough to get media coverage, and every outlet is selective. However, with persistence, authors can secure publicity even without their publisher making the call. It just takes months of persistence, of continually knocking on the door in a slightly different way for the same thing. This requires developing a variety of high-quality pitches that fit the style, tone, and needs of the media outlets you're pitching. And that means you have to take the time to research the outlets and know what each covers.

The most important thing to remember: Nobody cares that you wrote a book. So don't lead your pitch with the book. Lead with the hook or the story, and what your book will do for people. If you're pitching via email, the subject line is critical. Put the hook in the subject line, and keep your pitch short, about a paragraph. A lot of journalists and reviewers look at emails on their phones, so keep it succinct. Most of your targets won't say "no" to your pitch; they just won't answer. An effective, high-quality pitch process is time-consuming, so evaluate where your time and effort is best spent and decide if you could benefit from a publicist's assistance. A publicist's job is to stay on top of what's current and stay on top of news stories, and many authors don't have time for that.

For independent authors or those without much of a platform, regional marketing is a good place to start a publicity campaign. Authors can schedule events or tours in their city or area. Bookstores are perfectly acceptable, but look also at wine stores or restaurants or libraries, or other nonconventional places. (Be creative.) Then pitch media attention around the event you're holding. If you're aiming for national publicity, most publicists would advise that you get media training. Such training includes coaching on the use of talking points and behavior in front of a camera. Most media folks are not going to read your book, so whenever you deal with the media, you should go in with a cheat sheet for the journalist or interviewer.

Some authors are very good at finding news pegs for their book long after its release. If there are holidays, anniversaries, or current events that tie into your book's ideas or themes, then it's possible to get into the news again—*if* you can draw a strong connection for the media outlet. Some writers subscribe to HARO (Help a Reporter Out) to receive regular email alerts of journalists seeking experts or authors they can quote on specific topics. This can be a good way to keep your book visible in the media, especially for nonfiction authors.

SOCIAL MEDIA AND BLOGGING

Experienced publicists know that success in online marketing usually depends on what you start with: how big an online following you currently have, and how much energy you're willing to invest in pursuing sales. Some authors are interested in online marketing because they're building an audience for the long term. They may not be able to secure traditional media coverage anyway, so they'll focus on something easy and work up.

On social media, it's critical to use a gentle touch, always. Rather than pushing people to buy your book—to achieve a short-term goal—approach social media as a long-term investment. If you're struggling to figure out what to do, study authors you admire. What does their activity look like? What blogs or websites have they appeared on? What do they do on social media? Can you emulate those things?

With authors who think of blogging as a way to market their book, the chain of events goes something like this: A book nears its publication date. The author knows she needs to promote the book or build a platform, and hears that blogging is a good way to accomplish that. Only then does she ask herself, What should I blog about? It doesn't turn out well. While it's true that blogging can be an effective book marketing tool, doing it well requires practice, not to mention some level of respect for online writing as its own art form. I would not pursue blogging without a full understanding of the medium, especially if you only see it as a means to an end. (See chapter 18 for more on this topic.)

Blogging on your own turf isn't necessary for a book-marketing campaign, but major blogs and websites can play an important role in spreading word of mouth, which means it can be worthwhile to write guest posts, do Q&As, or otherwise try to get featured by bloggers who reach your target audience. It also helps to be an active participant or commenter on blogs where your readers hang out. However, it's a small number of websites that actually have influence and traffic; those that do, have tremendous publicity value and are just as picky as traditional media outlets in terms of what or who they feature. If you pursue marketing on any blog or website, make sure its audience is a good fit for you and your book so you won't invest too much time for too little return.

GIVEAWAYS

Giveaways can work if done strategically. One of the best-known venues for print book giveaways—especially for traditional publishers—is Goodreads, a social media site for books and reading with more than fifty million members. For self-publishers, the most popular option is BookBub, a daily email with millions of subscribers that features limited-time, deeply discounted or free e-books. Getting on BookBub—or running a special promotion—requires being able to cut prices during a specific time period, so traditionally published authors typically have to rely on their publisher to pursue such opportunities. Publishers do occasionally use the power of the giveaway (especially in advance of an author's new release), but more often they rely on deep discounting.

Because the market is currently awash in free e-books, some have argued that giveaways devalue all books and all authors' work. But that's not really true. Giveaways are popular for good reason; they're a classic, frictionless way to make people aware of new authors and new releases. Just about every industry has some way of using "free" to their advantage, particularly game, software, and app developers. If you can get a sufficient number of people in the door, and they like your work, you can build a relationship that leads to later sales. (See the "funnel" discussion in chapter 21.) There's also concern that giveaways attract low-quality readers. But they attract high-quality readers too. This is how business works. Some leads will be good. Other leads will be bad. Business-savvy authors learn over time how and where to use the giveaway incentive as part of a larger marketing strategy.

EMAIL NEWSLETTERS

Newsletter lists that an author develops and owns can have a significant impact on sales and word of mouth. New authors may not have such lists in place for their first book release. But successful authors—both traditionally published and self-published—affirm their importance, and most would recommend that you start building your email list early, through your own website and at events, in preparation for future releases. See chapter 20 for more on email marketing.

HOW TO BECOME A BEST-SELLING AUTHOR

A few years ago, a story broke about an author who hired a marketing firm to launch his book onto the *New York Times* best-seller list—and succeeded.[3] But when the firm's less than honest methods were uncovered, it resulted in scandal and embarrassment. The author had more or less paid this firm to purchase copies of his book in strategically important places.

Since that scandal broke, it's become harder to game the system in this way, though authors still look for shortcuts or secrets to best-sellerdom. Once you hit one of the major best-seller lists, that creates its own marketing momentum and additional sales. Arguably the *New York Times* best-seller list is most important, since it carries the most prestige and tends to get the most attention and publicity. But it can be the hardest list to hit; it gathers information from many different sales outlets across the country to determine what titles make the cut. It remains confidential which particular retail outlets are surveyed, but they include both physical bookstores and online sellers, such as Amazon.

The *New York Times* list is updated weekly, so publishers tend to concentrate sales efforts and launch events within a specific week to maximize the book's chance of making the list. Another quirk that factors into getting on best-seller lists, and makes the launch week or first week of sale the author's best chance of doing so, is that preorders made in the months prior to a release typically get counted when the book finally goes on sale.

Authors often ask how many book sales it takes to hit the best-seller list. It depends who you're up against in a given week. Your title will be competing against a lot of others. Some will sell in amazing numbers. But sometimes the threshold may be lower than you'd think. Some weeks, in some categories, you might get the last spot on the best-seller list with as few as a couple thousand copies sold.

So being a *New York Times* best seller doesn't actually tell you how many copies a book has sold. In the music industry, if a record goes platinum you know it's sold a million copies. But there are no such official designations in book publishing, and sales figures are almost never released. Furthermore, best-seller lists typically exclude what are known as "perennial sellers." For instance, the Bible is the best-selling book year after year in the United States, but you won't find it on any best-seller list. The same is true of books found on classroom reading lists, as well as test prep guides and self-published books. You might say the list is biased toward a certain type of book, and that's partly true. Some people argue that the list is unfair and arbitrary in its methodology and focus, but it is trying to give an accurate reflection of what relatively new titles are being bought and what the general public is now reading.

Before we discuss some of the ways books get launched onto best-seller lists, it may be worth raising the question of whether it's worth the trouble—since it requires a significant amount of time, money, and energy. When your book hits a major best-seller list, it does create a meaningful ripple effect   more people hear about it, more sales get triggered, more requests flow in to your publisher or agent asking about translations or film deals, and you're likely to get more invitations to do media or to speak. Not to mention you're in an excellent position to sign your next book deal.

The first principle most aspiring best-seller authors should adhere to is concentrating book sales as much as possible within the launch-week window, for the reasons just explained. Conduct an aggressive sales campaign that encourages everyone to buy the book during that specific week, or even on a specific day. Whether you can run such a campaign depends on where and how you've established yourself online as an author. For example, *New York Times* best-selling author Michael Hyatt literally asked people not to preorder or buy his book *Platform* until the week of his book launch. He was able to do this because he had thousands of people reading his blog and receiving his email newsletter, so when he gave his specific instructions, a large audience was listening. Furthermore, he offered them a significant incentive. If readers emailed Hyatt the receipt from their book sale (regardless of where or how they purchased it), he would send them several bonuses, such as access to his audiovisual curriculum and previous digital books. He began teasing this offer weeks before the pub date, encouraging people to wait. And it worked; he sold more than eleven thousand books during his first week on sale and hit the *New York Times* list.[4]

Of course, not everyone launching a book has Hyatt's resources. Aside from being a prominent blogger who reaches hundreds of thousands of people every month, he's the former CEO of Thomas Nelson, a major publisher. So he had connections few of us have. But his example does show you the power of making a focused and concentrated effort on getting your sales to hit within a specific timeframe.

It is possible to reach the *New York Times* best-seller list without specifically pursuing offline advertising, mainstream media, or publicity. One author who did so, and stayed on the list for months, is Tim Ferriss, author of *The Four-Hour Workweek*. His book was simultaneously number one on the *New York Times* list and the *Wall Street Journal* list. And he was a first-time author. How did he do it?

By his own account, he started by ruling out book signings or author events. He instead focused on creating word of mouth through all the best blogs. As a well-known blogger himself, this wasn't difficult. He was able to build a great deal of strategic buzz through other high-profile bloggers and online interviews, which led to offline media pursuing him for interviews and quotes. When the calls came, Ferriss was prepared. He had already invested in media training and had a reel that he used to establish himself as a viable guest to TV producers.

If you dig a little deeper into Ferriss's success story, though, you'll realize that he was focused on developing blog traffic and buzz for his book long before its launch, mostly through offline activities. He directed a lot of his time to attending and speaking at events attended by other bloggers, helping to ensure that when he needed their help, they'd remember him, feature him, and link to him.

Furthermore, despite his claims to have ruled out book signings or author events, Ferriss held a well-attended prelaunch party based on his in-person connections. He partnered with three friends to host a collective birthday party in San Francisco that doubled as a book launch. More than 250 people attended, many of them top bloggers in his industry. He gave away his book, signed copies, and offered lots of free booze, and buzz from the party alone led to media coverage. Ferriss is in fact a perfect example of how online and offline efforts build on each other to create success.[5]

PARTING ADVICE

Traditionally, one of the biggest values publishers have offered authors is the means to get their books into stores. Bookstore placement serves a marketing function, particularly when a book is selected for front-of-store display or for cover-out rather than spine-out placement. The more visible a book is, the better the chances a reader will stumble upon it—and talk about it with other readers. Ferriss attributed his staying power on the *New York Times* best-seller list to good bookstore distribution. The more his books appeared on shelves, the more books he sold. If more chains feature a book, or give it prominent placement, sales are nearly guaranteed to increase.

However, if fewer people are browsing bookstore shelves, publishers can't count on the serendipity of a visitor bumping into a front-of-store display and taking a chance on a new author. Amazon algorithms and discount deals and promotions (whether through Amazon or BookBub) now play an increasingly important role in how readers discover and decide what to read next. While publishers may be unparalleled in their ability to offer print retail distribution and mass-market branding campaigns, they are still catching up with direct-to-consumer marketing—by building consumer-facing book websites and email newsletter lists that offer discounts. As of today, some savvy authors are better equipped to reach readers than the average publishing house.

So where does this leave the average author? Probably the best thing you can focus on is what Hyatt and Ferriss focused on: if you build a network of readers you can reach directly, either online or offline, and they trust you, they will come when your book releases. Don't underestimate the difference your relationships can make. If you make connections, when it's time for your launch or event, you'll see a real and meaningful effect. While you might not be able to keep up with every changing nuance in digital marketing or book publishing, and you won't be able to control what your publisher does to support your book, you'll always benefit from building your own platform and reach to readership.

Part Five

HOW WRITERS MAKE MONEY

The number of writers who make a living off their writing *alone* has always been small. No one should expect to make a living through book publication alone, although it may be an important supplement or, over time, become the majority of a writer's annual income. Genre writers are often in a better position to realize the full-time book writing dream simply because they produce more work in a shorter amount of time. And that's true generally: having a prolific pen plays a role in the business model for a writer's career. The more work you can produce or the faster you can write, the more product you will have—this does matter. But for the more literary writer, it may not matter how prolific one is when the audience is small or market potential low.

We sometimes equate being paid for our words with being a "real" writer, but this is a product of the writer's ego—as well as writerly myths at work—and has no relevance when we talk about practical methods of making a living. Usually direct payments for your writing will not be enough to live on early in your career. The more experienced you become, and the bigger your platform, the more it becomes a possibility to support yourself through writing, if it's what you desire.

To get paid for writing directly, writers usually end up following one of two paths: securing money from publishers or securing money from readers. Obviously there is significant overlap: if you secure a book deal with a publisher, they'll pay you, but your earnings over the long term will be affected by the number of readers you have. Still, pitching and soliciting editors or businesses to pay for your writing involves a different mindset than approaching readers without a middleman. Some writers are adept at doing both, though the creative writing community tends to prefer being vetted and selected by editors and publishers, versus the more entrepreneurial path of self-publishing, blogging, or otherwise distributing material direct to an audience in exchange for payment.

In the beginning, most writers supplement their incomes through part-time work and day jobs that may or may not be related to writing, as they increase the visibility of and demand for their words. Some writers focus on the most highly paying opportunities—copywriting or corporate writing of some type—as they build an audience and seek opportunities for their other writing. (*The Well-Fed Writer*, a popular guide, essentially advises, stop trying to write for fancy magazines and get into commercial writing, which pays well.) The danger always is that this "shadow career"—a term from Steven Pressfield—will overtake the career you originally intended to pursue, because it offers more payment, easy success, or less resistance than your higher-risk creative endeavors. Still, this section focuses on how you can make money aside from writing and publishing your creative work—because these other methods are generally more feasible and sustainable.

Chapter 23 covers freelancing and related gigs—forms of income that you're most likely familiar with. Chapters 26 and 27 cover ways to obtain funding from organizations and your community of readers; such methods are useful for supporting specific, time-limited projects. Chapters 28 and 29 look at business models for online publications. You'll find that all of the skills covered up until this point—pitching, networking, understanding audience—surface again here as critical in how you will make money as a writer. Those who wish to focus only on freelancing for traditional print outlets should understand that those outlets have been decimated by the sharp decline in advertising dollars. If and when you hear negative messages about the future of journalism and freelancing careers, they typically come from people who enjoyed an era when newspapers and magazines were flush with advertising and it wasn't that difficult to establish a career working for them. Today, if freelancers are flexible in what type of work they produce, and where or how that work gets published, they can make a reasonable go of it, because there's still as much demand as ever for reliable contract help. Furthermore, in the digital era, there are more types of freelance activities one might undertake to assist others—such as online book marketing, social media management, website editing, and work as a virtual assistant—mostly outside the scope of this book, but skills often picked up in building one's own writing career.

Your experience and credentials as a writer may also help you pursue other sources of income that aren't strictly related to selling your words. Teaching, coaching, editing, and critiquing fall into this category, and are

Table 23.1 Business income during my first two years as a full-time freelancer with no conventional employment

	2016	2017
Affiliate marketing	7%	6%
Editing services	11.5%	30%
Speaking and events	3%	3%
Book sales/advance	5%	5%
Online teaching	32.5%	20%
Adjunct teaching	3.5%	4%
Freelance writing	11.5%	7.5%
Paid subscription newsletter	3%	11%
Consulting	23%	13.5%

covered in chapters 24 and 25. Writers who build a sizable online presence, with an engaged audience, can benefit from the attention they've captured through the use of online advertising and affiliate marketing; chapter 29 covers this area.

Successful artists of all types usually have multiple revenue streams, with the more profitable areas supporting the less profitable—just as happens at commercial publishing houses. While most writers are always striving toward a more ideal business model—one that allows them to do more of the work they find satisfying or fulfilling and less of the paycheck-driven work—by diversifying you usually have more choices and less vulnerability when one type of work dries up.

You'll need some self-awareness and vision to see which money-making methods are best suited to your personality and long-term writing goals. Fortunately, it's not hard to drop some methods and pick up others as one gains experience. I highly recommend reading artist Jessica Abel's website (jessicaabel.com), where she writes about how to identify your unique business model, and to lose the starving artist mindset that often gets in the way of making money. Sometimes the biggest barrier to a successful writing business is buying into prevailing cultural attitudes that say, "That's not how an artist/writer earns a living," or insist that you can't mix business concerns with art. This only serves to inhibit innovative thinking. Successful writers across history have bucked the trends and economic models of their time, and identified ways of sustaining their art that worked uniquely for them. I know that you can do the same, as you weigh your strengths, your available time, and what you're willing to compromise or sacrifice in order to earn a living. And because this is not a game that suits everyone, part 5 ends with a discussion of writing-focused day jobs.

23 : STARTING A FREELANCE CAREER

If you're considering freelance writing as part of your business model, prepare to hear many negative messages about how hard freelancing is these days, how you have to be prepared to hustle, how it's more competitive than ever, and how many publications and companies will take advantage of you, paying little or offering "exposure" in lieu of actual payment. If you are already inclined toward self-doubt or anxiety, you may all too easily internalize these negative messages. You may dwell on all the reasons you could fail: you don't like pitching, you're a terrible networker, you procrastinate. You could worry also that even with all the right qualities you may still not succeed.

To attempt a freelance career with little more than a college degree is likely to end in disappointment—or a very long start-up phase. Most people fresh out of college have not only a limited skill set but limited knowledge of the market and limited connections. To build your business, you need to offer something the market wants or will pay for, and be visible or known to the people who pay for it. New writers may still be exploring what skills they want to develop, or have an unrealistic idea of the value of their work. It bears repeating: You can't build a freelance career based on selling poetry, short stories, and personal essays to literary journals and magazines. A freelance career as discussed here means being self-employed and pursuing all types of writing and editing work, whether of the literary type or not.

Regardless of your experience level, each freelance career requires a bit of kindling, something to get a client base established or a steady stream of gigs that provide reliable monthly income. Here are the factors that most commonly come into play.

Mentors. An ambitious writer who is able to find one or two mentors willing to make the right connections for her can quickly gain momentum, assuming her work is marketable and she can produce work with a degree of spark and professionalism that invites further assignments. One might call this networking, but networking is different than having a person who is invested in seeing you succeed. Students whose only mentors may be full-time writing teachers should look for additional opportunities within their community that would bring them into contact with writers who freelance, if not companies who use freelancers. Mentors should ideally be ten or twenty (or more) years ahead of you, actively trying to pull you up the ladder by making introductions or recommending your work.

Networking. A freelancer's first clients often come from previous employers or an existing network. You tap the connections you already have, and build from there. Each job you successfully complete or each client you satisfy creates word of mouth. Each new editor you meet holds the seeds of new relationships with other editors. Former colleagues who believe in your work refer new opportunities your way. This is networking at its heart.

There are ways to nurture your network—like through literary citizenship, discussed in chapter 2. And there are ways to undercut it. You should stay in touch with important connections beyond just the times you perform work or ask for work. Be helpful and generous in connecting others. Avoid being that person who speaks ill of her clients or other freelancers. Build a reputation as being easy and professional to work with. If you can, commit to a weekly networking practice: Invite a new person to coffee or lunch (and offer to pay), or attend a networking event with the goal of building at least one new professional relationship. Don't meet only people who could give you work. Meet other writers, marketing people, tech entrepreneurs, and nonprofit folks. Allow network serendipity to work its magic.

Research industry events or conferences where you can meet people important to your freelance life. Invest in attending key events every year; go to see people and to be seen. Showing up where the opportunities are concentrated can be especially critical for those trying to build a freelance career outside of major cities.

Visibility. Visibility is about being seen continually and consistently by the people who are in a position to give you work. This is why some publications try to sell writers on "exposure." If you write for free for a publication that has millions of readers and reaches influential people, then your name is being put in front of people who could contact you about paying work. (See chapter 3 on generating leads.) But there are a multitude of ways to become visible to your intended audience aside from writing for free.

Consider a podcast, a highly visible volunteer position, a regular teaching gig, a reading or event series you organize, a witty Twitter account.

However, visibility, early in your career, means saying yes to just about every opportunity that comes your way, even if it's free labor. You may have to help people and organizations in ways that don't benefit your bottom line to strengthen your network and create testimonials for your work. But you don't have to say yes forever. If you produce quality work, word will spread, and you can start turning down the less desirable opportunities.

Time. Many experts advise writing or freelancing on the side until it overtakes your full-time work, to reduce your risk and experience a more seamless transition. Not everyone has the luxury of time, but if you do, then take small steps to build the assets above, not to mention your writing portfolio. You'll gain confidence and resources needed for freelancing—or you may realize that it isn't actually the dream you thought it was.

If you're already freelancing on the side, list these gigs religiously in a spreadsheet. How did these opportunities come to you? How much did you earn? How much time did you spend on the work in relation to what you earned? It's important to see and track where the work comes from as well as the profitability of the work.

DECISIONS YOU'LL FACE AS A FREELANCER

While you might aspire to a specific type of work, assume and plan from the outset that you'll accept many types of gigs as you build toward the more desirable opportunities. Here are a few of the business questions you'll face early on. (Be sure to read chapters 6, 7, and 17 for more background on these points.)

Generalist versus specialist. One of the most common debates in freelance circles is between generalists and specialists. Generalists are people who write and edit a wide range of material; they don't target any one market but play the entire field as much as possible. Specialists, on the other hand, go deep into a particular subject or field.

Before the internet, it was easier to be a generalist, due to the many and varied paying, general-interest publications seeking content and accepting pitches. Today, it typically benefits freelancers to specialize. Once your name becomes known and associated with a particular type of work, it will be easier to attract assignments. And once you can legitimately claim the title of expert, you can command higher rates.

Ultimately, it can be a question of personality. Some writers simply get bored writing or editing one type of thing for years on end. But a generalist needs to be prepared to do more work to get assignments. Writing and research are also more time-consuming when you switch topics or genres frequently.

Consumer versus trade outlets. Consumer publications are those read by a general audience. In the magazine market, think *Oprah, Real Simple, Popular Mechanics,* or *National Geographic.* Trade outlets are mostly unfamiliar to the general public and target specific niche audiences. Again, in terms of magazines, think *Publishers Weekly, Tire Review,* or *Funeral Service Times.*

General-interest or consumer outlets are perceived as sexier and more prestigious for a writer's career, but with fierce competition to break in, getting work usually takes patience and a knack for pitching. Specialized outlets, while low-profile and unknown to the general public, usually pay just as well (if not better) and can provide more reliable income.

There's nothing to say you can't play both sides of the field, but a freelancer who needs to prioritize earnings should look through resources such as *Writer's Market* to pinpoint publications that might provide an entry point to learning about a new field, gaining writing and editing chops, and earning an income. (*Writer's Market* lists only paying markets.)

Service versus journalism. Service writing is the bread-and-butter of many websites and women's magazines. Think of the pieces you see every day on health, beauty, relationships, and fashion. Publications that focus primarily on journalism include the *New Yorker, Harper's,* the *Atlantic,* ProPublica, Vox, and countless others. It's easier to get started writing and editing service pieces, and it typically requires less time, though it usually pays the same as journalism. However, literary writers and the publishing establishment tend to place more value on journalistic pieces than on service.

Native advertising and content marketing. Freelancers have to decide if they're willing to accept PR or publicity-related writing opportunities alongside traditional gigs. Many writers do both but rarely talk about the corporate-sponsored writing they do (which usually doesn't include their byline). See chapter 31 for background on this type of writing.

Participating in freelance marketplaces. A new freelancer willing to work for little payment can try entering the market at the low end, pitching for projects at Upwork, Fiverr, and other freelance marketplaces (even Craigslist), where the per-word or per-project rate is extremely low. There is a never-ending stream of companies looking for cheap writers and editors, and those who do well may build relationships and a track record that leads to better assignments. Some writers argue it's better to avoid these race-to-the-bottom marketplaces, but those who are very new might find it difficult to secure better-paying work.

A potential middle ground for new freelancers is to take online classes at places such as MediaBistro, and earn some credentials and contacts in freelance writing and editing. Invest in membership (and educational opportunities) with freelance associations such as the Editorial Freelancers Association, the American Society of Journalists and Authors, and other groups that provide member perks and private job boards. Also seek out freelance marketplaces focused on just writers and editors, which usually attract better-quality projects than broad, general-interest freelance sites such as Upwork. For example, Freelance Writing Jobs (freelancewritinggigs .com) is a long-running website that rounds up freelance gigs every weekday. Many of the jobs posted there are entry-level and good when you're just starting out.

SHOULD YOU LEAVE CONVENTIONAL EMPLOYMENT?

Until you commit to living without the security of a regular paycheck, it's hard to behave as a full-time freelancer would. Your head space, time, and energy remain consumed with traditional employment, and you can be blind to opportunities around you. At some point, you must leap and assume the net will be there. Inspired by Goethe, W. H. Murry wrote, in his 1951 work *The Scottish Himalaya Expedition*:

> The moment one definitely commits oneself, then Providence moves too. All sorts of things occur to help one that would never otherwise have occurred. A whole stream of events issues from the decision, raising in one's favor all manner of unforeseen incidents and meetings and material assistance, which no man could have dreamed would have come his way.[1]

I find that largely true, but be careful when asking other people's advice. By and large, people did not encourage me when I transitioned to freelance work. More often, they made me second-guess myself. Even when I announced I was leaving full-time employment, amid mostly positive messages I still received warnings: "You'll go from a full-time job to a 24/7 job." "Welcome to the cliff. No parachute, golden or otherwise."

The earlier you are in your career, the more patient you'll need to be in building a client base and consistent income. If you give yourself a deadline to reach some specified level of income, recognize that a year or two may not be enough. It can easily take that long just to lay the groundwork for a stable business and to establish a steady stream of leads. Ideally, you should have a financial cushion before quitting a day job so that you can weather dry spells and avoid monthly scrambles to pay the bills. It takes time to develop your freelance rhythm and anticipate where the jobs will come from, as well as to gain the confidence and skills to secure the right work at the right price.

24 : FREELANCE EDITING AND RELATED SERVICES

The work of an editor is often misunderstood, underappreciated, and maligned. This is partly because the roles editors play vary widely, even over the course of a single project and certainly across different types of publications. When working with a writer, an editor might act as coach, critic, champion, and wordsmith. Regardless of their role, a good editor must be respectful of the writer's voice and intentions—while also pushing the work toward its full potential, whether that's commercial potential or artistic potential (or often, both). An editor who leaves a project better than they found it is invaluable.

Writers interested in pursuing work as an editor should first understand the different stages of editing and where their skills can be best applied. Peter Ginna's book *What Editors Do* is a comprehensive look at the field and highly recommended for those who wish to pursue editing as a full-time career. In this chapter, we'll consider the basics of pursuing freelance editing work, primarily in the area of book publishing. But first, a caveat: Being a good writer does not make you a good editor. Aside from requiring adept use of language, writing and editing are quite different activities. As an editor, you have to help writers realize their own aims, and not just impose your will. Editors who can't step into the background aren't doing their jobs well, will likely run into conflicts with writers, and will probably eventually quit.

HIGH-LEVEL EDITORS

Developmental editing and content editing fall under the broad category of high-level editing. This level of editing inevitably leads to revision and substantive changes in the writer's work. If you work with a high-level editor, expect to do rewrites. Even if the editor assists in rewriting the manuscript to fix problems, the writer typically receives an extensive editorial letter and manuscript notations, with detailed advice for completing the revisions. In other cases the editor provides a more general manuscript assessment, which summarizes the strengths and weaknesses of a manuscript. An assessment doesn't offer page-by-page advice on revision, but a broad overview of how to improve the work.

Developmental editors are most commonly used for nonfiction work, especially by traditional book publishers. They focus on a book's structure and content, and if they work for a publisher, their job is to ensure the manuscript adheres to the vision set out in the book proposal or what everyone agreed to when the book was contracted. They get involved early, while the writing process is ongoing.

Content editing has more or less the same purpose as developmental editing—it's focused on structure, style, and overall development, for both fiction and nonfiction. However, content editors don't often work on an author's manuscript while it's still being written. You'll sometimes hear the term "book doctor" used in connection with this type of work. A book doctor is someone who performs developmental or content editing on a manuscript, usually on a completed draft.

In his essay "Developmental Editing," Paul McCarthy says, "A successful collaboration allows the author to feel sustained and liberated by knowing that she doesn't have to bear the burden of creation, development, and refinement alone."[1] A developmental or content editor offers the writer someone to trust and lean on. The editor's goal is always to produce the best book possible for the reader. They're concerned with narrative arc, pacing, and missed opportunities. They do their best to suggest solutions to any inconsistencies or structural problems, always with an eye to improving sales. Writers can of course be sensitive to feedback that leads to changing the book's structure or eliminating entire chapters. If the writer trusts her editor, then she'll be more likely to listen and accept that the editor may see things more clearly than she can.

To become a highly paid freelance editor typically requires some publishing experience—a combination of years spent at literary journals, magazines, or book publishers. Such editors may work for publishing houses or for writers. If hired by the writer directly, it's usually because the publisher or agent suggested the need for more help than either of them could provide. Other times, an author knows they need the work done before approaching an agent or publisher, or before self-publishing. Some writers are willing to pay thousands of dollars to work with an editor who has a New York trade publishing background and a track record of acquiring or producing best-selling authors. The more money that's on the line, the more the editor will be expected to offer industry-specific feedback and revision advice that will help the book succeed and compete in its genre. For this reason, most experienced editors specialize in specific genres or categories of work where they have in-depth knowledge and exposure to what sells. Until you have a proven track record, it may be difficult to secure the best-quality or best-paying clients.

SURFACE-LEVEL EDITORS

Line editors, copy editors, and proofreaders mainly focus on sentence- or paragraph-level editing. This work pays less than high-level editing and can be performed successfully by writers with little or no publishing industry experience. What is mainly required is expertise in grammar and punctuation, an eye for detail, and knowledge of style guides.

Line editing focuses on sentence structure, word use, and rhythm. Its goal is to create smooth and streamlined prose. Copyediting is generally more focused on correcting errors in grammar, syntax, and usage. Some copyeditors also fact-check and seek out inconsistencies or lapses in logic. Proofreading comes at the very end of the editorial process, after the book has been typeset. At this late stage, the proofreader is looking only for typos, formatting mistakes, and other egregious errors that shouldn't make it to publication.

Just because you're a writer who can produce error-free prose—or quickly catch a typo—don't assume this qualifies you as a surface-level editor. It's a specialized skill that necessitates some level of training or experience. MediaBistro offers courses in copyediting, and some universities do as well. These courses teach you grammar, etiquette for querying authors, how to apply house style and create a style sheet, and more.

RELATED WORK

In addition to editors, publishers of all kinds are in need of indexers, fact-checkers, and translators. There are also more technical editing jobs related to online or Web-based material that require knowledge of HTML and CSS. Nearly all of these areas require coursework or experience to pursue.

BUILDING AN EDITING BUSINESS

As discussed in chapter 23, knowing the right person, or seeking jobs from former employers, can help provide a starting base of repeat work. There are also associations that can be helpful to join and marketplaces where you can look for jobs. Here are two of the best known:

- **Editorial Freelancers Association.** This nonprofit, established in 1970 and based in New York City, is largely run by volunteers. It has chapters, events, and educational opportunities for members. One of its most important offerings is an online Job List; only EFA members can see the listings, but any individual can post a job for free (the-efa.org).
- **American Copy Editors Society.** Another New York–based nonprofit, started in 1997, ACES evolved from a community of newspaper copy editors. Similar to the EFA, you'll find an online job board, events, and educational opportunities (copydesk.org).

You can also ask publishing companies to add you to their pool of freelance editors. This typically requires taking a copyediting or proofreading test to prove you know what you're doing. You may have to dig through a publisher's website to find contact info or evidence of such a pool, if one is mentioned at all. As always, it helps to know someone or be referred by an existing editor at the company. Sometimes, if they're short on freelancers, publishers will post open calls for help at the EFA, MediaBistro, or PublishersMarketplace. Keep a close eye on those job boards, as such opportunities tend to receive quick response from freelancers.

The dramatic increase in self-publishing activity and services has produced a corresponding need for editors. Companies such as Author Solutions and Amazon employ a sizable pool of freelance editors who are typically paid a flat, per-word rate, and remain anonymous—they never have to interact with authors. You can also put out your shingle at one of the growing marketplaces for independent authors seeking professional editing help, such as Reedsy or Bibliocrunch. At such sites, you create a profile that describes your services and credentials; authors can search the freelancer profiles for the right fit and contact you with project proposals. Typically, the work you'll find through these marketplaces will pay a lower hourly rate than you might command elsewhere, but it can help you begin building a client base. Once you get the ball rolling, it gets easier over time, since new work often comes from word of mouth and referrals.

Regardless of the methods you use to find work, it's essential to have a website that makes clear who you are and the services you provide. (It can be the same site as your writer website; just make sure you point visitors to your editing services clearly in the navigation.) As you gain experience, post testimonials from happy authors or a list of clients you've worked with. You may have to ask for specific feedback from your clients to get your initial testimonials, and you shouldn't be shy about it; make it part of the overall editing process. Most people will avoid hiring an editor who can't provide evidence of quality past work.

WORKING WITH CLIENTS

In some cases, especially with publishing companies, being considered for your first job may require you to pass an editing test. But when a potential author looks to hire you, what kind of "test" makes sense?

Most writers are understandably anxious about paying someone a large sum of money for work that's subjective and difficult to evaluate. How freelance editors go about determining if there's a good "fit" between editor and author varies widely. In some cases—especially when it comes to higher-level editing—they may work on a sample chapter to help the author understand their approach and what value they offer.

As a general rule, the more credentialed and experienced the editor, the less likely they'll offer to edit a sample chapter—whether for free or for pay. Such a person simply doesn't need work that requires them to offer assurances of fit; they have a sufficient number of clients who trust them based on past experience, reputation, or referral alone. Less experienced editors may offer to work on a small sample, but charge the author for it—offering the author an economical way to test the waters. Those who are most proactive in securing new work and proving themselves are most likely to offer a free editing sample.

Whatever process you decide on, it's necessary to see some part of the manuscript before you agree to take on a job, so that you can understand the extent of the editing that might be required, see if you'll be comfortable doing the work, and give an accurate estimate of cost. Some editors charge by the page or by the word; others charge by the hour. If you charge by the hour, you'll have to determine how heavy or light the edit will be to offer an accurate quote. Sometimes clients—especially publishers—will advise you that the manuscript requires light, medium, or heavy editing, and offer a higher or lower flat fee (based on page or word count) based on their assessment of the editing required.

PARTING ADVICE

Whether you're a writer seeking editing jobs or a writer looking to hire an editor, understand that the current marketplace is overrun by mediocre and poor editors. As mentioned earlier, the growth of self-publishing has increased the number of people who are putting out shingles. There isn't any formal accreditation process for freelance editors; anyone can call themselves one, and many set up shop with little experience and few qualifications. Lots of people, then, can point to published works they've edited, but it's not all of very high quality.

So it may take time to distinguish yourself from the crowd. You may end up specializing in a particular type of editing or working with a particular type of client to get your start. Many writers combine some teaching work with editing. They build their client list by offering online or in-person courses, and continue to work one-on-one with students seeking help after the course ends.

25 : TEACHING AND ONLINE EDUCATION

In the 1980s and 1990s, it wasn't an unreasonable expectation that an MFA graduate in creative writing could, with just a little experience and a modest track record of publication, find a full-time or tenure-track job at a four-year university. According to the AWP "Guide to Writing Programs," between 1984 and 2004, the number of programs conferring undergraduate creative writing degrees grew from 10 to 86, while graduate programs increased from 31 to 109. It was a very good time to be looking for a job teaching creative writing at the university level. Today, the number of programs is still growing, if not at the same rate, and the market has become flooded with MFA graduates. In 2015, there were 171 tenure-track creative writing jobs offered in the United States, compared to 3,000 to 4,000 new MFA or PhD graduates.

At the same time, universities are using more part-time and adjunct instructors, and tenure-track jobs aren't as plentiful as they once were. Adjuncts typically earn between $3,000 and $7,000 per course taught, and benefits may be few. If you're interested in adjunct teaching, take a look at the *Chronicle of Higher Education*'s "Adjunct Project" at data.chronicle .com for an idea of pay near you, and seek out universities with adjunct unions, where benefits are likely to be better. Even if you manage to teach three or four courses per semester, the income rarely approaches the level of tenure-track salaries, especially given the potential lack of benefits.

Because of increased competition for any open position, even part-time and temporary jobs, creative writing programs have increased their requirements to the point that only a few are truly qualified to apply. To land almost *any* position in a creative writing program now requires a strong track record of publication, teaching experience, and the ability to cover classes in not just one core area of expertise but also a secondary area. Some programs are even beginning to require a PhD to apply. John Warner, an editor at *McSweeney's* and longtime contingent faculty member, bluntly stated, "There is no sustainable career path in academia for MFA holders in creative writing."[1]

If landing a tenure-track creative writing position is nonetheless your goal, then to be competitive, you'll need to focus on developing each of these components of your application package:

- publication of at least one book, with a steady and growing track record of other output
- teaching experience across multiple genres, at both undergraduate and graduate levels
- a stellar writing sample that will resonate with diverse members of a hiring committee

You should also follow the "Academic Jobs" wiki, studying the Creative Writing jobs page for the current year and past years to fully understand the landscape, what jobs are open, and what stage of the hiring process potential employers are at. AWP's "Career Advice" page is also useful for those new to the academic job market and application process (www.awp writer.org/careers/career_advice).

When you apply for a position, you'll often be competing against people who already hold teaching positions, usually as part-time or non-tenure-track staff. Other candidates may include recent graduates *and* well-established writers with award-winning work. To stand out will require much more than meeting the posted requirements. If this sounds daunting, what's an MFA grad to do? Depending on your background and experience, there may be other university teaching jobs or staff positions you're qualified for. Consider these possible opportunities:

- **Student publications or student media adviser.** Many universities have a full-time administrative staff or faculty member who oversees student media—newspapers, magazines, literary journals, and more. Sometimes teaching is part of the job, sometimes not.
- **Journalism, electronic media, or communications departments.** When I held a tenure-track faculty position, it wasn't in creative writing but in the electronic media division at the University of Cincinnati. Students there earned a BFA degree to prepare them for jobs in any facet of the media industry—from TV and radio to video-game production. My specialization was writing and storytelling across media.

- **Marketing and publicity.** Every university, and even some colleges within the university, have print and digital publications and marketing outreach that require skilled editors and writers.

Writers who wish to teach should also consider other types of schools and situations where an MFA degree can translate to a teaching or writing-related position, such as high schools, literacy programs, literary centers, and ESL programs. While you can start a teaching job search with well-known resources such as the AWP Job List, try casting a wider net by searching for "MFA in creative writing" or "writing teacher" on job aggregation sites such as Indeed.com.

OPPORTUNITIES IN ONLINE EDUCATION

Recently, there has been considerable debate in academia about MOOCs (massive open online courses). When I discuss online teaching opportunities, however, I'm not talking about MOOCs. I'm talking about online writing courses offered by nonprofit organizations, for-profit businesses, and individual authors. Think about the courses you see advertised by MediaBistro, *Writer's Digest*, The Loft, Gotham Writers Workshop, and *Creative Nonfiction* magazine, as well as other continuing education opportunities marketed to non-degree-seeking adults.

Online courses typically have a shorter duration than traditional university courses, and instructor pay is often based on a percentage of student registration fees. If the course is built to be scalable—meaning the instructor's work doesn't necessarily increase as more students enroll—then the return on investment of time is even greater. For courses that involve one-on-one student feedback, class sizes are generally kept manageable and offer competitive pay compared to adjunct positions, which usually carry higher workloads and more intensive time commitments. Many online courses are asynchronous, which means there are no set class times—the curriculum is available for students to read, study, or view on their own schedule. Instructors generally offer online office hours—interactive chat times—to answer student questions, but these too may be handled asynchronously through message boards.

For those who have never before taught online, it's helpful to get started by teaching with an established organization or business, so you can learn the basic tools and methods used to create a satisfying experience when students don't meet the instructor in person—and may not interact with other students. However, any writer with some teaching experience, once they know a few principles of online teaching, can get started if they have an effective way to market their course to prospective students. Today, there are affordable platforms with easy setup—allowing you to seamlessly accept payments and register students—so the technological barriers of even a few years ago are no longer a reason to avoid online teaching. (A few of the most popular platforms for online teaching are Teachable, Pathwright, and ZippyCourses.)

THE BASICS OF ONLINE TEACHING

The primary motivation for adult writers who take online classes is to acquire new skills, complete a project they've started, or receive personalized feedback and instruction. People value the motivation and accountability a class can provide, and also appreciate the immediacy of online education in serving their needs. Freedom and flexibility are often critical for adult students—more important than even price. Ultimately, as with all types of education, a course's success depends greatly on understanding or anticipating the needs of students, knowing how to teach them effectively about the topic at hand, and creating a structure around the material that leads to learning and engagement.

Deciding What to Teach and How

If you're new to online teaching, I recommend choosing a class you've already taught multiple times, where the curriculum is ready to go. It's also easier from a marketing perspective to teach topics you're associated with, that you have demonstrated success in, or that you know would interest your past students.

The first question you'll need to answer is how long will the course run. Unless you're enthusiastic about "boot camp"-style courses that run only a weekend or a week, I recommend a minimum of four weeks and a maximum of twelve weeks. The second question is how much personalized attention (critique, live sessions, office hours) will be involved? The more interactive the course, the more you can charge, but obviously the more time you'll need to commit as an instructor. These are the most common structures for online writing courses:

- **Lecture-oriented.** One lecture topic per week, with typically one large-scale project finished and critiqued by the end (e.g., first 25 to 50 pages of a manuscript, a completed personal essay, a book proposal, etc.). Lectures in an online environment could mean live video conference sessions (which require small classes), recorded video tutorials or lectures using software such as Camtasia or Screenflow, or written lectures.

- **Critique-oriented.** Alternate a lecture week with a critique/ discussion week; this works better when students are expected to produce 500 to 1,000 words at a time.

Discussions can take place asynchronously on a forum or through a private Facebook group. Keep in mind that discussions for the sake of discussion usually have low perceived value with online classes and are best when consolidated with feedback or critique of work. Critique or feedback can be offered in many ways, including traditional written critique by instructor (private), audiorecorded or audiovisual critique by instructor (private), and live interactive critique run like a traditional workshop, but this last option usually does not work well with an online course.

Developing Effective Video Lectures

If you choose to deliver curriculum via video, here are some of the best practices in the online education community:

Use visuals and don't be a talking head. Hopefully, you already use PowerPoint, Keynote, Prezi, or some other slide-based presentation tool as part of your curriculum. If not, I suggest you develop slides. Use summary lists, imagery, graphics, and other visuals to reinforce the points you're talking about. Images increase student engagement. If you give them just audio with a static visual (or a talking head), they tend to get bored and distracted. When you can't think of anything, add a cat GIF. Attention will skyrocket.

Be prepared to share your slides in PDF form. One of the first things students will ask for is a copy of your lecture. If you're uncomfortable sharing your slides, prepare a handout with the key ideas, lessons, resources, websites, or tips from your presentation. Having something in writing, like a tip sheet, is very helpful with online courses. Students appreciate not having to search through recordings to find that one minute when you referenced a particular resource.

Break up your lecture into three- to six-minute segments. It's less daunting to tackle a video lecture when things are broken down into their smallest steps or components. This is the model used by Lynda.com, one of the most successful online education sites, owned by LinkedIn. (Side note: Lynda is an excellent resource for learning any kind of software or technical skill.)

Whenever possible, build in next steps or actions. Students will learn better if they're given a specific task or action after watching a lecture or series of lectures. Make them put what they've learned to work, or get them writing. This may not apply to all types of writing courses, but be creative. When you incorporate action steps into your curriculum, satisfaction will increase, because people feel like they're accomplishing, creating, or learning something. Progress toward goals is inspiring.

Writing a Description of Your Course

For online courses, the description is critical in getting people to register. Write it in second-person, speaking directly to the students. The title and subtitle of your course should be as benefit-oriented as possible. Include specifics on what students will learn in the course—a bulleted list works great. Describe who should take the course; this gives prospective students confidence that your course is a good fit for them.

In addition to a week-by-week description of the course schedule or curriculum, offer a list of all the things the student will receive as part of the course: ten lectures, three critiques, handouts or worksheets, and so on. Offer testimonials or praise from past students, even if they're traditional students from a university setting. Finally, offer a bio that focuses on your qualifications to teach the course. If you need a model, follow the lead of established online course sites such as Gotham's WritingClasses.com.

Marketing Your Course

If you're not working with an established organization with a marketing list, this is the most difficult challenge (as it is with book marketing): how will you spread the word about your course and get people to enroll? The answers are as varied as writers. Most first steps include mentioning the course on social media, writing blog posts at relevant, well-trafficked sites (while course enrollment is open), and getting others who know your work to mention or recommend the course to potential students. One popular tactic is to offer a brief, free presentation (such as a single lecture or a one-hour tutorial) to promote course registration. The trick, however, is building awareness for the free offering—which usually requires the same tactics as getting enrollment in the first place, or promoting your work through the skills we covered in part 4. Once you've run a few online courses, you'll have a base of students who are interested in future opportunities in learning with you, and who will spread the word to their friends and writing groups if they had a positive experience.

26 : CONTESTS, PRIZES, GRANTS, FELLOWSHIPS

If you're a literary writer, working on projects in which artistic excellence is a top priority, there are thousands of prizes, grants, and fellowships you can apply for, including some that offer financial support. As you might expect, competition is fierce for the highest-profile awards (such as National Endowment for the Arts grants), but many others are within reach of new writers. As with so many things in the business of writing and publishing, it behooves you to focus on small and local awards first, and use each win as a stepping-stone to larger recognition or prizes. Let's first review the major types of opportunities:

- **Contests/competitions.** If you've ever flipped through a writers' magazine, you've probably seen a multitude of listings for writing contests, almost all focused on unpublished work. There's a competition for every conceivable genre and form, from commercial to literary, short to long. Most charge an entry fee. Some competitions are run as for-profit enterprises, while others are nonprofit and use entry fees to cover administration and judging costs.
- **Awards and prizes.** Published work may be eligible for a different range of awards, although you may not be eligible to apply for them. For the most prestigious awards, nominations may be restricted to publishers or guided by a formal process. It's rare to find a well-known prize in publishing that is also a for-profit endeavor.
- **Fellowships.** While this term is used for many different types of awards, it most commonly refers to positions offered by university creative writing programs to post-MFA students or published writers. Fellowships come with a significant stipend—possibly large enough to cover modest living expenses. Fellowships may be months-long or even years-long.

- **Residencies.** Residencies offer writers a specific place where they can spend focused time on their work, often for free. The length of the residency may be anywhere from a few days to a few months. The writer may be expected to interact with the community in some way, by giving readings or running workshops. Residencies can happen literally anywhere: universities, libraries, businesses, resorts—even airports and trains. (Amtrak announced writer residencies in 2014.[1])
- **Grants.** A grant is quite simply a gift of money. While an application process is required for nearly every opportunity discussed above, a grant application is typically a more formal and extensive document that can be daunting for the average writer to produce. Granting agencies may require a budget plan that outlines the specific funding required, even though the project may only be in the idea stage when the application is due.

Some of these opportunities offer very generous support for artists and writers, but you should never expect to sustain your writing life exclusively through financial awards, residencies, or fellowships. They may be essential for a particular project or provide economic relief over a period of time, but they're not reliable or dependable income over the long term of a career.

EVALUATING AND ENTERING CONTESTS AND COMPETITIONS

Writers should exercise caution when entering contests. The potential rewards may be very low, and the cost to enter high. Still, contests can play an important role in helping emerging writers get noticed and achieve recognition for work that might otherwise go unnoticed.

The reason contests can be so tricky is that anyone can start them (and anyone does!), and they can be profit centers for businesses that run them. When I worked for *Writer's Digest*, the revenue from competition entry fees approached a million dollars per year. The number of contest entries was a budgeted line item in the revenue forecast, and if the projected number was not achieved on time, the contest deadline was often extended to collect more entries.

While there's nothing inherently wrong or fraudulent about a contest that produces a profit, the prize should be meaningful enough to justify the entry fee the writer is paying, whether it's a monetary prize, a publishing contract, or something else. The ego boost from winning a contest is nice, but to make business sense it should advance your career or make you visible to the right people in the community.

Some writers love contests (and become a bit addicted to them) because they provide external motivation to complete work, plus there's the anticipation of possibly winning. A win can look good in a query or cover letter, and help indicate that your work stands out in a crowd. Whatever your reasons for entering contests, you must adequately research them before you submit your work, *even if there is no entry fee.* Here's what to look for:

- **Read the guidelines and fine print.** This is boring and tedious, but necessary. Some contests, especially those run by publishing companies and media organizations, claim all kinds of rights to your work, whether you win or not. By entering, you're agreeing to their terms, which are rarely negotiable after the fact. You may not care about such terms the day you enter the contest, but think about the ramifications down the road, if the work becomes publishable and of value, and a third party holds either exclusive or nonexclusive rights.
- **Are the guidelines clear and professional?** If the guidelines are confusing, contradictory, or seem hastily put together, avoid the contest. Sloppiness may carry over into the judging, prize fulfillment, and overall handling of submissions.
- **Who are the judges?** You want judges whose names you recognize or who are strongly associated with the type of work the contest is for. Be aware, however, that with large contests, entries are first screened by anonymous, low-level judges or staff, who winnow down the initial pool. This isn't a problem, but don't expect that the publicized judge will see your work unless you make it to the final round. Some contests that have multiple rounds will inform you of your entry's progress—or even send you the judge's comments— but such engagement takes a lot of administration work and usually means higher entry fees. In other cases, you won't know how far your entry made it.
- **How long has the contest been around?** Or, if it's a new contest, how long has the sponsoring organization or business existed? Do you trust the organization or business to run the contest well?

- **Compare the entry fees to the prizes—or other perks.** A high entry fee doesn't necessarily mean a contest is suspect. High entry fees may be justified when writers submit a lot of material for consideration, such as a full-length manuscript, or receive specific feedback. Significant monetary prizes, or multiple prizes (for runners-up), can also justify higher entry fees.
- **What has the contest done for past winners?** Have they gone on to secure book deals? Are they now accomplished authors? Or is the contest win the only accolade on their bio? Competition sponsors bear responsibility for publicizing the winners of the contest and helping them get recognition. Run Google searches on the contest and see what media outlets report on the results. If you can find no one talking about the contest or its results, that's not a good sign for the winners.
- **Is the prize a publishing contract?** It's not uncommon for small presses, university presses, and others that specialize in literary work to run contests that lead to a publishing deal. In such cases, it's critical to understand what the publishing contract looks like *before* you enter, assuming that it's not negotiable if you win the contest. Usually the advance is predetermined, as are royalties. Sometimes it's possible to have an agent negotiate the finer points, but don't expect it. Also study the books of past winners and see how they were distributed and publicized. Would you be happy with the same treatment?

It's becoming more common for literary journals to subsidize their operations by running regular, entry-fee contests, which may in fact be the primary way for writers to submit their work for consideration. Examples include *Glimmer Train* and *Creative Nonfiction*. Sometimes that entry fee also gets you a subscription to the publication. The staff reviews your submission within the framework of the contest, and "winning" results in publication and payment, just as if you'd submitted under normal conditions with a reading fee.

THE VALUE OF PRIZES

Prizes for published work can be desirable for more than just the prestige and recognition that comes with winning. Some include cash awards, and the better-known prizes can boost book sales over the long term. In a media landscape where it's increasingly difficult to get attention for one's work, prizes can offer a publicity shortcut to authors and publishers (it becomes an easy marketing and PR angle), but can also benefit readers (prize-winning work is more likely to be worth their while).

Prizes can be roughly divided into two categories: those for which authors can nominate themselves, and those that are open to publishers only. One of the best-known award series, the Pen Center USA awards, allows both authors and publishers to submit work for consideration. But some of the most prestigious awards, such as the National Book Award and National Magazine Awards, only allow entries or nominations from publishers.

Most people understand the value of winning a prize like the National Book Award. But what about prizes you haven't heard of—or new prizes? What about prizes for self-published work, which often require entry fees? Judging the value of prizes isn't so different from judging the value of a competition, as described above. Always look at the prize announcements and how much marketing and publicity the winners receive. Look at past winners and see how the prize is worked into their marketing copy, book covers, or author websites. Where and how extensively have prize winners been publicized? If the prize is highly valued by a particular community—such as teachers, librarians, professors, or professionals in a specific field—then it may help lead to better book sales and distribution.

Be careful about pursuing a prize (or a contest for unpublished work) that's operated primarily as a for-profit venture. The business or organization behind it may be playing to authors' desire for validation, and then making money off promotional packages marketed to finalists or winners. If you're pitched the "opportunity" to spend hundreds or thousands of dollars to buy advertising about your prize or to attend an awards ceremony, it's probably not a prize you'll benefit much from winning.

With any prize, contest, or competition, be cautious if it appears to be a new or unknown operation. Entry fees add up quickly, and you can easily spend hundreds, if not thousands, of dollars trying to win something. You can also end up wasting your time pursuing prizes that don't matter to anyone in your community. If someone hasn't heard of the prize, then the burden falls on you to explain its significance if you're to gain any marketing or career benefit from it. Be sure a contest or a prize will at least *potentially* open doors for you with the right people, and pursue it with a larger strategy in mind, rather than a validation-seeking one.

Some writers are incredibly astute and closely study what wins in specific contests, looking for bias that may be exhibited by the judges. It is indeed smart to avoid submitting work that doesn't align with the exhibited taste and proclivities of a contest. Look for an opportunity that will give your work the best chance possible—just as you do when submitting your work for publication.

APPLYING FOR FELLOWSHIPS, RESIDENCIES, AND GRANTS

As with publishing credits, it can be useful to get your feet wet and build a track record of success by applying for smaller, less well known residencies or grants (especially from local, regional, and state funding resources), rather than aiming straight for the top (National Endowment for the Arts).

Grants and other funding opportunities can usually be subdivided into those for emerging artists (those at the beginning of their career), and those for established or distinguished artists. Beyond that, programs may focus on supporting specific artistic projects; providing need-based funds; offering career fellowships; facilitating travel, research, or study; or other aspects of artists' careers. You can find listings of opportunities in writers' magazines, especially the *AWP Chronicle* and *Poets & Writers*, as well as by subscribing to Hope Clark's Funds for Writers (fundsforwriters.com) and following Mira's List on Facebook.

These opportunities often require a significant time commitment from the writer, both in preparing the application and in accepting the opportunity should it be offered. Sometimes they are life-changing events that require temporary relocation, and shouldn't be pursued unless you can take time away from traditional employment or family responsibilities. Here are the materials you'll likely need for an application:

- **Work samples.** The samples should showcase your best and most relevant work. Some applications require you submit only new work. It may seem obvious to say so, but it is next to impossible to apply for anything if you are not already producing quality work that can be read and evaluated. Still, some writers are under the mistaken belief they can receive awards based on intent alone. Don't wait for permission from an external source to get started on a project; committees and others who decide on awards always look at writers' motivation and dedication as a sign of whether they would be responsible and worthy recipients of resources or funds.
- **Letters of recommendation.** These should come from people very familiar with you and your work, who have been your advocates over many years. Some applications require letters from

someone within a specific field or with a specific background relevant to the opportunity. Sometimes you'll be asked only for a reference list; as with the letters, choose people who know your work well.

- **Curriculum vitae or resume.** It's smart to set a calendar reminder to update your CV and resume every three to six months. Adding new publications and other professional activities on a regular basis will help you avoid the painful process of trying to recall or research years' worth of activity.

Additionally, you may be asked for:

- **Project description or proposal.** This explanation of your writing project can be very straightforward—say, to finish a book manuscript, of which you're sending a sample. Other times, it may be quite complex, such as when you're seeking funding for an artistic collaboration or event.
- **Writer's or artist's statement.** This statement sets out your philosophy or purpose in writing. It can be challenging to write, but fortunately it doesn't have to be long—usually not more than 300 words. You can search online for examples and inspiration— but you'll know yours is close to the mark when nothing in it could be seamlessly inserted into someone else's statement.
- **Statement of need.** For opportunities that focus on providing funds or resources to artists in need, you'll have to provide details about your economic situation.
- **Budget.** When applying for a grant, you may be asked to provide a budget of how the money will be spent. (Yes, you are allowed to budget a stipend, salary, or other income for yourself.) While it can be difficult to draft a budget for something that does not yet exist, express yourself with a level of confidence. Don't slip into language that makes it sound like you're desperate and can't succeed without funds.

Your application has to express a coherent vision for your artistic project or career. Don't expect the committee to connect the dots as to your career path and goals; tell a convincing story that shows how the opportunity you're applying for is the most natural and strategic next step for your progression as an artist.

For more on putting together applications and proposals, I highly recommend Gigi Rosenberg's book *The Artist's Guide to Grantwriting*. Her advice works equally well for fellowship and residency opportunities and for traditional grant proposals. It also helps if you can possibly find past grant proposals that were successful; these are sometimes made available to applicants.

27 : CROWDFUNDING AND DONATIONS

In recent years, a new and encouraging response has appeared to the perennial question "Who pays writers?" The readers themselves have become key funders—through crowdfunding campaigns or regular donations.

By now, everyone has heard of Kickstarter. Such crowdfunding campaigns require a writer to mobilize a community or fan base, both to support the project and to spread the word to other potential supporters. How do you develop that sort of community or fan base in the first place? Typically, years of effort go into developing a readership—or at least a professional network. In other words, it's a strategy most appropriate for someone with a decent platform, especially online, as discussed in part 4.

First, we'll cover whether this is the right strategy for you, then look at different types of crowdfunding efforts, and finally discuss what's involved in launching a successful campaign.

IS CROWDFUNDING RIGHT FOR YOU?

First, a project being considered for crowdfunding should be easily defined and have a specific endpoint. People feel more comfortable supporting projects that have tangible goals. If your project is open-ended in its goals or its duration, then an ongoing donations model might be a better fit (see below).

Second, if you don't use social media, or you feel uncomfortable directly asking people for money, then you may not have a successful campaign unless you can enlist other people to do the asking for you. Most crowdfunding campaigns last thirty days, and each and every one of those days needs to be spent spreading the word about your project and asking people for money. It can't just happen once at the start of the campaign and once at the end. Most potential donors will need to see your appeal several times before it even registers in their memory—and not only that, they will likely need to be personally approached via email or social media and asked to donate. For some writers, this produces so much psychological stress that it's not worth the monetary reward.

Finally, the entire process will be easier if the marketing tools you're using are thoroughly familiar to you and you have established networks in place. If you sign up for a social media account (e.g., Twitter) only for the sake of your crowdfunding campaign, or start doing something online that's completely out of the ordinary for you, it's not likely to go well. You'll be too busy getting accustomed to the tools, and the community will resent you for showing up only to market to them.

TYPES OF CROWDFUNDING CAMPAIGNS

Crowdfunding services come in several flavors, and one of your first decisions will be what type of campaign you'll run:

- **Win it all or lose it all.** This is the classic Kickstarter model: if you reach the dollar goal that you set, you receive the full amount, minus fees (around 8–10 percent). If you don't reach the goal, you receive nothing.
- **Receive what you raise.** In this scenario, if you don't reach your goal, you still receive the amount you raised, but the administrative fees are higher. Indiegogo is one of the biggest players in this space.
- **Reach the goal and get published.** If you raise the required amount set by a publishing company—which provides you with the fundraising platform—then your book is accepted for publication. As of this writing, this model is limited to a handful of companies, including Inkshares in the United States and Unbound in the United Kingdom.

So why would anyone choose the "all or nothing" model? Interestingly, studies show that campaigns are more successful under that model—it tends to spur more donations and support, not to mention more commitment from the person campaigning.

Publishers that use crowdfunding are considered "hybrid publishers"—companies that mix self-publishing and traditional publishing approaches. Because such companies are only a few years old, the jury is still out on their value to authors and the larger publishing community. Authors considering them as a partner should look closely at their track record of getting coverage and sales through traditional trade outlets (bookstores, libraries, and mainstream media).

LAUNCHING A SUCCESSFUL CROWDFUNDING CAMPAIGN

With the classic Kickstarter model, the number-one factor in whether you reach your goal is whether you were smart about setting that goal in the first place. It seems obvious, but many people plug in a "nice to have" or otherwise arbitrary number that isn't based on a realistic calculation of what they might hope to raise given their current resources or network.

Bethany Joy Carlson of The Artist's Partner, a crowdfunding consultancy, recommends every author begin by quantifying the resources they have in hand when the campaign starts, including the size of their email list, the number of people they reach via social media, and confirmed donation amounts from known benefactors (even if it's your mom). Carlson says you can estimate somewhere between a 5 to 20 percent response rate on an email list, with a median campaign pledge amount of $25. For social media posts, she recommends assuming about a 1 percent response rate.[1] (Those who use Mailchimp or similar services should base their calculations on their list's average open and click rates, which will be most accurate for such projections.)

Before the crowdfunding campaign even begins, you should have a few "benefactors" lined up who will make donations within the first day after launch. This seed money inspires confidence in the campaign and encourages others who view your appeal to donate. Carlson's research shows that campaigns that reach 40 percent of their funding goal within the first day are far more likely to succeed.

There are many other factors that encourage people to donate, including the description that pitches your project (the marketing copy), a campaign video, perks for various donation levels, and your ability to gather influencers to help spread the word. Carlson offers a free, in-depth series about every major aspect of crowdfunding at her website, theartistspartner .com.

DONATIONS AND TIP JARS

If crowdfunding sounds difficult and time consuming, that's because it is. And, as indicated earlier, it's not appropriate for every type of project. Sometimes, it's better to pursue donations, whether passively (e.g., add a tip jar to your site) or more actively (mention donations as important to your work, frequently and briefly wherever you go, online and offline).

As a stellar example of a donations-driven operation, Maria Popova of Brain Pickings sustains herself through a combination of donations and affiliate marketing (see chapter 29). At her site and in her newsletter, readers are encouraged to donate on an ongoing monthly basis or to make a one-time donation via PayPal. Perhaps tellingly, she calls her donors "patrons," making them feel that they're supporting an important artistic endeavor or cause, not just paying for content.

Anyone from bloggers to podcasters to journalists can put a "donate" button on their site by simply signing up for a PayPal account and pasting some code into a widget. It takes little effort, but just having the button doesn't mean the donations will start rolling in. This approach makes the most sense, and yields the most benefit, when you are actively posting or distributing free content—as in the case of Popova and other bloggers like her. You can expect the amount of donations to be strongly tied to how much traffic your site receives, so this isn't a model that will work for people whose sites are ghost towns.

A more formal way to go about collecting donations is Patreon. While Patreon takes a cut of your donations (about 10 percent), it's a useful platform because it shows the cumulative amount of money that's been donated, which helps persuade others to join the circle of support. To encourage donations, you can offer perks or rewards to donors, similar to what's done through crowdfunding. A quick scan of successful Patreon users will generate ideas quickly about what's attractive: advance access to content, social media shout-outs, patron-only access to the authors/creators, and so on.

28 : MEMBERSHIPS, SUBSCRIPTIONS, AND PAYWALLS

The use of donations to encourage support of creative endeavors is an ideal approach for individual writers and small operations; it usually comes with low administrative costs and doesn't require special tools. For more complex operations with significant overhead, consistent and reliable revenue becomes desirable. Subscriptions or memberships offer ways of leveling up operations, and while well suited to the digital age, both business practices have been with us for centuries.

Subscriptions tend to be straightforward pay-for-content transactions. "Membership" is a more community- and relationship-focused approach, akin to patronage, that encourages levels of support that go beyond paying for a specific piece of content at a specific price. It engenders the notion of joining and supporting a group, a movement, or a philosophy, not just an individual or publication. As an example, in 2014 *Slate* rolled out Slate Plus, a membership program that offers early access to articles, exclusive newsletters, and discounts to live events.

There is ongoing debate as to whether large-scale, legacy print publications like the *New York Times* might do better as nonprofits with a membership model—whether "relationships" could reliably pay their bills. As of today, paywalls and formal subscription models are considered fundamental to such institutions' continuance. Paywalls, however, present a high-risk business model, given that few readers are willing to pay for online content unless it's so unique and vital that it can't be replaced by the mountains of readily available free content. Thus, paywalls have largely failed, especially for news-driven publications, whose content is likely to be undifferentiated or a regurgitation of what can be found elsewhere.

Individual writers can also be successful with formal membership programs or subscription plans. The lines between being a "member", a "subscriber", or a "donor" are in fact very blurry. Sometimes the differences are a question of marketing or an organization's status as for-profit or non-profit.

SUCCESSFUL MEMBERSHIP OR SUBSCRIPTION PROGRAMS

Launching a membership program requires an in-depth understanding of your target readership and what kind of benefits they would desire and consider meaningful. A venture with membership at its core usually requires an established reader base that can be studied and surveyed first.

An example of this type of progression can be found in the case of Ben Thompson's successful website *Stratechery*. In 2013 Thompson launched his blog-based publication, which focuses on informed analysis of the tech industry. His posts, offering unique, high-quality content, were well received and widely shared by the community, and he soon had a steady readership of about forty thousand unique visitors per week.[1] In 2014 he launched a subscription program. Exemplifying that blurry line I mentioned, it also exhibits qualities and benefits of a membership program—including three tiers of access:

- **Conversation ($5/month).** Ability to comment on articles and receive the full RSS feed.
- **Content ($10/month).** All of the above, plus access to Thompson's daily linked-list articles.
- **Community ($30/month).** All of the above, plus meet-ups with and email access to Thompson.[2]

Within about six months, Thompson had over a thousand subscribers and was earning more than $100,000 for his content, even though a portion of his content remained free. (He's now up to two thousand subscribers.) The churn rate of *Stratechery* is low—90 percent of his subscribers renew, a nearly unheard of renewal rate in traditional magazine publishing.[3] Thompson said about his success, "Stratechery . . . serves a niche, and niches are best served by making more from customers who really care than from milking pennies from everyone."[4]

For membership offerings tied to large-scale publications, such as Slate Plus, to offer something meaningful to their members often requires adding staff. *Slate* hired two full-time staffers to work on Slate Plus, and other staff also participate in generating exclusive content. Still, when surveyed, a considerable number of Slate Plus members said they joined because they like *Slate* and wanted to support its operations, not for the extra perks and benefits.

DEALING WITH TAX IMPLICATIONS

When you begin earning money from your website or online content, you'll quickly run into two big questions: How is this income reported to the IRS? and Do I need to collect taxes on digital products and services that I sell?

Some payment processors you may use (such as PayPal) report your income to the IRS and you'll receive a 1099 form during tax season. If you've ever received a book advance or freelance payment, the income is reported in the same way. The income is untaxed, and you must determine if quarterly payments are necessary. Some companies will not report your income to the IRS, but of course you still have to report it. I recommend using free accounting software such as Wave or ZipBooks to keep records if you're not doing so already.

As for taxes on digital content and services, tax law dramatically varies depending on what state you live in, what product or service you are selling, and even where the purchaser lives. Some third-party services will apply the correct taxes on your behalf (and possibly even remit them), and well-developed e-commerce solutions for Wordpress sites, such as WooCommerce, will calculate correct product taxes and help you stay on the right side of the law. But fair warning: This can be an enormous headache depending on the state you live in, and if you do need to collect taxes, you'll also need to secure a state license before you begin selling. To research tax laws in your state, visit www.taxjar.com/states. Finally, the European Union requires you pay taxes to them if you sell certain digital goods to EU residents; you may want to avoid selling to EU customers if you're not prepared to navigate that quagmire.

With or without a formal membership program, individual writers and publications should give some thought to how they cultivate and reward readers' loyalty and desire for involvement. For example, journalist Ann Friedman encourages a form of "membership" by asking people to pay $5 per year to receive the special edition of her email newsletter, which includes perks not included in the regular edition.

MAKING PAYWALLS PAY

For a paywall to work, the content it protects has to be worth paying for. Unlike membership programs, which can be introduced at any time and don't entirely lock out nonpaying readers, paywalls can be impossible to implement if the readership is accustomed to receiving your content for free. (*Slate* attempted to implement a paywall early in its history and had to abandon it—although not before losing a huge number of readers, who took a long time to return.)[5]

But this introduces a horrible Catch-22: if it's necessary to implement a paywall from the start, how do you get subscribers, people willing to pay for content sight unseen? Online marketing and publicity is also hampered when content can't be easily shared via social media: nonsubscribers may be intrigued by a posted link, but will hit the paywall as soon as they click to read.

Perhaps the most popular solution to this dilemma is the "porous" paywall: allow nonsubscribers a certain amount of access, then prompt them to subscribe as they near the specified limit. This model is used by the *New York Times*, the *New Yorker*, *Virginia Quarterly Review*, and many other publications. Another solution is to regularly make selected articles freely available outside of the paywall. This is the model used by publications such as *Harper's* and *n+1*, and is quite popular with literary journals. Additionally, some publications—whether they have a paywall or not—publish a range of online-only content that serves as a marketing and promotion tool for print or digital subscriptions. The *Paris Review* blog is an example; none of the journal's print content is available on its website.

Technology that supports paywalls and subscriber-only content is now widely available, regardless of an individual's or publication's budget. If a subscriber or member model is something you're serious about trying, there are countless plug-ins for Wordpress-based sites that can implement a paywall, or otherwise offer subscriber or membership functionality, such as Zeen 101.

29 : ADVERTISING AND AFFILIATE INCOME

As discussed in my overview of the magazine and online media industries (chapters 6 and 7), advertising has been the traditional means of sustaining both small, for-profit publications and large media conglomerates. The audience gains access to content for free or at reduced cost in exchange for being exposed to some type of advertising or sponsorship message. That model is now under tremendous strain. Advertising dollars are shifting away from traditional channels and into social media and mobile environments, while at the same time online forms of display advertising are perceived to have low value because of unlimited supply and low engagement. Ad-blocking software—which allows readers to prevent ads from appearing in a browser—has further exacerbated the problem and contributed to industry debate on how to deal with a readership increasingly avoidant of or even hostile toward ads. (Thus the no less controversial growth of native advertising and content marketing, discussed in chapter 31.)

Still, advertising can contribute some income—or a lot—to a writer who manages to accumulate significant readership, especially if the audience has qualities desirable to potential advertisers. And softer forms of advertising, such as affiliate marketing, also offer considerable money-making potential.

ADVERTISING CATEGORIES AND TYPES

There are three main categories of advertising you're likely to deal with:

- **Google Adsense.** This program, which anyone can participate in, grants ad space to Google on your site. The ad space automatically populates each time the site is loaded by a user, based on what Google thinks will interest that user or your audience. It's possible to disallow certain types of ads and control what the ad space looks like, to ensure it fits with your mission or brand. When visitors click on the ads, Google gets paid by advertisers, and you get paid by Google.

- **Ad networks.** Ad networks operate similarly to Adsense but usually specialize in a specific type of advertising client or content. For example, the Litbreaker ad network focuses on the publishing and literary community and claims to reach more than three million book lovers. Many publication sites you probably know and read serve ads from Litbreaker, including the *Paris Review, Guernica, The Millions,* and *The Rumpus.* You typically have to apply to be accepted into an ad network and abide by certain terms and conditions.
- **Direct placement.** If you have potential advertisers approaching you directly, you essentially become your own ad manager and salesperson, and can strike deals directly for whatever terms are mutually agreeable. Sites that use Wordpress can use plug-ins such as Ad Rotate to help automate ad management.

For low-traffic sites—or newcomers to the world of online advertising—Google Adsense is the first and best choice, and will train you in the language and customs of the online ad industry. Ad networks work well for all types of sites, from high-traffic sites to niche or specialized sites with loyal audiences. Direct placement is more likely in the case of niche or specialized sites, where an advertiser specifically wants to reach *your* audience.

The types of advertising you accept are limited only by your imagination and the types of ad vehicles you can create. The most common forms of advertising run on websites and blogs, but because this type of advertising is known to perform poorly, there's typically more growth and potential in areas such as email, video, and sponsorship. Here are some major types of advertising to be aware of.

Website Display Ads

Display ads use images, audio, or video to attract attention. The most common form of display ad may be embedded throughout the content you're trying to read, or may appear as a banner (at the top of the site) or a skyscraper (running the length of the site). Because display ads bog down the loading of a website, especially on mobile devices, ad blockers have become a popular method to prevent them from loading or displaying. Ads are paid for based on the number of impressions delivered, or number of clicks (known as PPC, or pay-per-click). When the number of impressions goes down, it hurts a website's ability to attain the numbers required for sustained ad revenue.

Pop-Ups and Road Blockers

These are perhaps the most despised form of advertising because they delay or impede a reader's ability to get to the content. However, pop-ups and other forms of blatant intrusion *do* work—not least because people accidentally end up clicking on them or giving in to whatever demand is being made.

Text-Based Ads

Envision the ads that appear in search engines—usually a headline with a few lines of text and a link. These are text-based ads, which are the most common form of ad after display ads. They are generally regarded as the least intrusive form of advertising, but they can be unattractive from an aesthetic perspective.

Email Advertising

Email newsletters may carry display advertising, text-based advertising, and/or classified-style advertising. Rates for advertising in email newsletters can be just as high, if not higher, than for website advertising, since email readers tend to be more highly engaged than website or blog visitors. Some publications also offer advertisers the opportunity to purchase a dedicated email blast, where the advertiser gets to send an entire email (that they write and design) to the publication's email list. Publications are typically cautious about striking such deals because they predictably lead to high unsubscribe rates from readers who consider such blasts to be spam.

Video Ads

Pre-roll and mid-roll ads may be inserted in videos and are quite similar to TV-style advertising. Such ads are usually no longer than 5 to 15 seconds, unless the video content is a long segment or show, in which case, a standard 30-second or one-minute spot may be used. It's also possible for text-based advertisements to be superimposed on a video while it's playing. Anyone with videos available on YouTube can give YouTube permission to place advertisements in their videos automatically, and then get a cut of the revenue. (YouTube is owned by Google.)

Sponsorships

What's the difference between a sponsorship and an advertisement? On the surface, there can be very little difference, but typically "sponsorship" refers to long-term or ongoing arrangements, rather than one-time placements. Sponsorship value is rarely tied to specific traffic or click rates, and can be attractive for bloggers and podcasters. Readers, too, may prefer the more elite or polished look and feel of a sponsorship line, especially if sponsor status is granted to one entity at a time, on an exclusive basis.

Sponsorships are also prevalent with nonprofits, such as NPR or PBS, which don't accept advertisements. (There are tax implications that are too complex to get into here. If you're operating a nonprofit, you'll need to study up on what qualifies as a sponsorship and what crosses the line into advertisement.)

Publications or individuals who have multiple ad vehicles to offer—such as print or digital publications, websites or blogs, apps, email newsletters, active social media accounts, or event sponsorships—should develop integrated advertising packages that offer a range of exposure for one price. For an example of how such packages work, study the Association of Writers and Writing Programs, which produces a detailed media kit and package for sponsors and advertisers, particularly related to its annual conference.

AFFILIATE MARKETING

Affiliate marketing is when you receive a financial reward (or something of value) for referring customers who then make a confirmed purchase or transaction. Amazon has the largest and most popular affiliate program in the world (known as Amazon Associates), and many people and publications make a sizable, full-time living based on affiliate marketing fees.

For example, let's say you run a book-recommendations website and are an Amazon affiliate. Whenever you mention a book, you would link to its purchase page at Amazon, using a unique link that helps track any eventual purchases back to you and *your* affiliate marketing account. Book purchases at Amazon offer a 4.5 percent affiliate payout, while sales of other merchandise may pay up to 10 percent or more.

To most customers, this affiliate relationship is completely invisible. Unless you tell them, readers don't necessarily know they're clicking on an affiliate link. If their purchase price is affected at all, it would be a promotional one—a lower price that the affiliate has special access to. The FTC does stipulate that affiliate marketers using affiliate links have a clear disclosure statement on their site.

To see affiliate marketing in action, take a look at *The Wirecutter*, a product-recommendation site owned by the *New York Times*. Every product mentioned links to Amazon with an affiliate link.

While Amazon has the most popular affiliate program in the world, it's not necessarily the most profitable one. Affiliate marketing is very popular in the tech and start-up world, and payouts or credits can be substantial for referring a customer. Well-known tech companies that run affiliate marketing programs include Mailchimp, eBay, and Bluehost. Website hosting services may offer up to $100, or even more, per customer referred. There are also dozens of affiliate networks you can join that regularly offer affiliate marketing opportunities with a range of companies.

To be a successful affiliate marketer requires a sizable audience whose members not only visit your site and read your content but trust your recommendations—and follow through with purchases. Reaching that stage can take years of effort, but you can create affiliate marketing accounts at any time, begin using affiliate links even with little or no audience, and let the income stream grow over time, especially as you see what methods work.

30 : PURSUING A PUBLISHING CAREER

I meet many writing majors who dream of a full-time career in book or magazine publishing. It evokes visions of reading all day, working to produce great literature, and spending time among writers. As is the case with many professions that are idealized, a publishing career has little in common with popular perceptions of it. A publishing career requires a strong stomach for business concerns and an ability to shape or market work in such a way as to bring success, attention, or profit to your employer. While nonprofit and literary ventures may put equal weight on artistic excellence or related concerns of quality, they are not free from the financial realities of the business. The focus of the financial calculus may simply be shifted, from what publication will produce a profit to what project will procure an NEA grant or large donation. In both cases, the sustainability of the operation depends on consistently wise project choices. Good judgment is essential, as is creativity in the use of limited time and resources.

One thing that surprises writers new to the publishing business is that marketing jobs, especially those in publicity departments, involve a lot more writing, at least for the public, than editorial jobs. They may even be a better fit for you—plus such positions often pay better!

I began my publishing career while I was still in college. I was editor in chief of the university literary journal and university newspaper, both of which had budgets that I managed; worked for a local publisher focused on military history; and interned at a midsize commercial publisher that later gave me freelance projects and hired me upon graduation. If you seek a publishing career, don't wait until you graduate to begin working in the field. Start with the publications closest to you, and experiment with a variety of positions if you can. You'll need experience and skills to land just about any entry-level job in publishing—it's an extremely competitive field that's more or less open to graduates with any major (though liberal arts degrees tend to predominate). While I held a BFA in writing, it was my practical publications experience that landed me jobs. It was also helpful to be schooled in AP style, which I learned as part of an undergraduate copyediting course. Today's students should look at acquiring digital media skills, such as image editing, social media marketing, and HTML/CSS knowledge. Never tell an interviewer or a potential boss that you want to work in publishing because you love to read or aspire to be a writer. You will be marked as naive at best.

While in school, I was lucky enough to have two professors with connections to prominent people in publishing. Both were actively publishing their own work or others' work, so they had significant practical experience, and they helped me secure my first publishing internship. If you lack professors who can help you find opportunities, look to the community for help—seek out nonprofit writing centers, reading series, or other organizations that focus on literary citizenship.

HOW AND WHERE TO START

For students who live outside of the largest publishing or media centers (New York City, Boston, Los Angeles, Chicago, Washington, DC), and who lack connections or internship experience, it will be easier to land a job with a local or regional media or publishing company, probably one that has little to do with mainstream books or magazines. Then, once you have a few years' experience, you can start planning your move to where you want to be. (It's very hard to land an entry-level, full-time job in a city where you do not live, especially New York City.) If you're bold or have the resources, you can proactively move to New York City if that's where you want to end up, but be prepared to work in a service job as you wait for luck and opportunity to collide.

To speed the process, those with money can take one of the well-known summer publishing courses. You'll learn a lot about the publishing business, but really you're paying to build a network and meet the people who might give you an entry-level job. If you're painfully shy, a bad networker, or unsure if you're able to stand out in a group, then these opportunities may have less to offer.

One of the most important attitudes you can adopt is that there are many roads to a job in publishing, and even if your goal is to be an editor at a big glossy publication or Penguin Random House, it's possible to reach that goal by starting as a social media editor at a newspaper, or a publicity assistant at a PR firm. Broaden your idea of publishing to include all forms of writing, media, and communication. Nearly any activity in these areas will give you experience and skills that will translate to a more traditional publishing job—or maybe you'll decide you like those media sectors well enough to stick with them. The best free job boards include BookJobs, run by the Association of American Publishers; PublishersMarketplace, a hub for book publishing insider news; MediaBistro, with the most diverse listing of jobs across all publishing and media; and JournalismJobs.com, excellent for anyone seeking writing positions at newspapers and small or regional publications. The AWP Job List can be useful, but is typically focused on jobs in academia, and requires an AWP membership.

IS PUBLISHING THE RIGHT CAREER CHOICE FOR YOU?

It's easy to assume that working in publishing is an ideal way to earn money while you pursue a writing career. But writers who end up in publishing, whether they succeed or not, may find that it drains them of the creative energy they need to produce their own work. You may not know if that will happen to you until you've experienced a publishing job and monitored your output. There *are* people who manage to pursue both a writing career and a full-time publishing job, but ultimately one will take priority, and more often than not it's the job.

Steve Jobs said, in a commencement speech at Stanford, "Every morning I look in the mirror and ask myself: If today were the last day of my life, would I want to do what I am about to do today?"[1] While it would be exhausting to undergo a thorough self-examination *every* morning, it's helpful to be attentive to recurring activities in your job and ask, "Am I enjoying this? Is this draining my energy?" I'm always tweaking what I do daily, as well as thinking long-term: OK, it took me five years to accomplish this, or ten years to reach that goal. Am I doing what's necessary today to achieve what I'm envisioning one, five, or ten years out? How does my work today serve where I want to be tomorrow? If I can't find a connection, I shed it.

Don't place high value on creativity or the muse. Time management is *vastly* more important. You have to make time to allow creativity to flourish. As John Cleese once said, "If you're racing around all day ticking things off lists . . . and generally keeping all the balls in the air then you are not going to have any creative ideas."[2]

31 : CORPORATE MEDIA CAREERS

Traditional publishing jobs—especially in editorial—can be very hard to come by. Most entry-level jobs related to writing and editing are likely to be in the realm of corporate media, digital media, and marketing. Here's an overview of what you need to know about such opportunities.

SOCIAL MEDIA EDITORS AND ONLINE COMMUNITY MANAGEMENT

One of the most prevalent entry-level jobs—across nearly every industry—is the social media editor position. The stereotype is that younger people understand and do better with social media, but in reality you find younger people in these positions because such tasks are considered lower-level, tactical roles that don't require as much as skill or experience as other positions.

Social media editors may not be called exactly that. Because the roles are commonly considered marketing communications positions, they tend to live within companies' marketing divisions, and the position title may be something like "marketing assistant" with primary responsibilities focused on social media accounts.

Despite the low-level nature of the positions, these can be challenging jobs that build your skills as a writer and editor. A social media campaign, to be effective, typically needs to develop a consistent voice and approach to customers that can be expressed and carried out across multiple types of accounts. It also requires considerable finesse—a capacity to communicate in public, often live or on the spot, in front of a diverse audience. The immediate feedback received on social media—both qualitative and quantitative—also makes it possible to improve and see tangible results from your efforts, which can be satisfying and motivating over the long term. If your goal is to leave social media management for other types of work, the role gives you, at the very least, specific outcomes you can talk about with future employers. There's clear evidence of what you did and the effect it had.

Online community management is another job function that has come into existence alongside the internet, especially with large-scale publications or websites that encourage interaction among visitors. If you've ever genuinely enjoyed the comments section of a website or blog (rather than being repulsed), rest assured that was no accident; active community managers are required for any site that hopes to have a productive, respectful, and insightful comments section. Community managers may be hired either to establish or nurture a community into being (no small task), or to cultivate and derive value from an existing one. Aside from moderating comments or message boards, they may be tasked with crowd-sourcing or curating material that arises out of the community, tapping specific community members to take on increased responsibility, or offering analysis and insight into the community for company executives or other higher-ups.

Social media roles are sometimes combined with community management responsibilities. Both require getting up to speed quickly. Until you understand the target audience, the spoken and unspoken rules within the community, and its shared knowledge or language, it's very easy to misstep. You may not fully share the values and priorities of the people you're communicating with, but it will be difficult to serve as a social media or community editor if you don't have some level of enthusiasm or interest in the target audience.

CONTENT MARKETING

Content marketing is among the more difficult publishing concepts to understand because, when executed well, it comes across not as marketing but as quality content—whether that content is a well-told story, a compelling video, an interesting infographic, or any number of other things. The big caveat is that the motivation for producing such content isn't derived from a "pure" editorial mission—it's connected to a business or sales mission.

Content marketing has been around for a very long time, only we didn't call it "content marketing" until recently. *Harper's Magazine* started in the mid-1800s with the purpose of publishing book excerpts and bringing attention to new releases—from the publisher of the same name.[1] That was classic content marketing: using great content with the goal of selling something. Or consider this: whenever someone suggests that you blog as part of a book launch, you're being asked to participate in a form of content marketing. Maybe a pitch or a sale isn't mentioned, or the sale doesn't occur for months (or years), but the potential and intent to instigate a purchase or a customer relationship is there. Content marketing rests on the faith that delivering great content to develop a trusted relationship with a potential customer will deliver value over the long term.

You can also think of content marketing as a more sophisticated or strategic method of handing out samples. For example, if an author gives away the first book in a series for free, it's a marketing strategy to get readers in the door, then sell them on the second and subsequent books. Or if a teacher offers a free workshop or course, they might follow up with a more advanced, fee-based course or offer one-on-one editing for students who desire more in-depth assistance.

Over the years, the practice has been called "customer media," "branded content," "custom publishing," and "custom content"—but "content marketing" is generally the preferred term today. As with more traditional marketing, content marketing falls under the domain of a company's marketing department.

Content marketing is used by all types of businesses. Retailers, restaurants, financial companies—you name the industry, you'll likely find some form of content marketing. In many cases, this content requires a high level of creativity, imagination, and storytelling chops, not to mention crackerjack writing. Businesses or organizations are responsible for creating the content (or hiring firms and freelancers to create it), then distributing, bringing attention to, and driving engagement with the content. Bottom line: they own the content and the space it's hosted on. (This will become important later, when we clarify the differences between content marketing and native advertising.)

Some of the most popular and well-known forms of content marketing are the active blog on a business's website; videos posted on its YouTube channel; photos and images posted to an Instagram or Pinterest account; free courses delivered via email; and free PDF guides, slidepacks, or white papers. Here are some specific examples:

- Anthropologie features cocktail recipes on its blog[2]
- Gold's Gym posted a video series telling stories of people who improved their health and quality of life through exercise[3]

- AMC Theatres created a Ron Burgundy "dress for success" infographic for the release of *Anchorman 2*[4]
- American Express created and manages OPEN Forum, with how-to articles for small business owners[5]

Some content marketing is flash-in-the-pan, intended only to promote a specific event, such as the release of a book, album, or movie. Other initiatives become critical to the brand's long-term community engagement and visibility, such as the OPEN Forum by American Express. To be worth the company's time, content marketing ultimately needs to trigger a response or reaction—there must be a way to measure the results so that future efforts can be improved or redirected.

The biggest content marketing challenge by far is that many businesses lack the in-house resources or expertise to produce consistently high-quality, engaging writing or stories. As a result, some companies have hired content strategy firms or freelancers to assist with the time-consuming and expensive work of producing valuable content. At the time of this writing, a couple of the best-known firms are Contently and Federated Media. You can also find traditional media companies, such as the *Atlantic*, creating special divisions to provide content for businesses—in addition to publishing content provided by advertisers, which brings us to native advertising.

NATIVE ADVERTISING

In some cases, companies don't *just* want someone to produce quality content; they want to gain access and visibility to a specific market or audience they don't own or control. And so we come to native advertising. "Native advertising" is when any business or individual pays a publication to post promotional material that appears much like editorial content and is delivered to readers in the same manner as the publication's "native" content. Some publications include disclaimers on such content, using a label such as "sponsored content." Others don't—and a reader might not know for sure if the content is pay-for-play.

Examples of obvious native advertising:

- On April 15, 2015, the *Onion*, a satirical news website, publishes "Complete Idiot Forgot to Shave Area between Nose and Mouth" (clearly labeled as sponsored by Schick).
- On August 5, 2012, *Fast Company*, a business publication, runs an

infographic titled "UPS's 2012 Change in the (Supply) Chain Survey" (sponsored by UPS).

These examples might be less obvious to the average reader unless she looked closely:

- On March 17, 2014, the *Atlantic* publishes "As Big Data Grows, a New Role Emerges: the Chief Data Officer" (written by IBM executive David Laverty, and sponsored by IBM)
- In June 2014, the *New York Times* publishes an article on why the male prison model doesn't work for female inmates, on the occasion of the second season premiere of *Orange Is the New Black* (sponsored by Netflix)[6]

Native advertising has been around for a very long time in the form, for example, of print advertorials, but in the digital publishing era, it started growing in importance as traditional print advertising declined and traditional banner or display advertising was shown to be ineffective. While BuzzFeed did not invent native advertising, it was one of the first digital media companies to be driven by its success.[7] Other companies, which long avoided such editorial-advertising collaborations (or kept them secret), have since started to pursue such opportunities. In 2014 the *New York Times* launched T Brand Studio to work with clients seeking to produce and distribute quality content that would be relatively indistinguishable from other *Times* content.

Such developments aren't without controversy, and people throughout the industry continue to debate the ethics of the practice—or how to make it as ethically acceptable as possible, since some outlets can scarcely afford not to pursue any and all available funding opportunities.

A Note about Content Strategy

You'll commonly see the term "content strategist" bandied about. Content strategy, which grew out of the web development field, is often mentioned in connection with content marketing, but it's a concept that extends further and includes both editorial content and marketing content. You'll find content strategists working in government, education, business, and non-profit organizations.

The Content Strategy Alliance, in its 2014 charter, defines content strategy as "Getting the right content to the right user at the right time through strategic planning of content creation, delivery, and governance."[8] Sometimes content strategists are seen as another form of editor, but a true content strategist encompasses a range of business concerns, such as how content is optimized, distributed, and delivered, and how it might be repurposed. Content strategy could easily command a whole chapter of its own. To learn more, I recommend *Content Strategy for the Web* by Kristina Halverson and Melissa Rach.

Higher-minded creative types, especially in the marketing and advertising industries, will talk about "storytelling" instead of content. The purpose for this change in terminology is twofold: "storytelling" foregrounds a need for skill and artfulness, and it connotes deeper meaning or experience, at least when compared to "content."

SKILLS TO ACQUIRE

Unsurprisingly, the writing you learn in a creative writing class won't, by itself, teach you how to be a great in any of the job areas discussed above, but it should give you a good grounding in storytelling, which is often the number-one required skill. Similarly, anyone with excellent journalism skills, especially those with proven research chops, will be highly prized.

Aside from those skills, copywriting is probably the first area you'll want to gain knowledge of. It'll teach you how to write great headlines, how to use storytelling to your advantage, and the psychology of persuasion. Of the self-training options, one of the best go-to sites is Copyblogger. Also, while not a copywriting guide, a favorite book of many entrepreneurs is *Influence* by Robert Cialdini, which lays out timeless principles for those trying to persuade.

Search engine optimization (SEO) is an ever-changing technical pursuit, but every writer should understand what factors tend to strengthen or weaken SEO. Understanding SEO helps you create content that turns up in relevant online searches and thus can be found more easily. Businesses like Yoast and Moz often offer beginner-level courses. (Learn about SEO basics in chapters 18 and 21.)

You'll become very valuable to any company you work for if you understand how to read and understand online metrics, such as those culled from Google Analytics. The data is useless unless you know how to make it tell a story about how customers are behaving, what content is successful and why, and what the business's next steps should be. Because of the mountains of data that are now available about every aspect of consumer behavior—through Google, Facebook, and other forms of social media—it's usually not from lack of data that companies suffer, but from a lack of attention to the numbers and of discipline to heed the story they tell.

It's also very useful to gain basic knowledge of user experience (UX) as it applies to website, mobile, and app design. In most cases, the context and design of where writing appears is just as important as the writing itself. For example, one of the biggest UX issues today relates to traditional display or paid advertising on publication websites and mobile apps—because such advertising can take a long time to load and end up detracting from the user experience.

Those who excel and climb the ladder in content development and social media jobs are strategists at heart. They can see the big picture and have a vision for how many, different types of content and social engagement can add up to a larger, compelling story.

WHERE TO SEEK JOBS

Content marketing and native advertising jobs can be found everywhere, from large-circulation publications (both online and off) to Fortune 500 companies to local or regional businesses that need help with the company blog. These jobs are business-focused endeavors that require a willingness, if not a desire, to write material and tell stories that, while they may tie into a larger do-good mission or philosophy, will first and foremost be good for a company's PR or publicity. Writers who feel uncomfortable telling stories for the benefit of business would not be a good fit in this field, or would need to choose carefully which companies they work for—preferably businesses that have core values matching their own, and a demonstrated, ongoing interest in something beyond the bottom line and quarterly financial results.

MediaBistro is one of the first places to check for jobs in the field. JournalismJobs.com also features a handful of listings. Expect titles such as marketing associate, content producer, or digital content specialist. Most entry-level positions involve lots of administration and scheduling, content management, and low-level writing. As you gain experience, jobs deal more with high-level strategy and campaigns, and may be called director of content marketing or content strategist. The highest-level role is typically chief content officer.

As you look at job postings, it's important to understand the difference between inbound and outbound marketing, which we touched on briefly in chapter 22. "Inbound marketing" aims to attract and capitalize on customers coming *into* your website or owned territory. Inbound marketing gains the attention of the customer and draws prospects to the website through great content or storytelling. This is the domain of content marketing. "Outbound marketing" involves more traditional marketing, for example, advertising. Most writers will want to focus on positions that involve inbound marketing, since they're far more likely to be qualified for and satisfied by them. (Nearly all companies do a mix of inbound and outbound marketing, with inbound marketing as the growth area.)

You'll also see the following terms used: earned media, owned media, and paid media. "Paid media" is pay-for-play placement, such as advertising, native advertising, or sponsorships. "Owned media" includes a business's website, blog, social media accounts, and anything related to content marketing. "Earned media" is when consumers do the marketing for you—the coveted "viral" video, for example, or fan-driven efforts that lead to publicity. While many organizations desire earned media, it is by definition out of their control, and can become negative. For example, in 2014, the New York Police Department tried a Twitter outreach campaign, putting out a call for photos of citizens and their friendly neighborhood cops. While some people responded as the department had hoped, the campaign quickly became an opportunity for people to criticize the NYPD with photos and stories reflecting police brutality and racial profiling.

For those with a high level of interest in the field, it's best to create and maintain a portfolio of work at Contently (one of the major firms in the content marketing industry) and to actively read its online magazine *The Content Strategist*. (It also publishes *The Freelancer*—just as useful.) Contently keeps tabs on the writers who register at its site and will sometimes proactively contact freelancers who look like a good match for a client. The site also has a strong repository of resources and case studies for writers seeking to broaden their knowledge and skills.

AFTERWORD

In this book, I have endeavored to convey sincerely what writers should know about building a successful career. Of course, some things about the writing life can only be learned through experience and by figuring out your own abilities and thresholds. Being open to experimentation, and accepting of uncertainty and failure, is enormously useful. If that doesn't describe you, try to fake it until it becomes natural.

For the most part, I have set aside any discussion of the life obligations that inevitably interfere with our best-laid plans. We're each faced with individual challenges that affect how and when we pursue the writing life. You may have family to provide for, and that must take priority above writing, or need a health care plan that only an employer can provide, or struggle with debt. Sometimes pursuing the writing life in the way you would like, or putting it at the center of your life, seems a tremendous luxury. Whatever your situation, if you're not making the progress you would hope for, and it's because life is getting in the way, my best advice is to take the pressure off yourself.

Early in my career, when I began speaking at writing conferences as an editor in the industry, I found it difficult to be among hundreds of writers who would often ask if I was a writer and what I was writing. Back then, I didn't have time to focus on my own work, but as a graduate of a writing program, I felt like acknowledging this was admitting failure. Once, when I'd made this guilty admission for what felt like the hundredth time, a kind woman took my hand and said, "Why, of course. You're exhausted." Finally, someone had given me permission to not be writing. I woke up to the unnaturalness of the expectation I had of myself, and stopped feeling guilty.

I spent fifteen years as an editor and teacher, mainly not focusing on my own writing, but they were not wasted years. I was building other skills and laying a foundation to earn a living that would support the writing life I now have—with more freedom and time. The struggle now is fear: fear of failure and not measuring up. (Those fears never go away, but one does become more adept at facing them when they appear.) One of the great secrets to building the writing life you want is to pursue a vision that is truly yours, rather than someone else's expectation weighing on your shoulders, and take what you're doing now—even if it's not what you planned—and use that as a stepping-stone to the next phase of your career. You will undoubtedly, as I have, experience a range of distractions and circuitous paths, but all experience can productively affect and contribute to your work.

APPENDIX 1: CONTRACTS 101

To negotiate a writing, freelancing, or publishing contract that serves your best interests, you need some familiarity with the legal language of publishing. Yet few writers and agents speak openly about contracts they've successfully negotiated or what standard terms look like—and most publishers or outlets don't make their contracts available for public scrutiny. Short of hiring a literary lawyer, which is impractical for most nonbook contracts, writers can be left muddling through on their own.

This section offers only a brief introduction. A comprehensive guide would require a book of its own. While I am not a lawyer, and this does not constitute professional advice, it should help you spot a rights grab or contract language that may do you long-term harm.

MUST-KNOW CONTRACT LANGUAGE FOR ALL WRITERS

The act of *granting rights* in a contract does not traditionally mean giving up your copyright. The moment you write something, or put ideas into tangible form, it is protected under the US Copyright Law, and you own the copyright. "Granting" rights to your work simply means you are licensing or granting permission to a person or a company to publish a specific piece of your work—that you own copyright in—under certain circumstances, in certain formats and venues, for a stated amount of time.

Exclusive and *nonexclusive* are critical words you should look for and carefully consider in every contract. Broadly speaking, "nonexclusive" works in your favor and gives you more flexibility; you are "sharing" the rights with a publisher, and you can share them as well with other people and continue to profit from the work in any way you like. "Exclusive" means you commit the work to a single publisher, at least for the time specified in the contract. That ties up your rights and abilities; it means the publisher is the one and only party that can use, publish, or distribute the work in question. Exclusivity, therefore, traditionally comes with better compensation. Some contracts will list exclusive and nonexclusive grants of rights separately, for clarity.

Work-for-hire contracts assign all rights to the material you write, including copyright, to the person or company that is paying you. You lose any ability to reuse or resell that material. The contract may not say "work for hire," but instead say that your work is the "sole and exclusive property" of the publication. It may also slip the phrase "all rights" into a complex sentence with multiple clauses that is hard to unpack. If you sign such a contract or agree to give up all rights to a piece, make sure the compensation is appropriate for the nature of the work, because you'll never be able to earn another dime off it, or even use it in a future collection of your own work, unless you negotiate a contract provision that grants you that permission.

MAGAZINE, LITERARY JOURNAL, AND ONLINE PUBLICATION CONTRACTS

The first thing you should look for is the grant of rights clause, often at the beginning of the contract, which specifies what rights you are granting or licensing to a publication. Before the internet, a typical contract for a magazine article in the United States asked for "first North American serial rights." Essentially, this granted the magazine first dibs on publishing your work in print, in North America. Often the writer would also need to promise not to resell that piece, or repurpose it, for a specified time after publication. If the magazine wished to reuse the work (for example, reprinting the piece in a special issue), a reprint fee would have to be paid or negotiated. This is still how many print-based contracts work. Here is a generic example of what this looks like in a typical contract:

> Writer hereby grants and assigns to the Publisher exclusive first North American print rights for ninety (90) days after the Publisher's first publication of the Work. . . . In the event Publisher reprints the Work in any of its products, Publisher shall pay to Writer an additional sum of 10% of the original Compensation for each such reprint.

If you agreed to the language above, you would be giving the publisher an *exclusive* right to the material, in print in North America, for 90 days. If they want to reprint it, they would need to pay you 10 percent of your original rate each time they do so. If they want to publish and distribute it on another continent, they'll need to negotiate a new contract or clause with you. (Note that this clause says nothing about online or digital rights; with print contracts, those areas are often covered separately, sometimes in a subclause. We'll get to that in a minute.)

What's a reasonable period of exclusivity? It depends on the frequency of the publication, as well as the nature of the material. A quarterly publication might reasonably ask for 90 to 180 days of exclusivity, while a weekly should ask for a fraction of that. The longer and more important the piece—and the more the publication has invested in it—the more justification it may have to ask for a longer period of exclusivity.

It's now nearly impossible for a writer to sign a print-based article contract without also granting some digital rights to the material. By law, a print publication is allowed to include your work in its digital replicas. "Digital replica" refers to a version of the print issue in digital form, in which the print presentation remains intact—including advertising, article order, and so on. For example, when the *New Yorker* released its entire archive of issues going back to 1925 in digital form, it did not need to secure further rights or pay the contributors, because it was distributing replicas of the print issues.

Writers have more room to negotiate digital rights when it comes to how their work is made available outside the context of a full issue. "Out of context" usually means (1) on the publication's website, whether available for free or to subscribers only, and (2) as part of online database access, such as through libraries. The most favorable scenario for the writer is a nonexclusive arrangement. This allows the publication to keep your article available as part of its online or digital archive for as long as it wishes, but not to prevent you from reselling or reusing the material elsewhere.

It pays to study up on how the publication markets and promotes content from the print issue online. While some writers may value exposure over exclusivity, you want to ensure you're getting paid appropriately for how your work is used. At the same time, you don't want to miss out on good marketing and promotion, or word of mouth, because you refused to give the publication any permission to use your work in an online context. Each writer weighs these choices differently: scarcity may sometimes increase a piece's value in the long run, but it's also nice if your mom (or a potential new editor) can read your article online.

Here is a generic example of what an online grant of rights might look like:

The Author agrees to grant to the Publication: (a) nonexclusive worldwide online rights after first publication of the Work; and (b) the perpetual, worldwide right to reproduce, display, and distribute the Work in digital, individually retrievable, form via a website or database associated with the Publication identified above.

Agreeing to this clause allows the publication to keep your work available on its website or other online properties, in individually retrievable form (out of context of the full issue), as long as such sites are associated with the publication. However, it's a nonexclusive grant, so it also allows you to reuse and resell the work however you wish. Note the word "worldwide"; with very few exceptions, worldwide online rights must be granted (since most publications make their online media accessible to the world), but this doesn't affect the limiting of print rights to North America.

Typically, an online-only contract—in cases where there is no print publication, and *especially* when you're being paid little or nothing—will ask for limited exclusivity (generally 90 days or less), and nonexclusive rights thereafter. Online publications that are high-profile and pay well may be in a position to demand long periods of exclusivity. Either way, many online-only contracts may ask for blanket, nonexclusive rights to reuse or repurpose your material for e-books, digital collections or anthologies, special digital magazine issues, and so on. If the publication would profit off such use, consider using that as a negotiation tool to ask for more money, or see if you can strike such reuse from your contract if you don't see any benefit to your work being repurposed in that way. At the very least, you should ask to be notified when reuse occurs.

BOOK PUBLISHING CONTRACTS

If you're offered a deal with a traditional book publisher, your contract will follow one of these three conventions:

- **Life-of-copyright contracts.** This describes the typical traditional print book publishing contract. The author grants the publisher rights to publish the work, potentially for the duration of the work's copyright (life of the author plus 70 years, in the United States) unless specific conditions are met under which rights revert to the author.
- **Fixed-term contracts.** These contracts grant rights to the publisher for a set time limit (e.g., five years), after which all rights revert to the author.
- **Work-for-hire contracts.** As with all work-for-hire agreements, author gives up all rights to the work, including copyright.

None of these contracts is necessarily more favorable than the other; much depends on the work being contracted, the compensation, and the author's goals. Life-of-copyright contracts should be expected from most traditional publishers. Fixed-term contracts are used more often by e-book or digital-only publishers. Work-for-hire is common with publisher-developed series, book packagers, and ghostwriting projects.

While it sounds ominous, "life-of-copyright" contracts are not expected to last until the copyright expires. Rather, the contract typically remains in effect for as long as sales occur. The reversion-of-rights clause details specific conditions under which rights can revert to the author, and may even state the sales figure that must be sustained for the publisher to keep the rights to sell and distribute the work. Here is a generic example of what a life-of-copyright grant of rights looks like:

> The Author hereby assigns to the Publisher the exclusive right to publish, reproduce and distribute the Work and derivatives thereof in all languages in any and all forms/media whether now known or hereafter invented and to exercise and grant to third parties any of said rights to the Work, throughout the world, for the full term of copyright available to the Work.

Any good literary agent would tell you that this example is not very favorable to the author, but if the advance and royalties were right, it could be acceptable. Most agents would negotiate for an amended clause that limits the publisher's claim to the rights enumerated, or at the very least puts a limit on how long the publisher can exploit certain rights—meaning the author can get rights back within a short timeframe if the publisher has not sold or made use of them.

For any life-of-copyright contract, it's essential to review the termination or rights-reversion clauses. You need to ask for specific sales minimums that would automatically trigger reversion of rights, so the publisher can't sit on your book indefinitely by arguing that a translated edition selling in Mongolia constitutes being "in print," even if the book isn't selling a single copy in English. Worst-case scenario: US law does allow for authors to sever a life-of-copyright contract after thirty-five years when certain conditions are met. Fixed-term contracts can be easier for an author to review and negotiate since the term is clear-cut.

Book contracts are far more complicated than most magazine contracts. If you don't have an agent, consider becoming a member of the Authors Guild, which offers contract review services. Also, there are "literary lawyers" you can hire on an hourly basis; run a search on the term to begin uncovering potential people you can hire, or try asking the industry watch-dog site Writer Beware for guidance on finding one.

NON-COMPETE CLAUSES AND WORK-FOR-HIRE AGREEMENTS

If you sign a non-compete clause while working with an employer, publi-cation, or publisher, you hamper your ability to work with others—or even for yourself. Thus, you should hesitate before signing one. Here's a typical, very restrictive non-compete clause in a traditional book contract:

> While this Agreement is in effect, the Author shall not, without the prior written consent of the Publisher, write, edit, or publish, or cause to be written, edited, or published in any format, any other competing work that is of a similar character on the same subject matter or that is in the judgment of the Publisher likely to interfere with or injure the sale of the Work.

In plain English, this means: While your book remains under contract (which might be decades, remember), you cannot publish any work (book-length or otherwise), in print, digital, or any other form, for any other publisher or publication—or on your own—that would be categorized as similar to your book or that the publisher thinks might hurt the present book's sales. This type of restriction has serious implications for a writer trying to make a living off her writing. It can create a dependency on this one publisher either to give her sufficient work or to grant her leeway to produce her work for others.

It's most important that you be able to continue making a living in a way that's fair and reasonable. A publisher of a single book or article shouldn't prevent you from doing the work you normally do, unless, of course, the publisher is contracting you for work that might constitute a new full-time living. If you're working with an agent, make sure you're on the same page about your writing and publishing over the long term, so that your contract doesn't leave you stuck, unable to publish future work, or in a breach-of-contract situation.

Once fairly innocuous, the non-compete clause is becoming a hot-button issue for writers who work for established media companies and media-tech start-ups, either full time or on a contract basis. The non-compete clause often goes hand in hand with a work-for-hire agreement, which means that any and all work you produce during your contract or employment automatically becomes the property of your employer. That may include your social media accounts, any creative work you do outside the office, book contracts, and any branding your employer creates that's associated with your name.

New and young writers looking for their first job or big break may not think twice about signing contracts that grab all of their intellectual property rights and temporarily prevent them from doing creative work once they sever ties. Even if you have very little negotiating power, try to push back in these ways:

- Reduce the term of the non-compete. Can you reduce it to three or six months? You can make a reasonable argument that you need to be able to make a living when your contract or employment terminates.
- Always define what constitutes a "competitor." If possible, list the specific names of competing companies that you cannot work for or be affiliated with during the term of the clause. This reduces the most immediate threat for your employer or publisher, who is probably worried about you defecting to some particular place that's known for poaching high-value employees and contributors.
- Spell out specific types of work you are allowed to engage in or keep your rights to. Maybe you're writing and maintaining a blog on a specific topic that shouldn't fall under the purview of your employment or contract, or maybe you want the freedom to teach or speak at events without needing to seek permission. Think through all possible scenarios and put in writing what you want the freedom to do. When new opportunities arise, create a paper trail that indicates the company said it was OK for you to engage in those activities and that you own rights (if applicable) to any work created.

PARTING ADVICE

Whenever presented with a contract, assume everything is negotiable. Don't be shy about asking what the language means if you don't understand it clearly, and ask to modify any boilerplate agreement you're given. The worst that could happen is that the publication or employer says no. Remember that nearly every publisher's or employer's contract is built to protect its interests, not yours. Stick up for yourself, and be wary of any editor or manager who tells you, "Oh, you don't need to worry about that clause. That never happens." Don't trust anyone's reassurance that the contract language doesn't matter. It's in the contract for a reason, and it has the potential to affect you, your work, and your earnings potential.

- **For more in-depth guidance on contracts and contract language, see businessofwriting.org.**

APPENDIX 2: LEGAL ISSUES

With more writers than ever publishing on their own, whether online or in print, legal issues now arise far more frequently as part of everyday business. Having an experienced agent or editor on hand can be of incalculable value, but as with contracts, writers have a responsibility to educate themselves on a few key issues, to ensure they understand their own rights and the rights of others. Pleading ignorance is not an effective defense should you find yourself in hot water.

COPYRIGHT AND PROTECTING YOUR WORK

Writers can be particularly concerned about how to prevent their unpublished work from being stolen by unscrupulous people. While I am not an attorney, years of experience in publishing have shown me that writers can be overly anxious, if not paranoid, about this issue. Many warnings you might run across are unnecessary and counterproductive. My goal in discussing your rights as an unpublished author is to give you information based on the actual likelihood that something bad will happen to you. (Note: The following advice is directed toward writers of prose and poetry. Screenwriters or playwrights should consult the Writers Guild of America website for registration information specific to their field.)

First, it is not possible under current US law to copyright or protect an idea, and you'll inevitably find other writers with ideas similar to your own. Chalk it up to the cultural zeitgeist. Ideas are a dime a dozen, and everything depends on execution. So share your work with trusted mentors or critique partners, send it to publishing professionals for consideration, and talk about aspects of it when you're networking at conferences. It's not worth the energy to worry about the small chance an idea will be stolen. In any case, you can't work professionally as a writer for very long without pitching your ideas to others.

No matter how valuable you think your idea is, do not tell an editor or agent that you can't disclose the details until they sign a nondisclosure agreement (NDA). They will reject you outright for withholding information that would help them decide whether to do business with you. You have to be up-front and clear about every aspect of your project. Don't expect anyone to go out of their way and create a special business agreement with you because you're nervous about idea theft. Such anxiety is more likely to hurt you in these situations than protect you.

When it comes to protecting your actual writing—including unpublished manuscripts—you do not have to officially register it with the US Copyright Office for it to be protected under the law. Nor do you need to put the copyright symbol anywhere on your work for it to be protected. As US copyright law is currently written, as soon as you express your work in tangible form, it is protected. You will, however, need to register the work if you find infringement and wish to sue.

The frank truth is that no one sees unpublished writing as an untapped gold mine. It's hard work to profit from a piece of writing—especially writing from an unknown writer. Therefore, the threat of infringement is very low when you're submitting to already very busy agents and editors. However, if you self-publish your work or otherwise begin selling it publicly, then you should officially register it with the Copyright Office.

PERMISSIONS

Permissions allow you to quote or excerpt other people's copyrighted work within your own. Obtaining permissions requires contacting the copyright owner (or their publisher or agent) and requesting permission to use the work. You may be charged a fee for the use, anywhere from a few dollars to thousands of dollars.

But it's not always necessary to seek permission. Some quotations of copyrighted work are regarded as "fair use." So how do you know if your use is fair? The most common "rule" you'll find, if you search online or ask people, is "Ask explicit permission for everything beyond X." And what is "X"? Some people say 300 words. Some say one line. Some say 10 percent of the original work's word count.

In fact, there is no legal rule stipulating what quantity is OK under fair use. Major legal battles have been fought over this question, but this remains one of the grayest areas of copyright law. Any rules you find will be based on a general institutional guideline or a person's experience, as well as their overall comfort level with the risk involved in quoting or excerpting work. (There's also a risk to asking permission. Once you do, some publishers or copyright owners will take the opportunity to ask for money or refuse permission, even in cases where the use would actually be considered fair.) It's important to recognize that crediting a source does not remove the obligation to seek permission. It is expected that you will credit your sources regardless of fair use; otherwise, you are plagiarizing.

But while there is no black-and-white rule you can apply, there are principles. And there are, fortunately, a few clear-cut cases in which you do *not* need to seek permission:

- When the work is in the public domain. This isn't always a simple matter to determine, but any work published before 1923 is in the public domain. Some works published after 1923 are also in the public domain.
- When simply mentioning the title or author of a work.
- When you are stating unadorned facts. If you copy a list of the fifty states in the United States, you are not infringing on anyone's copyright. Those are straightforward facts.
- When you are linking to something online. Linking does not require permission.
- When the work is licensed under Creative Commons. Such a license should be prominently declared on the work itself.

Principles of Fair Use

There are four criteria for determining fair use, which sounds tidy, but it's not. The criteria are vague and open to interpretation. Ultimately, when disagreement arises over what constitutes fair use, it's up to the courts to make a decision. The four criteria are as follows:

- The purpose and character of the use (e.g., commercial versus not-for-profit/educational). If the purpose of your work is commercial (to make money), that doesn't mean you're necessarily in violation of fair use. But it makes your case less sympathetic if you're borrowing a lot of someone else's work to prop up your own commercial venture.
- The nature of the copyrighted work. Facts cannot be copyrighted. For that reason, more creative or imaginative works generally get the strongest protection.
- The amount and substantiality of the portion quoted in relation to the entire original work. Again, the law does not specify any percentage or word count. If what you quote is considered the most valuable part of the work, even if it is comparatively brief, you may be violating fair use.
- The effect of the use on the potential market for or value of the quoted work. If your use of the original work reduces the likelihood that people will buy the original work, you can be in violation of fair

use. That is, if you quote the material so extensively or in some other way such that the original source is no longer required, then you may be affecting the market for the quoted work. (Don't confuse this criteria with the purpose of reviews or criticism. If a negative review dissuades people from buying a publication, this is not related to the question of fair use.)

Some writers wonder if these fair use guidelines still apply to copyrighted work on websites, blogs, and other digital publishing platforms—given the rampant infringement that is typical on the internet. Yes, the law still applies, but attitudes online tend to be more lax, which of course confuses matters further. When online publishers and writers aggregate, repurpose, or otherwise excerpt copyrighted work (whether it originated online or offline), they typically view such use as "sharing" or "publicity" for the original author rather than as copyright violation, especially if it's for noncommercial or educational purposes. I'm not talking about wholesale piracy here, but about extensive excerpting or aggregating that would not be considered OK in other contexts. It's a controversial issue that's outside of the scope of this book.

A final word of warning: Because song lyrics and poems are generally so short—and because songwriters and music publishers are more formally organized, represented, and at times litigious—it's dangerous to use even one line without asking for permission, even if you think the use could be considered fair. However, it's fine to use song titles, poem titles, artist names, band names, movie titles, and so on. (Titles aren't protected under US copyright law.)

MENTIONING BRANDS OR TRADEMARKED ENTITIES

Generally speaking, you do not need permission to mention branded or well-known products in your stories, whether fictional or not. Your character can smoke Camels, drive a Jeep, and binge on Goetze's Caramel Creams without any risk—and it's not necessary to use the copyright or trademark symbol when mentioning them. Your writing is considered a noncommercial context when it comes to such mentions, which relieves you of any legal obligation.

DEFAMATION: LIBEL AND SLANDER

Writers are at risk of being sued for defamation when they communicate a false statement that harms the reputation of another person, a business, or even a nation. Slander is spoken defamation; libel is defamation in writing.

If what you write is the truth, that's the best defense of all against defamation. There are other defenses available, but a writer who prefers to stay out of court will at all times seek and write only the truth to the best of their knowledge. Unfortunately, if what you write displeases someone, truthfulness can't prevent your being sued; it only helps ensure that you win what can easily be an expensive and prolonged legal battle.

Defamation doesn't apply only to journalists, freelancers, and other nonfiction writers. It affects *all* writers. If a novel features a character who is recognizably based on a real person, and that person is portrayed negatively, that person can sue the writer for defamation. That's why fictionalizing a true-to-life story is not a reliable method to avoid lawsuit. Additionally, defamation laws in other countries can be less favorable to writers, meaning you could find yourself sued by someone in another country even if your work wouldn't be considered defamatory in a US court. Writers can protect themselves through the following measures:

- When writing fiction based on real people or even businesses—if the portrayals might be perceived in a negative light—change identifying characteristics so that they can't be recognized.
- Stick to the facts, and let readers come to their own judgments. If writing nonfiction about specific people or companies, relate verifiable details or your experience, avoiding accusations of deviance or criminality. Let the reader decide—the old "show, don't tell" rule.
- Don't write anything to get even.
- For freelancers, journalists, or others who publish regularly: review your contracts; does the publication bear any responsibility should a lawsuit arise? If not, it's wise to buy media libel insurance from the Authors Guild, the Freelancers Union, or another organization.

Fortunately, writers are rarely sued and defamation claims are hard to prove, since they require proof that a reputation has been harmed. Still, the safest strategy is to avoid writing and publishing something that might provoke a lawsuit from someone with the financial resources to fuel a legal battle.

INVASION OF PRIVACY

Here's where things become more complicated. Writing and publishing the truth doesn't protect you from invasion-of-privacy lawsuits. If you disclose embarrassing or unpleasant facts about an identifiable, private person that aren't of public interest, then you could be accused of invasion of privacy. However, public conduct is not protected, especially today when cameras are everywhere.

Invasion of privacy can also apply to public figures and celebrities. For example, you may have heard of the lawsuit former wrestler Hulk Hogan filed against online publisher Gawker, which posted a sex video of Hogan. Gawker argued that Hogan had lost his expectation of privacy by discussing his sex life in public, but Hogan's lawyers successfully argued that publishing the video was an invasion of his privacy. Another example is J. K. Rowling's victory in the UK against paparazzi taking photos of her son; the court ruled that the children of famous parents should be protected from intrusive media attention.

RIGHT OF PUBLICITY

You cannot use someone else's likeness, name, or identifying information for commercial purposes—and it doesn't matter whether the person is a private or public individual. The law can even apply to using the likeness or name of a dead person. In practical terms, this means you shouldn't merchandise or sell anything (whether a book, T-shirt, or freelance service) with the likeness of another person without their explicit permission. However, it is perfectly acceptable under the law to write about famous and historical figures if the use is expressive—which of course includes journalistic and creative writing. It's also OK to write about people when it's in the public interest, assuming your work doesn't constitute defamation or invasion of privacy.

APPENDIX 3: RECOMMENDED RESOURCES

PRACTICAL GUIDES TO GETTING PUBLISHED

Published every year since 1920, the Writer's Market annual directories offer instruction and information on how and where to get your work published. The biggest one is *Writer's Market*, which covers all paying markets in both book publishing and magazine publishing. For fiction writers, *Novel & Short Story Writer's Market* is a more comprehensive, focused listing that includes smaller presses and literary journals that may pay very little, or even nothing. *Children's Writer's & Illustrator's Market*, as it name implies, is specifically for writers seeking to publish anything in the juvenile market, from picture books to young adult novels. *Poet's Market* lists places to publish individual poems as well as full collections. *Guide to Literary Agents* lists hundreds of literary agents, mostly US- and UK-based.

The Writer's Digest Guide to Query Letters (2008) by Wendy Burt-Thomas offers instruction in basic query writing and includes query letter examples for each major genre and category.

The Essential Guide to Getting Your Book Published (2005) by Arielle Eckstut and David Sterry is the most comprehensive guide you'll find on the topic—written by an agent and an editor.

How to Write a Book Proposal by Michael Larsen, a literary agent, is the industry-standard guide to book proposal writing. It first appeared in the 1980s and has been updated regularly ever since.

Thinking Like Your Editor: How to Write Great Serious Nonfiction and Get It Published (2002) by Susan Rabiner and Alfred Fortunato is a now-classic guide for any writer seeking to publish a nonfiction book, by a well-respected New York editor and agent and her freelance editor husband.

Formatting & Submitting Your Manuscript (2009) by Chuck Sambuchino offers visual examples of how to format your submissions materials—by genre, category, and purpose.

Get a Literary Agent (2014) by Chuck Sambuchino is a straightforward guide to literary agents, including how to query and pitch.

The First Five Pages (2000) by Noah Lukeman shows with clear examples how agents and editors can tell within the first five pages if a manuscript is worth reading further.

The Forest for the Trees (2000) by Betsy Lerner is a New York editor's sage and timeless advice to writers who seek publication. (She's now an agent.)

The Fine Print of Self-Publishing (2006) by Mark Levine is regularly updated and has become the go-to guide for self-publishing authors in the age of e-books and online retail.

APE: Author, Publisher, Entrepreneur (2012) by Guy Kawasaki is an easy-to-digest guide to the self-publishing process, for absolute beginners.

AUTHOR PLATFORM AND BOOK MARKETING AND PROMOTION

Platform (2012) by Michael Hyatt is a *New York Times* best-selling book on how to build your author platform.

Your First 1,000 Copies (2013) by Tim Grahl is a short, helpful guide on how to sell your self-published book, by a professional marketer who has helped best-selling authors.

THE BOOK PUBLISHING INDUSTRY

"The Business of Literature" by Richard Nash (*Virginia Quarterly Review*, Spring 2013) discusses what the digital era augurs for the business of publishing.

Merchants of Culture (2010) by John B. Thompson is an engagingly written history of US and UK trade publishing in the twenty-first century, by a Cambridge professor.

The Late Age of Print (2009) by Ted Striphas is helpful for understanding where book publishing has been, and how it is changing (or might change) in response to the digital era.

MAGAZINE WRITING AND FREELANCING

The Essential Guide to Freelance Writing (2015) by Zac Petit is a comprehensive guide for beginners, written by the editor in chief of *PRINT* magazine, who still works as a freelancer on the side.

For highly practical information on making a living from freelance writing, two of the best resources are Make a Living Writing (www.makealivingwriting.com) and The International Freelancer (www.theinternationalfreelancer.com). FreelanceWritingGigs.com is also a rich source of leads for writers trying to establish a client base.

LEGAL ISSUES

The Copyright Permission and Libel Handbook (1998) by Lloyd Jassin and Steven M. Schechter is one of the few guides to sorting through legal issues in written work, particularly those pertaining to permissions.

Kirsch's Guide to the Book Contract (1999) by Jonathan Kirsch is a reference book that every agent has on their desk.

ACKNOWLEDGMENTS AND CREDITS

This book would not exist were it not for the encouragement and proactive efforts of its editor, Mary Laur, who has been such a wonderful advocate and sharp reader. I would also like to thank Joel Score for his meticulous copyediting; Lauren Salas for her marketing and promotion support; Richard Nash, who provided early guidance on the book's scope and direction; and Jay Swanson, for his useful feedback as a working writer.

For her help during the drafting process, I am indebted to Kelly Figueroa-Ray, who was indispensable in her research and organizational support to prepare this manuscript for publication. Finally, my partner in all things, Mark Griffin, has been unfailingly patient and cheerful as I spent countless weekends engulfed in writing and editing this book. Most writers only dream of having someone so supportive and understanding.

Portions of this book are adapted from material first posted at Jane Friedman.com.

A portion of chapter 5 is adapted from "The Book P&L," *Scratch* magazine (Spring 2014).

Portions of chapter 8 are adapted from "The Future Value of a Literary Publisher," published in *Literary Publishing in the Twenty-First Century* (Minneapolis: Milkweed Editions, 2016); "The Future of the Gatekeepers," in *The Little Magazine in Contemporary America* (Chicago: University of Chicago Press, 2015); and a symposium on the future of literary publishing, in *Boulevard*, nos. 92–93 (2016).

Appendix 1, "Contracts 101," is adapted from the "Contracts 101" series in *Scratch* magazine.

NOTES

PART ONE

1. Dr. Edward Eggleston, quoted in "Poetry," *Literary World* (Boston), 21 (1890): 88.

2. Richard Nash, Twitter, September 13, 2016, 12:01 a.m., https://twitter.com/R _Nash/status/773370482007638018.

3. "Dana Gioia on the Close Connection between Business and Poetry," Knowledge@Wharton, May 30, 2007, http://knowledge.wharton.upenn.edu /article/dana-gioia-on-the-close-connection-between-business-and-poetry.

CHAPTER 1

1. Mark Rose, *Authors and Owners: The Invention of Copyright* (Cambridge, MA: Harvard University Press, 1993), 4.

2. Elizabeth Hyde Stevens, "Borges and $: The Parable of the Literary Master and the Coin," *Longreads* blog, June 14, 2016, https://blog.longreads.com/2016/06 /14/borges-and-money/.

3. "Ira Glass on Storytelling," part 3 of 4 (Public Radio International, 2009), https://www.youtube.com/watch?v=X2wLPoizeJE, 0:30–1:12.

4. "Advice on Writing from the *Atlantic*'s Ta-Nehisi Coates," *Atlantic*, September 27, 2013, https://www.theatlantic.com/video/index/280025/advice-on-writing -from-i-the-atlantic-i-s-ta-nehisi-coates/, 3:16–3:37.

5. Rosamund Stone Zander and Benjamin Zander, *The Art of Possibility* (Boston, MA: Harvard Business Press, 2000), 1.

6. Paul Graham, "How to Do What You Love," January 2006, http://www.paul graham.com/love.html.

CHAPTER 2

1. Clay Shirky, *Cognitive Surplus: Creativity and Generosity in a Connected Age* (New York: Penguin Books, 2010).

2. Daniel Lyons, "Has Arianna Huffington Figured Out the Future?," *Newsweek*, July 25, 2010, http://www.newsweek.com/has-arianna-huffington-figured-out -future-74833.

3. George Packer, "The Struggling Writer: Gissing Had It Right," *New York Times*, October 13, 1991, http://www.nytimes.com/1991/10/13/books/the -struggling-writer-gissing-had-it-right.html.

4. "Ira Glass on Storytelling," part 3 of 4 (Public Radio International, 2009), https://www.youtube.com/watch?v=X2wLPoizeJE, 1:35–1:37.

5. Here I am partly indebted to Michael Margolis, "The Resume Is Dead, The Bio Is King," *99U*, May 11, 2011, http://99u.com/articles/7025/the-resume-is-dead -the-bio-is-king.

6. Michael Ellsberg, "How to Connect with Powerful and Influential People," March 6, 2014, http://www.ellsberg.com/awesomeness-fest.

7. Chris Guillebeau, "279 Days to Overnight Success: An Unconventional Journey to Full-Time Writing," 2009, 31–32, http://chrisguillebeau.com/files/2009/04/279days.pdf.

8. Becky Tuch, "All Work and No Pay Makes Jack a Dull Writer," *Various Small Flames*, May 24, 2014, https://variousmallflames.wordpress.com/2014/04/24/all-work-and-no-pay/.

9. Paul Graham, "How to Do What You Love," January 2006, http://www.paulgraham.com/love.html.

10. Richard Wiseman, *The Luck Factor: Changing Your Luck, Changing Your Life: The Four Essential Principles* (New York: Miramax/Hyperion, 2003).

CHAPTER 3

1. With thanks to Kevin Smokler.

2. Jane Friedman, "An Interview with Richard Nash: The Future of Publishing" (blog post), September 22, 2015, https://janefriedman.com/an-interview-with-richard-nash/.

3. Roxane Gay, *Hunger: A Memoir of (My) Body* (New York: HarperCollins, 2017).

4. Debbie Ridpath Ohi, "Inkygirl," Instagram, accessed July 4, 2016, https://www.instagram.com/inkygirl/.

5. Robert Lee Brewer, "Poetic Asides" (blog), *Writers Digest*, accessed June 17, 2016, http://www.writersdigest.com/editor-blogs/poetic-asides.

6. Jane Friedman, "Book Publishing Statistics," Pinterest, accessed June 17, 2016, https://www.pinterest.com/janefriedman/book-publishing-statistics/.

7. Austin Kleon, *Show Your Work! 10 Ways to Share Your Creativity and Get Discovered* (New York: Workman Publishing, 2014), 23.

8. Friedman, "Interview with Richard Nash."

9. See TheJohnFox.com and CliffordGarstang.com

10. Yiyun Lee, "A Letter from Yiyun Lee." A Public Space. Oct. 1, 2013. http://apublicspace.org/blog/detail/a_letter_from_yiyun_li

11. Rosamund Stone Zander and Benjamin Zander, *The Art of Possibility* (Boston, MA: Harvard Business Press, 2000).

CHAPTER 5

1. George Haven Putnam and John Bishop Putnam, *Authors and Publishers: A Manual of Suggestions for Beginners in Literature* (New York: Knickerbocker Press, 1904), v.

2. For an example of the type of conversation that occurs after every merger/acquisition, see Boris Kachka, "Book Publishing's Big Gamble," *New York Times*, July 9, 2013, http://www.nytimes.com/2013/07/10/opinion/book-publishings-big-gamble.html.

3. Author Earnings (website), "Apple, B&N, Kobo, and Google: A Look at the Rest of the Ebook Market," October 2015, http://authorearnings.com/report /october-2015-apple-bn-kobo-and-google-a-look-at-the-rest-of-the-ebook-market/.

4. "Traditional Print Book Production Dipped Slightly in 2013: New Report Also Shows Print-on-Demand Experienced a Steep Decline after Years of Stunning Growth," ProQuest press release, August 5, 2014, http://www.bowker.com/news /2014/Traditional-Print-Book-Production-Dipped-Slightly-in-2013.html.

5. Porter Anderson, "Glimpses of the US Market: Charts from Nielsen's Kempton Mooney," *Publishing Perspectives*, May 20, 2016, http://publishingperspectives .com/2016/05/us-market-kempton-nielsen/.

6. For the Nielsen BookScan 2004–2013 report, see "Kids Books Matter More in Print and in Store, as Teens Warm Up to eBooks—and Lose Interest in Reading," *Publishers Lunch*, January 13, 2014, http://lunch.publishersmarketplace.com/2014 /01/kids-books-matter-print-store-teens-warm-ebooks-lose-interest-reading/.

7. Daniel Menaker, "What Does the Book Business Look Like on the Inside?," *New York Magazine*, November 16, 2013, http://www.vulture.com/2013/11/daniel -menaker-on-publishing-industry-insanity.html.

8. Jane Friedman, "Book Publishing P&L Statement," Google Docs, posted August 8, 2016, https://docs.google.com/spreadsheets/d/1UvtNSvsrT7YrYTjHId _rmjLAuUbQizSaTvnk7tLehlU/.

9. Michael Meyer, "About That Book Advance . . . ," *New York Times*, April 10, 2009, http://www.nytimes.com/2009/04/12/books/review/Meyer-t.html.

10. Lucien Febvre and Henri-Jean Martin, *The Coming of the Book: The Impact of Printing 1450–1800*, trans. David Gerard, ed. Geoffrey Nowell-Smith and David Wootton (London: Verso, 1976), 161.

11. "Sold by Subscription Only," on website for the exhibition *The Business of Being Mark Twain*, 2010, http://rmc.library.cornell.edu/twain/exhibition /subscription/index.html.

CHAPTER 6

1. Stuart Elliott, "Magazine Association Renames Itself," *New York Times*, July 30, 2010, http://www.nytimes.com/2010/10/01/business/media/01adco.html ?_r=0.

2. Lyon N. Richardson, "Biographical Note," in *The American Magazine; or, A Monthly View of the Political State of the British Colonies* (New York: Columbia University Press, 1937).

3. John William Tebbel and Mary Ellen Zuckerman, *The Magazine in America, 1741–1990* (New York: Oxford University Press, 1991), 60–62, chap. 7.

4. Ibid., 141.

5. Ibid., 246–47.

6. Jeffrey A. Trachtenberg, "Magazines Try New Tactic: Money Back If Ad Fails to Deliver," *Wall Street Journal*, October 12, 2015, http://www.wsj.com/articles /magazines-try-new-tactic-money-back-if-ad-fails-to-deliver-1444683026.

7. "US Online and Traditional Media Advertising Outlook, 2016–2020," MarketingCharts (website), June 14, 2016. http://www.marketingcharts.com/traditional/us-online-and-traditional-media-advertising-outlook-2016-2020-68214/.

8. "Digital Will Represent 37% of US Total Media Ad Spending," eMarketer.com, September 13, 2016, https://www.emarketer.com/Article/US-Digital-Ad-Spending-Surpass-TV-this-Year/1014469.

9. Kenneth Olmstead and Kristine Lu, "Digital News—Revenues Fact Sheet," in *State of the News Media 2015*, Pew Research Center, April 29, 2015, http://www.journalism.org/2015/04/29/digital-news-revenue-fact-sheet-2015/.

10. Michael Rosenwald, "The Digital Media Industry Needs to React to Ad Blockers . . . or Else—," *Columbia Journalism Review*, October 2015, http://www.cjr.org/business_of_news/will_ad_blockers_kill_the_digital_media_industry.php.

11. David Griner, "U.S. Newspapers Make $40 Billion Less from Ads Today Than in 2000," *AdWeek*, October 24, 2014, http://www.adweek.com/news/press/us-newspapers-make-40-billion-less-ads-today-2000-160966.

12. Jeffrey A. Trachtenberg, "Prevention Magazine Takes Radical Step: No Print Ads," *Wall Street Journal*, April 3, 2016, http://www.wsj.com/articles/prevention-magazine-takes-radical-step-no-print-ads-1459714328.

13. Matt Weinberger, "BuzzFeed Pays Facebook Millions of Dollars to Promote Its Clients' Ads," *Business Insider*, August 12, 2015, http://www.businessinsider.com/buzzfeed-native-advertising-is-paying-off-2015-8.

14. William Pfaff, "The Decline of the New Yorker," *Chicago Tribune*, March 10, 1998, http://articles.chicagotribune.com/1998-03-10/news/9803100023_1_new-yorker-magazine-newhouse.

15. Tebbel and Zuckerman, *Magazine in America*, 320–21.

16. Jeremy W. Peters, "Web Focus Helps Revitalize the Atlantic," *New York Times*, December 12, 2010, http://www.nytimes.com/2010/12/13/business/media/13atlantic.html.

17. Tim Baysinger, "Old New Yorker Stories Are Being Turned into Compelling Short Films for Amazon Prime," *AdWeek*, February 16, 2016, http://www.adweek.com/news/television/old-new-yorker-stories-are-being-turned-them-compelling-short-films-amazon-prime-169650.

CHAPTER 7

1. "*Salon* (website)" (under heading "Business Model and Operations"), Wikipedia, June 24, 2016, https://en.wikipedia.org/w/index.php?title=Salon_(website)&oldid=726731038.

2. Mark Hoelzel, "Video Ad Spending Is on a Tear—Here Are the Most Important Trends Shaping the Industry," *Business Insider*, March 6, 2015, http://www.businessinsider.com/digital-video-advertising-aggressive-spending-and-growth-2014-9.

3. Mary Meeker, "2016 Internet Trends Report," Kleiner Perkins Caufield Byers

(website), June 1, 2016, http://www.kpcb.com/blog/2016-internet-trends-report, slide 44.

4. On the challenges of ad-supported digital publishing, read Glenn Fleishman, "Why Isn't the Magazine Free with Ads? Volume," *Glenn Fleishman Writes Words about Things* (blog), October 24, 2013, http://glog.glennf.com/blog/2013/10 /24/why-isnt-the-magazine-free-with-ads.

5. Dao Nguyen, "How BuzzFeed Thinks about Data, and Some Charts, Too," BuzzFeed, February 18, 2016, http://www.buzzfeed.com/daozers/how-buzzfeed -thinks-about-data-and-some-charts-too.

6. Thompson has also written some of the most insightful posts on changing business models for internet-era publications. Start with his "Popping the Publishing Bubble," *Stratechery*, September 16, 2015, https://stratechery.com/2015 /popping-the-publishing-bubble/.

7. Cited in Martha Woodmansee, *The Author, Art, and the Market: Rereading the History of Aesthetics* (New York: Columbia University Press, 1994), 28.

8. Chad Wellmon, "Why Google Isn't Making Us Stupid . . . or Smart," *Hedgehog Review* 14, no. 1 (Spring 2012), http://www.iasc-culture.org/THR/THR_article_2012 _Spring_Wellmon.php.

9. Marc Fisher, "Who Cares If It's True?: Modern-Day Newsrooms Reconsider Their Values," *Columbia Journalism Review*, March 3, 2014, http://www.cjr.org /cover_story/who_cares_if_its_true.php?page=all.

10. Jane Friedman, "An Interview with Bo Sacks on the Magazine Industry" (blog post), Spring 2014, https://janefriedman.com/an-interview-with-bo -sacks/.

11. ProPublica, https://www.propublica.org/; *Pacific Standard* magazine, https://psmag.com/.

CHAPTER 8

1. Martha Woodmansee, *The Author, Art, and the Market: Rereading the History of Aesthetics* (New York: Columbia University Press, 1994), 28.

2. Hamilton Nolan, "The Problem with Journalism Is You Need an Audience," Gawker, January 14, 2016, http://gawker.com/the-problem-with-journalism-is-you -need-an-audience-1752937252.

3. John William Tebbel and Mary Ellen Zuckerman, *The Magazine in America, 1741–1990* (New York: Oxford University Press, 1991), 249–50.

4. Ibid., 22.

5. "The Business of Literary Publishing in the Twenty-First Century" (panel S248), AWP Conference, Seattle, WA, March 1, 2014, https://www.awpwriter.org /awp_conference/event_detail/1784.

6. Elizabeth Day, "Will Self: 'I Don't Write for Readers,'" *Guardian*, Aug. 5, 2012, https://www.theguardian.com/books/2012/aug/05/will-self-umbrella-booker -interview.

7. Will Self, "The Novel Is Dead (This Time It's for Real)," *Guardian*, May 2, 2014,

https://www.theguardian.com/books/2014/may/02/will-self-novel-dead-literary
-fiction.

8. Travis Kurowski, "In Exile and against Criticism: *The Paris Review* and the Branding of Contemporary Literature," in *Paper Dreams: Writers and Editors on the American Literary Magazine*, ed. Travis Kurowski (Madison, NJ: Atticus Books, 2013), 191–206.

9. Cited in "6Qs: Richard Eoin Nash, Social Publisher," interview by Guy LeCharles Gonzalez (blog post), September 29, 2009, http://loudpoet.com/2009 /09/29/6qs-richard-eoin-nash-social-publisher/.

10. Chris Fischbach, "Literature Is Not the Same Thing as Publishing," *Virginia Quarterly Review* blog, May 23, 2014, http://www.vqronline.org/essays-articles /2014/05/literature-not-same-thing-publishing.

11. See comment section in Joy Lanzendorfer, "Should Literary Journals Charge Writers Just to Read Their Work?," *Atlantic*, October 25, 2015, http://www .theatlantic.com/entertainment/archive/2015/10/why-writers-are-paying-to-get -published/411274/.

12. Richard Nash, "What Is the Business of Literature?," *Virginia Quarterly Review* 89, no. 2 (2013), http://www.vqronline.org/articles/what-business -literature.

13. Michael Nye, "Stubbornly Submitting to a Literary Magazine Is Good," *Missouri Review* (blog), April 28, 2015, http://www.missourireview.com/tmr-blog /2015/04/stubbornly-submitting-to-a-literary-magazine-is-good/.

14. Susan Gabriel, Facebook comment, May 17, 2015, https://www.facebook .com/jane.friedman/posts/10153292595297417?comment_id=10153300251037417.

CHAPTER 9

1. Chad W. Post, "Three Percent: The Nonfiction Gap," September 19, 2011, http://www.rochester.edu/College/translation/threepercent/?id=3613.

CHAPTER 10

1. William Heinemann, "The Middleman as Viewed by a Publisher," *Athenaeum Journal of Literature, Science, the Fine Arts, Music, and the Drama*, no. 3446, November 11, 1893, 663.

2. Mary Ann Gillies, *The Professional Literary Agent in Britain, 1880–1920* (Toronto: University of Toronto Press, 2007).

CHAPTER 12

1. Rebecca Ruiz, "'Fight for What You Believe In': How Best-Selling Authors Battled Rejection," *TODAY*, August 22, 2013, http://www.today.com/popculture /fight-what-you-believe-how-best-selling-authors-battled-rejection-6C10971491.

2. Jessica Strawser, "The Market for Memoirs," *Writer's Digest*, October 5, 2010, http://www.writersdigest.com/writing-articles/by-writing-goal/get-published -sell-my-work/the-market-for-memoirs.

CHAPTER 16

1. Gettysburg Review, "Guidelines," accessed July 8, 2016, http://www.gettys burgreview.com/submissions/guidelines/.

CHAPTER 17

1. Charles P. Daly, *The Magazine Publishing Industry* (Boston: Allyn and Bacon, 1997), 7.

2. "Writer Submission Guidelines," *Runner's World*, December 20, 2006, http:// www.runnersworld.com/about-runners-world/writer-submission-guidelines.

CHAPTER 18

1. Felix Salmon, "The Problem with Online Freelance Journalism," Reuters, March 5, 2013, US edition, http://blogs.reuters.com/felix-salmon/2013/03/05/the -problem-with-online-freelance-journalism/.

2. Alexis C. Madrigal, "A Day in the Life of a Digital Editor, 2013," *Atlantic*, March 6, 2013, http://www.theatlantic.com/technology/archive/2013/03/a-day-in -the-life-of-a-digital-editor-2013/273763/.

3. Jakob Nielsen, "How Little Do Users Read?," Nielsen Norman Group (web-site), May 6, 2008, https://www.nngroup.com/articles/how-little-do-users-read/.

4. Farhad Manjoo, "You Won't Finish This Article," *Slate*, June 6, 2013, http:// www.slate.com/articles/technology/technology/2013/06/how_people_read _online_why_you_won_t_finish_this_article.html.

5. Michael Barthel et al., "The Evolving Role of News on Twitter and Facebook," Pew Research Center, July 14, 2015, http://www.journalism.org/2015/07/14/the -evolving-role-of-news-on-twitter-and-facebook/.

6. Jesse Mawhinney, "37 Visual Content Marketing Statistics You Should Know in 2016," *Hubspot*, January 13, 2016, http://blog.hubspot.com/marketing/visual -content-marketing-strategy.

CHAPTER 19

1. Kevin Kelly, "1,000 True Fans," "The Technium" (blog), March 4, 2008, http:// kk.org/thetechnium/1000-true-fans/.

CHAPTER 20

1. Tad Friend, "The One Who Knocks: How Bryan Cranston Made Himself a Star," *New Yorker*, September 16, 2013, http://www.newyorker.com/magazine/2013 /09/16/the-one-who-knocks.

CHAPTER 22

1. Roger C. Schonfeld and Brian F. Lavoie, "Books without Boundaries: A Brief Tour of the System-Wide Print Book Collection," *Journal of Electronic Publishing* 9, no. 2 (August 31, 2006), doi:10.3998/3336451.0009.208.

2. Mary Houlihan, "A Novel Approach," *Chicago Sun-Times*, June 10, 2013.

3. Jeffrey A. Trachtenberg, "The Mystery of the Book Sales Spike," *Wall Street Journal*, February 22, 2013, http://www.wsj.com/articles/SB10001424127887323864 304578316143623600544.

4. Dorie Clark, "Make Your Book a Bestseller: Platform Building Tips from Michael Hyatt," 2014, http://dorieclark.com/make-your-book-a-bestseller-platform -building-tips-from-michael-hyatt/.

5. Tim Ferriss, "How Does a Bestseller Happen? A Case Study in Hitting #1 on the New York Times," August 6, 2007, http://fourhourworkweek.com/2007/08 /06/how-does-a-bestseller-happen-a-case-study-in-hitting-1-on-the-new-york -times/; Darren Rowse, "Tim Ferriss Interview—Part I," *ProBlogger*, April 26, 2007, http://www.problogger.net/tim-ferris-interview-part-i/.

CHAPTER 23

1. Cited in Meredith Lee, "Popular Quotes: Commitment," Goethe Society of North America (website), March 5, 1988, http://www.goethesociety.org/pages /quotescom.html.

CHAPTER 24

1. Paul D. McCarthy, "Developmental Editing: A Creative Collaboration," in *Editors on Editing: What Writers Need to Know about What Editors Do*, ed. Gerald Gross, 3rd ed. (New York: Grove Press, 1993).

CHAPTER 25

1. John Warner, "To Potential MFA Students: There Are No Academic Jobs," *Inside Higher Ed*, September 14, 2014, https://www.insidehighered.com/blogs/just -visiting/potential-mfa-students-there-are-no-academic-jobs.

CHAPTER 26

1. "Writers Selected for Amtrak Residency Program," *Amtrak Stories* (blog), September 24, 2014, http://blog.amtrak.com/2014/09/writers-selected-amtrak -residency-program/.

CHAPTER 27

1. See Jane Friedman, "Q&A about Crowdfunding for Authors with Bethany Joy Carlson" (blog post), May 24, 2016, https://janefriedman.com/qa-bethany-joy -carlson/.

CHAPTER 28

1. Mathew Ingram, "Can a Little-Known Blogger Turn His Site into a Business by Selling Memberships? Ben Thompson Is Sure Going to Try," April 17, 2014, https://gigaom.com/2014/04/17/can-a-little-known-blogger-turn-his-site-into-a -business-by-selling-memberships-ben-thompson-is-sure-going-to-try/.

2. Ibid.

3. Mathew Ingram, "Ben Thompson: The One-Man Blog Isn't Dead, It's Better Than Ever," *GIGAOM*, February 2, 2015, https://gigaom.com/2015/02/02/ben-thompson-the-one-man-blog-isnt-dead-its-better-than-ever/.

4. Ben Thompson, "Blogging's Bright Future," *Stratechery*, February 2, 2015, https://stratechery.com/2015/bloggings-bright-future/.

5. Andrew Beaujon, "Jacob Weisberg: 'The Confusion about Paywalls Is Bad for Sites like Ours,'" *Poynter*, December 18, 2012, http://www.poynter.org/2012/jacob-weisberg-no-paywall-for-slate/198639/.

CHAPTER 30

1. "'You've Got to Find What You Love,' Jobs Says" (video and text of commencement address), Stanford University (website), June 14, 2005, http://news.stanford.edu/2005/06/14/jobs-061505/.

2. Maria Popova, "John Cleese on the Origin of Creativity," *Open Culture*, September 23, 2009, http://www.openculture.com/2010/09/john_cleese_on_the_origin_of_creativity.html.

CHAPTER 31

1. John William Tebbel and Mary Ellen Zuckerman, *The Magazine in America, 1741–1990* (New York: Oxford University Press, 1991).

2. For example, "Fleurs Du Friday: Marigold Cocktail," Anthropologie (blog), February 27, 2015, http://blog.anthropologie.com/112232890213/.

3. "Stronger with Gold's Gym" (playlist), 2013, https://www.youtube.com/watch?v=vitmlBLK3Wg&index=1&list=PLZoykXxVooGghufBhxALKnQkpK_McuCIo.

4. Justin Gardner, "Ron Burgundy's Guide to Dress for Success—An Anchorman 2: The Legend Continues Infographic," 2013, originally posted at https://www.amctheatres.com, since reposted at numerous sites.

5. American Express Company, "OPEN Forum," accessed July 6, 2016, https://www.americanexpress.com/us/small-business/openforum/.

6. The URL for the IBM-*Atlantic* item includes the directory "sponsored"; the domain in which the Netflix-*Times* article is posted begins with the term "paid post": Melanie Deziel, "Women Inmates Separate but Not Equal," June 2014, http://paidpost.nytimes.com/netflix/women-inmates-separate-but-not-equal.html.

7. By Andrew Rice, "Does BuzzFeed Know the Secret?," *New York Magazine*, April 7, 2013, http://nymag.com/news/features/buzzfeed-2013-4/.

8. "Content Strategy Alliance Charter," posted July 5, 2014, http://contentstrategyalliance.com/the-beginnings/csa-charter/.

INDEX

content strategy, 200–203; careers in, 273–74, 274–76

contests, 245, 246–47

contracts: agents', 93, 97; article, 280–82; book, 282–84; literary journal, 280–82; publishers', 128; terminology in, 279–80

conversion: defined, 199; measuring, 204

copyright, 287–88

copywriting, 201, 202, 274

cover letters, 144–45, 148, 247

craft, developing, 12, 37

creative nonfiction, 86

creativity, business vs., 8, 11, 26, 41

crowdfunding, 253–55

databases, agent and publisher, 100–101

day jobs, 11, 231–32

deadlines, publisher, 129

defamation, 290–91

demand, generating, 28–30

digital media: business models for, 64–66, 67–68; earned vs. owed vs. paid, 276

disaggregation, 60–61, 67, 74

discoverability, 72–73

donations, 255–56

earned media, 276

earning out, 48

editors associations, 235–36

editors: freelance, 233–38; relationships with, 128–29

email newsletters, 178, 181, 190–91, 193–94, 219

engagement, 162, 171, 188–90, 197–98, 206–7

escalators, 50

essays, 87, 143–49, 152–53

exclusive readings, 114

expectations, unreasonable, 43

exposure, working for, 28–30, 32

Facebook, 187–90

Facebook Ads, 205

fair use, 289–90

fees: agents', 91; contest entry, 248, 249; reading, 76, 146–47

fellowships, 245, 250–52

Ferrante, Elena, 171

Ferriss, Tim, 221–22

fiction, literary vs. commercial, 83–85

freelance editing, 233–38

freelance writing, 150–59, 227–32

freelancing, guides to, 294

funnels, 161, 198–200

gatekeepers, 17–18, 77–79

Gay, Roxane, 30, 87, 202–3

genre, 83

giveaways, 218–19

Glass, Ira, 12

Google Analytics, 203–4

graduate degrees, 36–39

grants, 246, 250–52

headlines, online, 65, 161, 162–63; SEO and, 163

hero's journey, 84

homepage, author's, 183–84

hook, in queries, 108, 155, 157

humor, 87, 153

Hyatt, Michael, 220–21

income, sustainable, 2, 36, 143–44, 223–24

indexing, 235

influencers, 17–18, 167

Ingram, 138

invasion of privacy, 291–92

keywords, 127, 163, 165

Kindle, 46

leads, generating, 28–35

legal issues, guides to, 295

Li, Yiyun, 33–34
libel, 290–91
licensing, 133
link shorteners, 205
literary agents. *See* agents
literary citizenship, 19–21, 32–33, 175
literary content, short, 143–49
literary fiction, 83–85
literary journals: business models for, 76; contracts with, 149; as lead generators, 33–34; researching, 147–48; submitting to, 144–48
literary publishing, 71–79

magazines, 53–63; business models of, 53, 54–55; consumer, 58
marketability vs. quality, 22
marketing, 22; by authors, 123–25, 134–35, 136; inbound, 209, 276; lack of by publishers, 20, 130, 136; outbound, 209, 276; plan, 123–25, 134–35, 195; publicity vs., 209; by publishers, 103, 130–31, 133–36
media, digital: business models for, 64–66, 67–68; earned vs. owed vs. paid, 276
media-agnostic publications, 61–62
memberships, 257–59
memoir, 86–87, 111
MFAs, 36–39
micropayments, 66
micro-publishing, 30–31, 176
middle-grade books, 88
monomyth, 84

narrative nonfiction, 85–86, 118
Nash, Richard, 8, 29, 31, 75, 77–78
native advertising, 57–58; careers in, 272–73, 274–76
networking. *See* relationship building; *see also* literary citizenship
newsletters, email. *See* email newsletters
niche publishers, 74–75, 97

non-compete clauses, 284–85
nonfiction: book proposals, 110, 117–27; creative, 86; essays, 87, 143–49, 152–53; memoir, 86–87, 111; narrative vs. prescriptive, 85–86; poetry, 143–49. *See also* freelance writing; platform
nonprofit publishing, 71
note-taking, 99
novellas, 89

obligations, life, 277
online teaching, 241–44
online writing, 32, 160–69; visuals with, 164, 192–93
orphaned books, 130
others, focusing on, 19–21. *See also* literary citizenship
owned media, 276

P & L (profit and loss) statements: book, 47–49; magazine, 55
paid media, 276
patronage, 9, 29, 41
paywalls, 66, 257, 259–60
permissions, 288–90
persistence, 12
picture books, 88
pitching, 21–26; magazine articles, 153, 154–59; to media, during book launch, 216–17; nonfiction, 106; novels, 106
platform, 111, 118, 123–24, 173–74; components of, 176–77; fiction and, 175; guides to, 294; nonfiction and, 174–75; outsourcing, 177; prioritizing, 178
POD (print on demand), 102, 138
poetry, 143–49
premise, in queries, 108
prescriptive nonfiction, 85–86
prestige, trap of, 14
prestige content. *See* literary publishing

print on demand (POD), 102, 138

privacy, invasion of, 291–92

prizes, 245, 248–50

profit-and-loss (P & L) statements: book, 47–49; magazine, 55

projections, sales, 48–50

pub board, 47

publication, guides to, 293–94

publicists, 209–12

publicity: marketing vs., 209; right of, 292. *See also* literary citizenship; relationship building; social media

publishers: Big Five, 43–45, 91, 133; choosing, 90; contracts, 128; digital-only, 102; largest US book, 44; largest US magazine, 59; marketing budgets of, 46–47; niche, 74–75, 97; purpose of, 132–33; relationships with, 52, 73, 128–29; researching, 98–105; small, 45, 97, 102–3 (*see also* niche publishers); vanity, 138

publishing: book, 83–90; careers in, 266–68; literary, 71–79; nonprofit, 71

quality vs. marketability, 22

queries, simultaneous, 110, 146

query letters, 106–14

readership. *See* audience

rejections, 46, 78, 81–82, 96, 116, 158

relationship building, 17–19, 197, 198; with agents, 93–95; with author events, 212, 214; for book launch, 222; as freelancer, 218. *See also* audience; platform

relationships: with editors, 128–29; with publishers, 52, 73, 128–29

researching: agents and publishers, 98–105; market, for book proposal, 117, 119–20; outsourcing, 98

residencies, 246, 250–52

reviewers, 131

reviews, 215–16

revisions, 116, 128–29, 148–49

revolutions in publishing, 7

right of publicity, 292

rights, exclusive vs. nonexclusive, 279

royalties, 50–51, 92–93

sales-driven communication, 197–98

sales projections, 48–50

samples, editing, 237

satire, 87

search engine optimization. *See* SEO (search engine optimization)

search engines and aggregators, 161

self-publishing, 109, 137–42

SEO (search engine optimization), 163, 204, 274; author websites and, 184–86; blogs and, 165

service content, 59–60

short stories, 143–49

simultaneous submissions, 110, 146

slander, 290–91

slush pile, 143

small presses, 45, 97, 102–3. *See also* niche publishers

social media: careers in, 269–70, 274–76; and book launch, 217–18; digital publishing and, 66–67; engagement and, 206–7; hard sells via, 18; marketing via, 186–87; micro-publishing via, 30–31; networking via, 18–19; platform and, 176, 177; for research, 104

software, note-taking, 99

spoilers, in synopses, 114, 116

sponsored content. *See* native advertising

submission fees, 76, 146–47

submission guidelines: for literary journals, 145; for magazines, 155; for publishers and agents, 101

submissions: book, 90; simultaneous, 110, 146; on spec, 154

Submittable, 146–47

subscriptions, 257–59

synopses, 106, 114–16

taxation, 259

teaching writing, 36–37, 239–44

tip jars, 255–56

titles, book, 129

tours, author, 212–13

trade publications, 154

trademark, 290

trends, writing to, 23

vanity presses, 138

visuals, 164, 192–93

websites: for authors, 180–87; for free-lance editors, 236–37; writing for (*see* online writing)

word count, 89

WordPress, 181

work-for-hire, 279–80, 284–85

writing: as commercial product, 9, 29; consistent production of, 12, 16; content vs. 62; for free, 28–30, 32; freelance, 150–59, 227–32; magazine, guides to, 294; teaching, 36–37, 239–44

young adult (YA) books, 88